Man-E

Tales of Lion and Ti

Man–Eater

Tales of Lion and Tiger Encounters

edited by

Edward Hodges-Hill

Cockbird Press
HEATHFIELD

First published 1992
Cockbird Press Ltd
P O Box 356, Heathfield, East Sussex TN21 9QF

British Library Cataloguing in Publication Data
Man-Eater: Tales of Lion and Tiger Encounters
I. Hodges-Hill, Edward
599.74
ISBN 1 873054 03 3

Designed by Peter Guy
Typeset and Produced by Book Production Services
Maps by Denys Baker
Printed and bound by Richard Clay Ltd, Bungay, Suffolk

FOR BOOT, GEORGE, NICO AND TOM

Contents

Acknowledgements

The publisher acknowledges the huge debt owed to those who assisted Edward Hodges-Hill with valuable suggestions about which material to include in this edition. Locating out-of-print text was often difficult and special thanks in this regard are due to Dr Hubert Hendrichs at the University of Bielefeld, Guy Mountfort and to Dr C J Hails of the World Wide Fund for Nature. Staff at the London Library, British Library, Natural History Museum Library and the Heathfield branch of the East Sussex County Library have also been most helpful and patient in finding often very obscure material. A debt of gratitude is also due to Andrew Cook, Map Curator of the Oriental and India Office Collections, British Library, whose expertise was much appreciated in tracing the location of numerous Indian place-names and, for clarifying certain text details, to Bill Mouland at the *Daily Mail* and also Dick Lyon. Thanks are particularly due to Linda MacLachlan for her research efforts and to our editor Sue Mertens who, from the start of this enterprise, has shown great energy as reader and copyist.

Permission for the use of text under copyright has kindly been given by: HarperCollins*Publishers* Limited, copyright © George Allen & Unwin, for two extracts from *Man-Eaters and Jungle Killers* and an extract from *Tales from the Indian Jungle* by Kenneth Anderson; International Publishers (Pakistan) Limited for extracts from *Man-eaters of Sunderbans* by Tahawar Ali Khan; and Oxford University Press for extracts from *The Man-Eaters of Kumaon* (1944) by Jim Corbett. Every effort has been made to trace copyright holders but if any have been inadvertently overlooked the publisher will be pleased to make the necessary arrangement at the first opportunity.

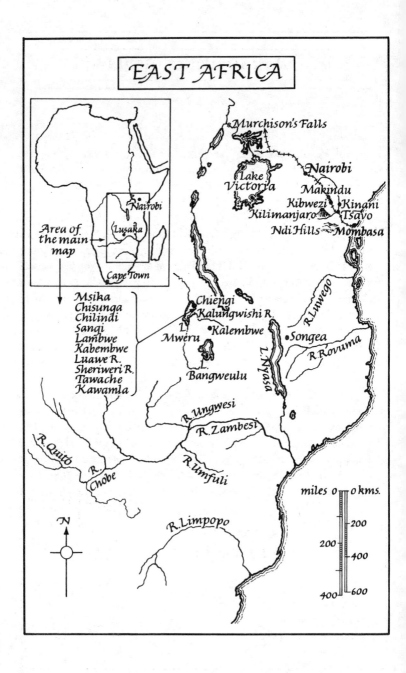

EAST AFRICA

Murchison's Falls

Nairobi

Lake
Victoria

Makindu
Kibwezi · Kinani
Kilimanjaro · Tsavo
Ndi Hills · Mombasa

Nairobi

Area of
the main
map

Lusaka

Cape Town

Msika
Chisunga
Chilindi
Sangi
Lambwe
Kabembwe
Luawe R.
Sheriweri R.
Tawache
Kawamla

Chiengi
Kalungwishi R.
· Kalembwe
L.
Mweru
· Songea

R. Luwego

L. Nyasa

R. Rovuma

Bangweulu

R. Ungwesi

R. Zambesi

R. Quito

R. Chobe

R. Umfuli

N

R. Limpopo

miles 0 ⊤ 0 kms.

200

200 ⊤ 400

400 ⊥ 600

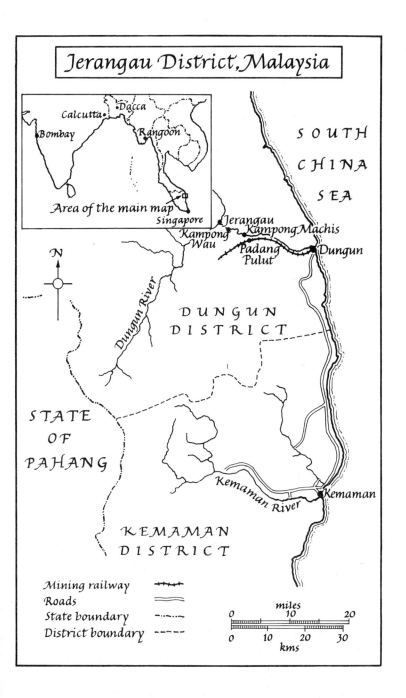

Jerangau District, Malaysia

Calcutta
Dacca
Bombay
Rangoon

Area of the main map

Singapore

SOUTH
CHINA
SEA

Jerangau
Kampong Machis
Kampong
Wau
Padang
Pulut
Dungun

N

Dungun River

DUNGUN
DISTRICT

STATE
OF
PAHANG

Kemaman River
Kemaman

KEMAMAN
DISTRICT

Mining railway
Roads
State boundary
District boundary

miles
0   10   20

0   10   20   30
kms

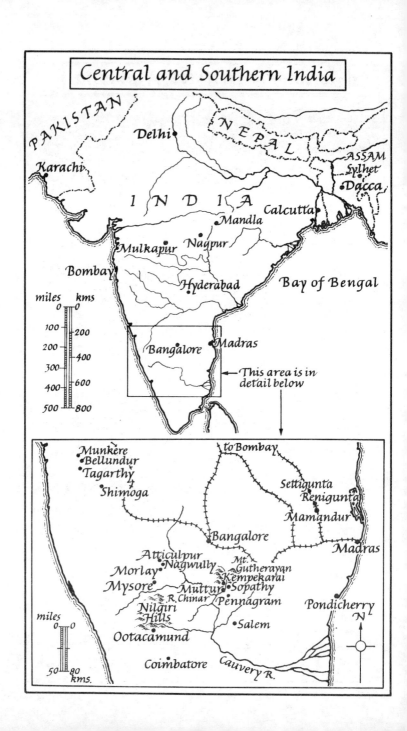

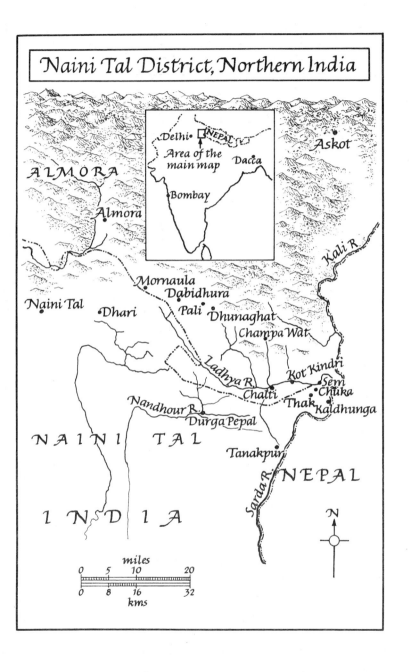

Naini Tal District, Northern India

ALMORA

Askot

Kali R.

Almora

Delhi• ☐NEPAL
Area of the
main map   Dacca

•Bombay

Mornaula
Dabidhura

Naini Tal   •Dhari   •Pali • Dhunaghat

Champa Wat

Ladhya R.   Kot Kindri
Sem
Chalti   Chuka
Nandhour R.   Thak Kaldhunga
Durga Pepal

N A I N I   T A L

Tanakpur

I N D I A   Sarda R. NEPAL

N

miles
0   5   10   20

0   8   16   32
kms

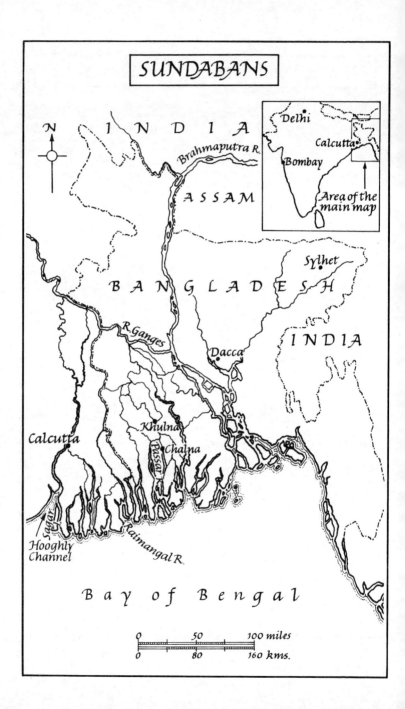

SUNDABANS

N

I N D I A

Brahmaputra R.

A S S A M

B A N G L A D E S H

Sylhet

R.Ganges

Dacca

I N D I A

Calcutta

Khulna

Chalna

Passar

Hooghly
Channel

Raimangal R.

Sagar

B a y   o f   B e n g a l

Delhi

Calcutta

Bombay

Area of the
main map

0	50	100 miles
0	80	160 kms.

Tyger! Tyger! burning bright
In the forests of the night…

Introduction

IN 1971 ATTACKS BY TIGERS on human beings in the Sunderban region of the Ganges river delta accounted for the lives of 91 Indians and Bangladeshis. In this region of swamps and low-lying tidal islands no year passes without there being at least some deaths by tiger attack reported from amongst villagers who enter the mangrove forests to cut firewood, fish and collect honey for their livelihood.

The Sunderbans is the last area in south Asia in which a significant number of human beings still live under the constant threat of man-eating tigers. Elsewhere, as with lions in east Africa, human deaths from attacks are comparatively rare, still more so from animals formally declared as persistent man-eaters. Even in the parts of present day India which are the tiger's remaining habitat, only very few tigers a year are confirmed as man-eaters and which, as such, then have to be captured by game wardens or, however reluctantly, hunted down and destroyed.

Concern about the survival of the lion and the tiger in the face of the continued erosion of their natural habitat by the encroach-ment of man is, today, a widespread and legitimate concern. Modern day nature films and television documentaries bring such issues to the notice of every home with their often remarkable portrayals of animal life in the wild.

It is perhaps inevitable that the familiarity that such exposure brings should also blunt our perception of the lion or tiger as a dangerous animal, while concern about conservation make it more difficult for us to conceive of there having been a time not so long ago when these animals constituted a substantial threat to man.

The encounters with man-eaters related in these pages are mostly from earlier eras this century and before when lions and tigers, particularly in east and central Africa and in northern India, were sufficiently abundant to constitute a distinct challenge to the way of life and sometimes continued existence of the human population that lived alongside them sharing the same habitat.

There are numerous accounts describing the depredations of man-eaters which for over three centuries, and no doubt much longer than that, terrorised the lives of African and Indian villagers. 'People living in the perfect safety of their homes in a Western country have no conception of the insecurity that is felt by blacks in their kraals in the interior of Africa' concluded a hunter, James Sutherland, in 1912. 'The cause of this feeling of insecurity is chiefly the man-eating lion, and no other animal of the forest inspires such terror into the black man's heart. In villages far in the heart of the pori, where the white man is never seen, not hundreds but thousands of Africans are annually killed by these monsters'.

In parts of India, the tiger has been a similar menace for the native population. One observer has remarked that 'at one time in parts of India at the beginning of the 19th century man-eaters were so numerous that it seemed to be a question of whether man or tiger would survive.'

Countless Indian villagers down the ages would not have found that an exaggeration. As the tiger authority Richard Perry has noted, those who lived in a man-eater's country, on leaving their village at daybreak, could never be sure of returning home in the evening. A tigress in one district might be killing two villagers every month over a period of four years; in another district fifteen people in a single month; in a third district forty-eight people in twelve months.

At one time villages in the United Provinces (modern day Uttar Pradesh) were protected at night by lines of fires, while other villages in the Central Provinces and in Bengal were protected at all times by high stockades. 'The villagers only stirred abroad when necessity compelled in large bodies, covered by armed men, and beating drums and shouting as they passed along the road' noted a 19th century Indian Government Officer, J Forsyth. 'Many villages had been utterly deserted and the whole country was evidently being slowly depopulated' by the activities of a single man-eater.

Another writer of the same period describes how the Bengal Rajahs attempted to reduce the number of tigers which were terrorising areas by setting fire to ten and twenty mile stretches of jungle in order to drive the tigers into nets for capture. In one area village after village, or rather the sites where they stood, lay 'wholly uncultivated and deserted. Whenever a tiger carries off a man near a public road or footpath, a stick with a coloured cloth, or white triangular flag on a bamboo staff ten or twelve foot high, is erected as a warning to travellers; and every passer-by throws a stone on to the heap, which soon become large heaps in great abundance.'

Such death cairns were to be seen throughout the last century in many areas. In Mysore, central India, they were located at quarter-mile intervals along roads skirting the jungle, every stone in every cairn carrying a prayer from a passing traveller that he not share the fate of the victims commemorated by the cairn.

In regions where man-eaters operated it was the constant suspense of being defenceless against sudden and horrible death by day or night, over a period of months if not years at a time, that broke the spirit of villagers just as much as the actual number of deaths among them, though the latter were terrible enough.

The statistics of man-eater depredations over the years show that such abject fear in native villages was more than justified. Tigers were estimated to be accounting for between 1000 and 1600 souls per year in India as late as the 1930's, not appreciably less than the estimated human mortality of 1300 to 2000 victims annually in the 1860's. Loss of life was, if anything, greater in Africa, where the lion was more abundant than the tiger in India by the early part of this century, at which time human deaths from man-eaters were approaching 2500 annually.

These bare statistics hardly suggest the scale of human misery which they represent. 'There is no more terrible thing than to live and have one's being under the shadow of a man-eater' concluded Jim Corbett, who spent more than sixty years in India's jungles earlier this century, over one-half of them hunting man-eaters.

One or more man-eaters operating in a specific district some-times accounted for large numbers of victims. More than four hundred people were reported to have been killed over just a few years at the town of Bhiwapur in India in the mid-18th century, with the town subsequently abandoned. A hundred years later similar figures were still being recounted: 350 deaths over four years at Kardeish, between two and three hundred deaths annu-ally in Jubbulpore. In 1907 a four year reign of terror by one tigress in the Kumaon district of northern India accounted for 236 victims.

Amongst the accounts of man-eaters which follow, the descrip-tion of the tigress of Thak shows how one man-eater, in addition to terrorising the resident villagers, kept a forestry labour force of fifteen thousand men, working over an area of fifty square miles, sitting up night after night with large fires, shouting and drum-ming. Total paralysis of the district was brought about by this one tigress, with every one of the hundred or more inhabitants of Thak fleeing and taking their livestock with them, until Jim Corbett - after great courage - was able finally to meet up with her.

The Thak man-eater's power to immobilise a whole district was mirrored by the activity of a pair of man-eating lions at the beginning of this century in east Africa which, by their infallible attacks on workers' camps, succeeded in interrupting work on the construction of the Uganda railway for a period of months. Only after the death of twenty-eight workers, together with an un-known number of villagers, were these two man-eaters eventu-ally killed.

The fact that one man-eater would range over many square miles meant that the activities of a relative few could paralyse whole districts. Probably less than one percent of lions or tigers became habitual man-eaters and it has been estimated that at the beginning of this century there were less than a thousand and perhaps no more than 300 man-eating tigers, for example, oper-ating throughout India. While the tiger and lion populations were greatly reduced in India and east Africa through hunting, particularly in the last half of the 19th century through to the 1930's, it is noticeable that annual deaths from man-eaters through this period did not fall appreciably. The expanding human and cattle population in central and northern India and east Africa during this same period exerted an inexorable pressure on the natural habitat, increasing the contact between man and the lion and tiger which was taking place in a steadily contracting environment.

The universal spread of firearms over this period saw a progressively higher proportion of the lion and tiger population becoming wounded and maimed and, unable to pursue their normal prey, turning to the native human population for food. Incapacity, as well as old age, has always been one main cause for man-eaters, though men are not the only agents for lion and tiger wounds. Thorns in the pad from diverse sources can cripple an animal sufficiently to start it on a man-eating career and there are numerous recorded instances of porcupine quills being found responsible for wounds which prevented a tiger from hunting its natural prey. In such instances, turning to the domestic herds of cattle, and from them to the herdsmen who interfere in protection of their stock, is a progression which has been repeated countless times. Emboldened by the success, and losing its fear of man, the nascent man-eater also turns to stalking the villages, particularly at a time when cattle may be scarce as pastures are seasonally changed, or the number of cattle decrease for reasons of drought, famine or plague.

A human being is not the natural prey of a tiger or lion but once an animal becomes a regular man-eater, even though it is in its prime and suffers from no injury, it is then likely to prefer human flesh to that of its normal prey. Few man-eaters, however, exist solely on human flesh for the reason that they are not able to kill sufficient numbers of men to satisfy their hunger. An average human being weighs one-third or one-quarter of a wild buffalo or a villager's cow, even if entirely consumed and the palms of the hands and soles of the feet, together with the skull, are not rejected, as often is the case.

Cattle killing is only one route in the descent towards a career of man-eating. There is also a large 'accidental' element in the development of a man-eater. Jim Corbett has suggested how one tigress' chance encounter with a human being, and the change over in diet from animal to human flesh, led to a subsequent career of man-eating.

A tigress was lying up in a patch of grass, when a woman from a nearby village selected this particular patch to cut fodder. At first the tiger took no notice of her, but when the woman had cut the grass right up to where she was lying, the tigress struck out at her, crushing her skull with one blow. Although starving from a porcupine quill injury, the tigress left the body where it had fallen, and limped away to take cover under a fallen tree. 'Two days later a man came to chip firewood off this fallen tree, and the tigress who was lying on the far side killed him. The man fell across the tree, and as he had removed his coat and shirt, and the tigress had clawed his back when killing him, it is possible that the smell of the blood trickling down his body as he hung across the bole of the tree first gave her the idea that he was something that she could satisfy her hunger with. However that may be, before leaving him she ate a small portion from his back. A day later she killed her third victim deliberately, and without having received any provocation. Thereafter she became an established man-eater and had killed twenty-four people before she was finally accounted for'.

Lions and tigers are eaters of carrion. Therefore any catastrophic event, or religious or funeral rites, which results in human bodies being left exposed can also lead to lions and tigers becoming introduced to human flesh, subsequently killing deliberately in order to continue the diet. The Second World War provides one example. In 1942 one hundred thousand Indians were evacuated from Burma into western Bengal ahead of the advancing Japanese army, some four thousand Indians dying on the journey through the wilderness of jungle and mountain passes. Tigers fed upon the corpses and became addicted with the result that several years later deaths from man-eaters were reported by Allied troops passing through the area: fourteen west African troops were reported seized and the 82nd Division also lost a number of men.

The man-eaters responsible for these atrocities were found to be healthy, virile animals. Hunger and starvation through injury or old age, or an initial chance encounter with human flesh by other means, have undoubtedly been dominant causes for lions and tigers turning man-eater, and there is also the question of man-eating through example, and the possibility that grown cubs of man-eating parents will sometimes kill men because they have lost their instinctive fear and are familiar with men's ways and eating their flesh. It cannot be shown conclusively, but the persistence of man-eating tigers decade after decade in areas like the Sunderbans strongly suggest this possibility.

A lion or tiger on a fresh kill, or wounded, or a female with small cubs will sometimes kill human beings who disturb them. These animals, or those who get the better of hunters who pursue them, cannot be termed as man-eaters; the stories which follow are about lions and tigers which have, for whatever reason, turned to human beings as a preferred and regular diet.

These encounters with man-eaters are largely by professional men living in the country as doctors, engineers, district commissioners, military personnel, or travellers and sportsmen visiting the area on a temporary basis. The full-time game warden is a comparatively recent phenomenon and even the two most successful pursuers of man-eaters in modern times, Kenneth Anderson and Jim Corbett, were both full-time forest wardens who had first to obtain leave of absence from their employer before embarking on their hunting activities. Accounts by both men are included in this anthology.

Pursuit of a man-eater takes great courage. Common to all these stories is a terrifying degree of personal risk, accepted in full knowledge of what was being taken on and invariably written down in the narrative. Often the hunter is operating alone, knowing that he would only succeed by coming to close quarters with a man-eater whose innate cunning and natural caution could dramatically reverse the role of the hunter and the hunted.

On the trail of a man-eater every bush, every tree, every dip and bend in the path through the scrub or jungle has to be approached with extreme caution. Anywhere the animal could be lying in wait. Great knowledge of jungle craft is needed and, if the man-eater is ranging over a wide area, the problem of pursuit is formidable. If any pattern has developed to its behaviour or the animal has been prowling in a certain area, the hunter could lie in wait, perhaps in a hide over a bait. But the man-eater may not come, vanishing only to reappear thirty miles away where it might kill again. All reconnaissance work must then begin afresh and meanwhile village life, or railway construction work, or other human endeavour over the whole area remains paralysed.

It was in such an environment that many of these encounters with man-eaters took place.

CHAPTER ONE

Glow-worms In The Night: Three Man-eater Sieges

FEAR-GRIPPED COMMUNITIES, with all life paralysed over a wide region by the depredation of one or two man-eaters, is a common theme to these accounts. They are three examples of reigns of terror which were repeated countless times in Africa and India. The stories differ only in detail and in the type of terrain and vegetation in which they took place, and which largely dictated the means by which a man-eater had to be pursued.

I. The White Lion

James Dunbar-Brunton tells of experiences from when he was a doctor in east Africa earlier this century.

There is a fifty mile strip of territory in north-east Rhodesia [now part of Zambia] which lies north of the Kalungwishi River, bordering Lake Mweru, which is a favourite haunt of lions and of man-eaters as well. This strip is narrow, having a high range of continuous mountains on one side, while on the other is the water of the lake. This mountain range is the boundary of a large game reserve and there is no doubt that, while all game is increasing rapidly, the lions are also increasing and wander into the country around. In the old days this strip of land was densely populated, but now the villages are few and the population very small.

With the lessening of the population, the lions have possibly increased in boldness, as they are now found everywhere in the neighbourhood of these villages. There is no one to control them as shooting in this part of the country is forbidden to hunters, not only because of the big game reserve, but because, owing to the presence of sleeping sickness, the district is closed to all but the officials who are concerned with its suppression. These officials have little time to spend in lion-shooting. The hills which rise behind are full of ravines which contain bushes and tangled grass, giving excellent shelter for lions, leopards and hyenas.

The following is an account of the depredations of a man-eating lion in this district. It was in January, 1909, that the first of what was to prove a long series of deaths caused by a lion was reported by the natives to us at Chiengi station. A lion described as a large male, very light in colour, had taken a woman from a village called Msika, not far from Lake Mweru. A few days afterwards another woman was taken from the same village; both were killed at sundown.

A week later a man and his wife had just left Msika to visit friends at a neighbouring village, when they met the lion in the road at eight o'clock in the morning close to a small stream which crosses the road. The lion sprang at the man, who tried to defend himself, while his wife climbed a tree and screamed for help from the village which was about a quarter of a mile away, its gardens extending to the stream. None of the villagers ventured to approach and the man was killed and devoured almost before his wife's eyes.

A few days later, about 5.30 p.m., a woman was grinding corn at the next village, called Chisunga, working under the eaves of her hut with another woman beside her. The 'white' lion, as it came to be called by the natives, sneaked round the hut and killed both the women, carrying off one of them. At the same village a man who had been recently in my employ was working in his garden in the afternoon when the same lion was seen to spring upon him and kill him, carrying away his body. The lion then left the shores of Lake Mweru and made for the hills, for his next appearance was at a small isolated village high up on these hills, called Chilindi.

There had been a shower of rain, which had passed off, and the natives had built numerous little fires throughout the village at which they were sitting warming themselves. The lion came into the village and, before all the natives could seek safety in their huts, he sprang upon one of the women and carried her off. The next village to this is a small one some four miles away, called Sangi, the headman being a brother of the chief of Chilindi. Sangi has about fourteen huts and is exceedingly untidy, with anthills amongst the huts and rough high grass growing right up to the edge of the village. Here the lion took a woman from her door.

On February 17 in the same year I pitched my tent in this village to stay the night. At six o'clock it started to thunder and rain, and became rapidly dark. My native assistant, a very clever mission-educated man, both talking and writing English well and for whom I had a great regard, had just left me after receiving his orders. He seated himself beside the camp-fire where he started talking to my gun-bearers and some of the carriers. About fifteen minutes later I got into my hot bath, which was placed as usual in a glass shelter at the rear of my tent.

I was just drying myself when I heard a lion's roar within a few feet of me. This was at once followed by a wild outcry from my men at the camp-fire, with shouts of 'A lion! A lion!' and my tent was rushed and filled in a minute with terror-stricken men. I scrambled into pyjamas and slippers, shouting for silence and calling for all the candles and my gun. Unfortunately I had no lantern so we lit torches of dried grass torn from the inside of the hut roofs. On arriving at the place from where we had heard the lion roar, on the other side of the fire from the tent and only thirteen yards away from the tent door, we saw that a man had been taken. In the wet ground was the imprint of a man's body, in addition to the marks of the lion's paws.

The lion had been standing on a tobacco bed and had sprung upon the man as he left the fire and passed between the bed and the hut. Close by I picked up a piece of blue calico which was at once recognised as belonging to my native assistant. Some of my men shouted his name loudly in the darkness, hoping against hope that he might answer, but of course no reply came. I had just started to follow the track of the lion through some long wet grass when the rain again came down and extinguished candles and torches, leaving us in darkness. I fired two shots along the track taken by the lion as I left. There was no sleep that night for either myself or the men. The latter were terror-stricken and I, besides being horrified at the loss of my assistant, was kept awake by the talking of the men. They were sitting huddled together under the protection of my tent, firmly convinced that the lion would come back some time during the night for another victim, and they could not be assured otherwise.

At daybreak I started out with my 450 to kill the lion if I could. I was following the track through the wet grass when unfortunately one of the natives suddenly shouted out and startled the lion, which had evidently been lying eating the body quite close to the village. The place it had recently vacated was quite warm and the grass was smeared with blood with a few broken bones strewn about. On hearing the man shout the lion had evidently picked up the body and was carrying it off in front of us, but I could not get a sight of the animal owing to the long grass.

At a slight rise in the ground we found it had put the body down, and had walked round behind a tree to get a sight of its pursuers. It had then picked up the body and gone off, mounting a hill consisting of very rocky ground. As I got to the top of this hill I saw something brown quite close to me, lying amongst some bushes and weeds, and was just on the point of firing, thinking that it was the coat of the lion, when one of my gun-bearers shook me by the arm and said, 'Don't fire, it's a body.' On getting a better view I saw that the brown was the khaki-coloured uniform tunic of my native assistant.

The poor fellow was lying peacefully on his back, right arm crossing his chest, the left extended as though he were asleep. He was in no way disfigured, having been killed by a bite on the neck. His right leg was entirely eaten off by the hip, and the back of his left knee was also eaten. The lion had gone off, finding the chase too hot, and so had left the body hidden, as it thought, no doubt with the intention of returning later to complete its meal.

I left the body where it was and took up the trail again. This was now most difficult to follow, as the ground was exceedingly rocky and it was only occasionally that I could pick up a footmark here and there. I followed these as best I could for half a mile, till they led into a ravine filled with huge boulders and grass some ten feet high, and numerous thorn bushes. Wading into this and climbing a boulder then gave me some command of the sides of the ravine, this being of no great extent and sloping upwards towards the hills. I then instructed the natives, of whom there were about fourteen, including my two gun-bearers who were carrying a loaded rifle and shotgun, to beat the grass for me. But this they refused to do, in spite of threats and offers of reward, and not even the explanation that the lion wanted to escape would encourage them. The most they would do for me was to throw stones into the grass.

These people belonged to an old slave tribe called Watabwa, who are not only deficient in physical courage, but are strongly possessed of the belief that a man-eating lion contains the spirit of a dead chief, and that if this one lion is slain the spirit will divide itself among other lions, which will become man-eaters also. Thus they were really against my finding and shooting this lion, a fact I found out later. The native who shouted out had been instructed by his companions to do so, in order to warn the lion and thus prevent my killing it.

It may be interesting to relate a curious prophecy which had been made by their paramount chief, who had died a few days before the first victim was taken by this man-eater. The chief, who was an old man, had expressed himself aggrieved by being reproved by the district administration for his treatment of some of his people. On his deathbed, a few days afterwards, he told several of his headmen that he was dying, but that he would come back as a lion and revenge himself upon the people who had worried him, killing and eating them. The dead chief's prophecy was well known throughout the country, and this was no doubt influential in deterring the natives who had accompanied me from rendering any assistance in shooting this lion.

I left the animal in possession of the ravine with great reluctance, because I knew that the result of my having failed to kill it would be yet more tragedies. We then returned and picked up the body of my assistant, which we buried close to the village. I heard afterwards a lion had tried to dig it up. I have regretted ever since that I did not leave the body where I first found it amongst the rocks. If instead of trying to follow the lion I had waited until it returned, I should have had an excellent opportunity of shooting it.

For two nights the lion wandered about this village and then followed the line of hills to another village called Lambwe, where it took a boy right from the middle of the village in the afternoon, though many people were standing close by. After this it took two men in quick succession from a miserable little village called Kabemwe, close to Lambwe. The lion was next seen close to Lake Mweru again, upon the banks of the Luawo river which runs into the lake and where there are several villages close together. From one of these it took a man, following this act up promptly by taking two women and then another man from two other villages. By this time it had discovered that it was quite an easy matter to kill people whenever it wanted food, and it used to make one meal only, never returning twice to the same body. The trap-guns and poisoned meat put out for it in the various villages only succeeded in destroying leopards and hyenas.

Finding no more victims here for four days, as the natives shut themselves up in their huts early in the afternoon and did not venture out till well after sunrise the next morning, the man-eater trekked for ten miles along the road to a village called Sheriweri, five miles from Chiengi government house. Here it took a sick woman who was living in an isolated hut just outside the village who had been sitting at her hut door.

The man-eater then went up the hills, returning to Sangi, where it had killed my native assistant. Finding the natives still wary, for they had seen its pad marks one morning amongst the huts and had kept themselves well shut up, it came down again and killed a man at sunrise in the centre of the village one mile behind Chiengi station. The natives, who were all about at the time, shouted and drove it off from the body of the man who was, however, quite dead his neck having been broken by a blow from the lion's paw. The animal then travelled down the main mail road along the lake side to the Kalungwishi river, where it inaugurated a panic by taking people from village after village and even when walking along the main road, so that it became unsafe for any native to walk about towards sunset. Trap-guns put down again proved useless.

At this time I was transferred to a new district a hundred miles away. The next thing I heard of the man-eater was that it had been seen one evening just outside the government house at Chiengi. Luckily that night the servants, returning after their work to their native quarters, saw it and ran back to safety into the house. The lion, baulked of its prey, went off, in its rage pulling up some sticks which had been put in to mark the lines of a new path leading from the house to the office on the hill.

The next night it returned and, as three boys left the house, it sprang from behind some grass which had been piled for thatching purposes, taking the kitchen boy who was in the middle. It swung this boy over its shoulder by his left arm, going off towards the hills with him. One of these boys had been armed with a gun by Mr Sealy, the native commissioner at Chiengi, but he was so frightened at the sight of the lion that although he fired, and was only two yards away, he missed; this boy was an Awemba, a much braver race than the Watabwa.

The next morning the track of the lion was followed by a crowd of natives, one of whom was armed with a rifle. They found the leg of the poor boy, which had been bitten off below the knee, a few hundred yards from the place from where he had been taken. The boy had possibly been hitting the lion over the eyes with his right hand when the animal threw him down and bit off his leg, probably killing him at the same time. The track led for another three miles up the hills.

As the natives mounted the hill, the man with the rifle leading the way, they suddenly came upon the lion twenty yards away, standing over the body of its victim. The native immediately fired his rifle, and of course missed the lion, which then stole contemptuously away. It was unfortunate that these natives had started to follow the lion, for had they waited for Mr Sealy it would have been shot and in consequence several lives would have been saved. As it was, when Mr Sealy arrived at the place where the body of the boy lay, accompanied by Mr Scott of the Mbereshi Mission, they found an excited crowd of natives but the lion had already made off.

The man-eater haunted Chiengi for some time after this and then returned towards the Kalungwishi river. About a week after this last occurrence I had occasion to travel to Chiengi from my new station, in connection with the sleeping sickness work. Some twenty miles from Chiengi I stopped for lunch at a village called Tawache. While I was eating under the shade of a tree, the chief of the village came up to me saying that he had had a terrible time of it during the night with a lion, and asked me to go and see his hut. When I got there I found a large part of the wall broken down on each side of the door posts and the door loosened on its fastenings.

The chief told me that the lion had attacked his hut in the early hours of the evening and that he and a young wife with a baby had to sit and watch the work of destruction going on, having no spear or knife with which to defend themselves. Every now and again the paws of the lion would come breaking into the holes which were gradually growing larger as it was endeavouring to claw its way in through the dried mud and sticks which formed the walls of the hut. At last it got its head and one forepaw in, the hole not being sufficiently large to enable the whole of its body to pass through. The young wife then, with great presence of mind, pulled burning wood from the fire with which she hit the lion about the head, finally forcing it to retire. They spent the rest of the night in fear and trembling, unable to sleep, expecting the return of the lion at any moment. However, they were left in peace.

I advised the chief to go to a large town some miles away and borrow spears for his and his people's protection, and this advice certainly saved the lives of two other men in this village.

The following night the lion took a man from the next village a mile away. Two nights afterwards it then returned to Tawache where it had tried to break into the hut of the chief. It again tried this new game of hut-breaking to get at the people inside, but by this time the people had taken my advice and got spears. Two young men were inside the hut it attacked, and as the lion pushed its head through a hole it had torn in the wall they jabbed at it with their spears until it retired, growling with rage, carrying off one spear stuck in its neck. This spear it pulled out with its teeth as it was found a hundred yards away the next morning much damaged. The blade was of soft iron of native manufacture and had probably only penetrated the skin.

For two days after this the man-eater was neither seen nor heard of. By this time Mr Lyons of Kawamba had sent out a trusted hunter armed with a service rifle. This man also put down numerous trap-guns round these villages as well as poisoned meat. On the third day after the lion had been jabbed with the spear I was travelling back from Chiengi, and on arriving close to the village of Tawache, I came upon a large pool of fresh blood in the middle of the road close to where a trap-gun had been placed. On arriving at the village I heard that the native hunter had put down part of a dead sheep beside the trap-gun, and that the lion coming along the road had pulled at the meat with its paw and had fired the trap-gun, wounding itself badly.

The gun was an old-fashioned Snider loaded with heavy ball. The natives on hearing the gun ran out, hoping to find the man-eater dead, but though they saw it staggering away badly wounded none of them had enough courage to finish it off with spears. One of the men went off to the next village to call for the native hunter, who followed the trail of the lion for five miles to some thick bush where he was afraid to follow further. This lion was then seen no more for six weeks. We all hoped that it had died from its wound, but we were doomed to disappointment. Three people were promptly killed in quick succession from a village called Kalembwe nine miles south from Chiengi on the same road as the other villages. The people were again in despair. That it was the same lion was confirmed by several of the villagers who had seen it, its very light colour being unmistakable.

From this time onward the lion's boldness and ferocity seemed to increase. One afternoon it came into Chiengi station in broad daylight, but everyone saw it in time and took refuge. The lion then lay outside the carpenter's house for some time, growling, but did not try to break in. Another day it came into the station about five o'clock in the afternoon and was seen by some natives lying on the verandah of the office, evidently waiting for the native clerk who was working inside, to come out. It was fired at and wounded by a native armed with an old gun, and also fired at by the native commissioner, but again managed to get away.

It then left Chiengi, taking natives from time to time from other villages. A couple of weeks later it entered a village close to Chiengi in the afternoon and killed the chief and his brother, who were sitting beside a small fire on the edge of the road. Within a week of this, the lion with two others rampaged through the administrative town of Chiengi for several nights, trying to break into the houses. One night they jumped over the wall which surrounded the Commissioner's house, around which they then prowled, roaring and growling for several hours but they were unsuccessful in finding a victim.

Shortly after this latest episode Mr Lyons, the magistrate of Kawamba, paid a visit to Chiengi. He spent several nights waiting up for the lions, not succeeding in getting a sight of them even though one night while he was waiting upon his platform a man was taken and carried off from less than a hundred yards away. After this, trap-guns were put down upon every path. Strings were attached to the triggers which were stretched across the path on the chance that the lion, on entering the village by one of these paths, might touch one of the strings and discharge a gun, killing or wounding it seriously.

This plan proved to be immediately successful. During the following night two of these guns went off. One destroyed the man-eater with a shot through the ear. The other wounded a second lion on another path which managed to escape into the bush, leaving a blood trail behind it.

Naturally there was great rejoicing on the part of all the natives at the destruction of the enemy which had terrorized them for so long and had taken so many victims. It was an old lion, evidently unfitted for the active pursuit of game, but it certainly showed great intelligence and great vitality in the way it recovered from its previous wounds. In its stomach, when it was cut open, were toe and finger nails of its last victim.

It is curious that this lion should have escaped destruction so long, for besides the occasions I have already indicated when it was fired at, it was once also missed by an ex-sergeant of police, in broad daylight, a short distance away from a stockaded camp. As soon as the shot was fired the lion made off into the bush uninjured. This man was armed with a 303 rifle and, had he had the sense to refrain from firing and to call to Mr Sealy, the native commissioner, who was actually sitting in his tent at the time, many subsequent victims might have been saved.

II. The Tigress of Iyenpur

A generation earlier there were similar man-eater stricken communities in south-central India where G P Sanderson was a government officer at Mysore.

When I pitched camp at Morlay in September 1873, to commence the elephant kheddahs, the countryside was in a state of considerable alarm from the attacks of a man-eating tigress. This tigress's fits of man-eating seemed to be intermittent as, after killing three or four persons some months before, she had not been heard of till about the time of my arrival at Morlay, when she killed two boys attending goats. I anticipated some trouble from her in our kheddah work, as it would be unsafe for one or two men to go alone through the jungles. But whether it was from the disturbance caused by seven or eight hundred people at work, or other reasons, we heard nothing of her for some time.

On November 30th, when the work people had dispersed, news was brought in that a man, returning to the village of Nagwully (about six miles from Morlay) with cattle, had been carried off the evening before. From an account of the place where the mishap had occurred I knew it was useless to look for the tigress after a lapse of eighteen hours, as she would have retired to impracticable jungle. I urged the people to bring news of further losses at the earliest possible moment.

On December 19th another man was carried off close to the village of Iyenpur, five miles from Morlay, and I took an elephant and some trackers in hopes of learning something of the tigress's habits. The unfortunate victim's wife, with her three small children, were brought to me as I entered the village. The woman, with the strange apathy of a hindu, related what she knew of her husband's death without a tear. I gave her some money as, before she would be admitted into her caste's villages, she would have to expend a small sum, in accordance with caste usage, to rid herself of the devil on account of her husband being killed by a tiger. Then, accompanied by the headman and others, I went to the scene of the last disaster.

A solitary tamarind tree grew on some rocks close to the village. There was no jungle within three hundred yards, only a few bushes in the crevices of the rocks. Close by was a broad cattle track into the village. The unfortunate man had been following the cattle home in the evening, and must have stopped to knock down some tamarinds with his stick which, together with his black blanket and a skin skull-cap, still lay where he was seized. The tigress had been hiding in the rocks and in one bound had seized him and dragged him to the edge of a small plateau of rock, from which she jumped down into a field below, and there killed him. The place was still marked by a pool of dried blood. She had then dragged her victim half a mile to a spot where we found his leg bones.

After searching about for two hours with the trackers in the hopes of seeing recent marks of the tigress, but without success, the village cattle were sent for and herded into the jungles in the hope of attracting her, if she were near. The poor beasts were, however, so frightened by the constant attacks of tigers that we could scarcely get them to face the jungle, and a partridge rising suddenly was too much for their nerves and sent them, tails up, to the village before they had been out half an hour. After some time they were got back. About 1 p.m., as they were feeding near a cover in a hollow encircled on three sides by low hills covered with bamboo, a wild scurry took place as a large tiger rushed amongst the foremost of them. Strange to say they all escaped, two only being slightly wounded; a few plucky buffaloes were in advance, and interfered considerably with the tiger's attack, as these animals never hesitate to do.

Up to this time I had been walking, rifle in hand, amongst the cattle, but the heat was considerable, and at this unlucky moment I was some little distance behind getting a drink, or I might have had a shot. As the herdsmen were not certain that the tiger had not secured something in his rush, we went in force to look through the cover. We only found footprints, however, and knew they were not those of the man-eater, but of a large male who was a well-known cattle-killer about the place. We shortly heard a spotted-deer bark over the saddle of the hill to our left; the tiger had moved off in that direction. We saw nothing more of him that day, nor of the man-eater, and I returned to camp by moonlight. It was so cold that I was glad of an overcoat. A good camp Christmas dinner was awaiting me and, had I only been lucky enough to bag the man-eater, I should have been able to enter this amongst my red-letter days.

After this nothing was heard of the tigress for a week, until the trackers and I were going to look after some wild elephants, and at the ford in the river below the Koombappan temple we found a tiger's pugs which were immediately pronounced to be hers. I sent back two men on my riding-elephant to warn the people of Morlay that the tigress was again in our jungles, as her usual hunting-grounds were to the east of the river, and the people on our side were liable to be off their guard. We tried to follow her, but she had crossed open dry country, in which tracking was impossible, and we had to give her up. During the day I made arrangements for hunting her systematically next day should she still be in our jungles.

Whilst at dinner that evening, I heard voices and saw torches hurriedly approaching my tent, and could distinguish the words *naie* and *nurrie* (dog and jackal) pronounced excitedly. The Canarese people frequently speak of a tiger by these names, partly in assumed contempt, partly from superstitious fear. The word *hooli* (tiger) is not often used amongst jungle-men, in the same way that, from dread, natives usually refer to cholera by the general terms of *roga* or *jardya* (sickness).

The people were from Hurdenhully, a village a mile and a half away, and had come to tell me that their cattle had galloped back in confusion into the village at dusk, without their herdsman. Only one man had been with them that day as there was some festival in the village. We suspected he had fallen a victim to the tigress, but it was useless to attempt a search that night. The cattle had been two or three miles into the jungles, and we had no indications where to look for the unfortunate herdsman who now was probably half devoured. So ordering some rice for the men, I sent them to Morlay to tell the trackers, and to sleep there and return with them in the morning.

At dawn we started on the back-trail of the cattle from Hurdenhully till we found the point where they had begun to gallop, just below the embankment of a small channel drawn from the river near Atticulpur, and supplying the Hurdenhully tank with water. The ground was hard and much trodden by cattle and we looked for some time for the tigress's tracks in vain, till the distant caw of a crow attracted us to the place where we found the man's remains. Only the soles of his feet, the palms of his hands, his head and a few bones were left. We lost no time in taking up the tigress's track, and used every endeavour to run her down, as we had over a hundred men ready at camp to beat her out could we but mark her into some practicable cover. But, though she had eaten much, she had recrossed the river as usual and had gone into the jungles towards the hills where there was no chance of finding her.

About a week after this the priest of a small temple ten miles due west from Morlay was jogging along on his riding bullock one morning and in comparatively open country where a tiger had not been heard of for years. He was on his way to sweep out and garnish the small jungle temple in which he officiated, and to present to 'Yennay Hollay Koombappah' the offerings of the simple villagers whose faith was placed in that deity. Suddenly a tigress with her cub stepped into the path. The terrified bullock kicked off his rider and galloped back to the village, whilst the tigress – for it was the Iyenpur man-eater, far out of her ordinary haunts – seized the hapless priest, and carried him off to the bed of a deep ravine near.

Upon hearing next day of this my men and I thought it must be some other tiger, as the man-eater had managed with such cunning up until then that we did not know that she had a cub. It was not till we found this out subsequently that we traced this death to her also. Up to this time she must have left her cub in the thick jungles along the hills, making her rapid hunting forays alone, as the cub had never been with her. This accounted for her invariably crossing the river and making for the hills after a raid. The absence of the tigress from the vicinity of Morlay during September and October was probably caused partly by her keeping out of the way when this cub was very young.

The next death was of a horrible description. Several villagers of Ramasamudrum were grazing their cattle in a swampy hollow in the jungle near the temple, when the tigress pounced upon one man who was separated from the others. She in some way missed her aim at his throat, seized the shoulder and then, either in jerking him, or by a blow, threw him up onto a thicket several feet from the ground. Here the wounded and bleeding wretch was caught by thorny creepers, whilst the tigress, as generally happens when any contretemps takes place, relinquished the attack and made off. The other men and the cattle had fled at the first alarm. The village was some distance away and there was not time before nightfall for a party to search for the man, who was not known to be still alive.

Next morning the lacerated wretch was found. In his mangled state he had been unable to release himself. He was moaning and hanging almost head downwards amongst the creepers and he died soon after he was taken down.

Before long the tigress visited my camp, but fortunately without doing any mischief. Close to my tent (my bungalow was not built then) was a large banyan tree. Every night a fire was kindled near it and here I sat and discussed plans for work or sport with my men. One morning when the trackers came to wake me early, they found the man-eater's tracks leading down a path close to the banyan tree in question. As we thought she might still be on our side of the river, I accompanied the men to examine the vicinity and to ascertain if she had recrossed it towards the hills. If not, we intended to hunt the different covers on its banks during the day.

Upon reaching the river we walked down the sandy bed overshadowed by drooping Indian beech trees. The scene at early morning was very pleasant. Gaudy kingfishers fluttered and poised over the pools and shallow runs of clear water into which the river, which was a considerable stream in the rains, had now shrunk. At a bend we came upon a troop of lungoor monkeys feeding upon some fallen fruit, running nimbly across the sand to the sanctuary of the large trees when we appeared. In one stretch a spotted stag and several graceful hinds were drinking at the cool stream. The cooing of doves, the scream of a toucan, and the cheery and game cry of a jungle-cock completed the tranquil scene.

The trackers moved quickly and silently along. We passed two or three pugs, but these elicited no notice, except one into which Dod Sidda drove the butt-end of his spear without a word. This was the night's track of the tigress to our side of the river. We had nearly got to the temple, below which it was not likely she would have crossed, and were in hopes of not finding her out-going trail, when a single track across an unblemished stretch of sand caused an exclamation of disappointment, and one glance showed it to be the unmistakable small oval pug of the man-eater. We felt our chances of finding her that day were very small, but there was nothing like trying; so sending for an elephant to come to the temple and there await my return, we cast ahead towards the hills and again hit off the trail.

After several hours' work, now and then finding tracks in the sandy beds of ravines but all leading to a country where the cover was continuous, we were obliged to give it up as useless as we could neither keep the trail, nor have done anything about driving such extensive cover had we even found where the tigress lay hidden. We were forced reluctantly to return, consoling ourselves with the hope of finding her in more favourable country soon and vowing to leave no stone unturned till we bagged her. It had become quite a point of honour with the trackers. They had never been played such successful tricks before by any animal and said the tigress was 'throwing dirt into their mouths'.

We got back to the temple late in the afternoon. Here I found the elephant and several of my people, and a man with a note from a captain of the Revenue Survey who was in camp a few miles from Morlay. I started the messenger back with a reply, and though we were pretty certain the man-eater was miles away, it was a nervous job for him to get through the jungle till he reached open country on the far side. He left us, already casting furtive glances around him, to the great amusement of my men (who had not the job to do themselves).

Before he had got far, one of them, who was a bit of a humorist, called him back. The man came, when the wag, assuming a concerned air, said: 'Keep a good look-out ahead of you - never mind the rear; if the tiger seizes you from behind, you can't do anything about it anyway. But you can see her if she is coming for you from the front, and you might try a run for it. Good-bye! Koombappah be with you! And don't delay, it's rather late as it is!' The poor villager grinned painfully at the joke, which the rest enjoyed immensely. But I saw he was in such a fright that I sent half-a-dozen men (the joker amongst them) to see him safely into the cultivated country on the other side.

Shortly after this work took me to Goondulpet, twenty-five miles from Morlay on the Nilgiri road, and I returned on the 14th January 1874. As I rode into camp about midday the trackers were waiting for me, and informed me that they had heard the 'death-cry' raised at a small village called Bussavanpur below the Ramasamudrum lake, some two miles from Morlay, that morning. On inquiry they found a woman had been carried off by the man-eater out of the village during the night, but that they had not followed the tracks as I was not with them.

Bussavanpur was a small hamlet situated in the middle of open rice fields, then bare as the crop had been cut. There was no jungle to cover the man-eater's advance and a tiger had never hitherto been heard of near the village. This attack was therefore all the more terrifying to the villagers.

Immediately breakfast was over and an elephant ready I started and soon reached Bussavanpur. The attack had been most daring. At one end of the single street of the village stood a shady tree round the base of which a raised terrace of stones and earth had been built as a public seat; within ten yards of this tree the houses began. From the marks we saw that the tigress had crouched upon this raised terrace from which she commanded a view of the street. The nearest house on one side was occupied by an old woman, the one opposite by her married daughter. The old woman, it appeared, sometimes slept in her own house, sometimes at her daughter's. The night before she had been going to her daughter's and as she crossed the street, only a few feet wide, the tigress with one silent bound seized and carried her off. No one heard any noise and the poor old creature was not missed till morning.

When I arrived the son-in-law came forward, and with the other villagers gave an account of the mishap. The son-in-law's grief was really painful to witness and, when he told me how all his efforts to find any trace of his mother-in-law had been unsuccessful, he gave way to the most poignant outbursts. Now, knowing pretty well how little store is placed upon an old woman in India, I could not but regard this display of feeling by the fat young son-in-law as rather strange. A mother-in-law is not usually so highly esteemed that her loss is deemed an irreparable calamity. When I further noted that the afflicted youth could only give a shaky account of his exertions in looking for the body, I thought something was wrong and had him taken along with us.

The tigress had gone towards the river. Though cattle and people had been over the fields, and it was now afternoon with the sun hot and a strong wind blowing clouds of dust about, the trackers carried on the trail very cleverly, pointing out that several footmarks had followed it before us, for which the prostrated son-in-law found some difficulty in accounting.

After passing through a field of standing rice in which the broad trail was very distinct and where in the soft mud we got a fair impression of the tigress's pugs, and through some bushes where strips of the woman's blue cotton cloth were hanging, we came to a coconut garden near the river and here, amongst some aloe bushes, we lost the drag. There was a place which looked as if the tigress had lain down, probably to eat as there were marks of blood, but there were no remains. Her trail continued across the river, which we followed.

The trackers soon thought something was amiss, as no trace of the body being dragged could be found. One of them remarked that the tigress would hardly eat the whole at once and, had she carried off the remainder in her jaws, she must have had to lay it down at the pool in the sandy bed where she had drunk. There was no trace of her having done this. We returned to the aloe bushes. After examining these for some time one of the men looked inside a thicket. With an exclamation, he then turned upon the son-in-law and demanded 'what he meant by it'. 'It' was what the villagers had followed along the track with horns and tomtoms earlier that morning (as we subsequently learned). They had burnt the woman's remains to avoid a police inquiry, the dejected son-in-law acting as chief mourner. The ashes of a fire which the tracker now pointed to inside the thicket sufficiently explained the affair.

The woman was of good caste. Had her death been reported, the remains would have been handled by out-castes, and have formed the subject of a sort of inquest by the police at Chamraj-Nuggar. To avoid this, the relatives had burnt the remainder of the body as soon as it was found. What could be done when foolish villagers either brought us news too late, or acted in this way? We sent the chastened son-in-law back to the village, and finding that the tigress had gone east we returned to Morlay, it being useless to follow her in that direction.

This latest death caused great consternation. The villagers concluded that they would now not be safe in their houses at night and some of the outlying hamlets were likely to be temporarily abandoned if the tigress lived much longer. But our chances of killing her seemed still as remote as ever.

Next day, the 15th January, I determined upon a more organised plan of hunting her. I arranged that Bommay Gouda and three trackers should go to Iyenpur, at one end of the tiger's usual range, while I remained at Morlay. In case of any one being killed near Iyenpur the men were to let me know immediately; and I supplied them with strychnine, and a gun charged with powder, as a safeguard in their jungle wanderings. The four men started early in the afternoon.

About an hour afterwards one of them came running back, pouring with perspiration and covered with dust. I feared some accident had happened until he found breath to say that the party had met the tigress, and that she was then in Karraypoor Guddah, a small hill two miles from camp. This hill rose to a height of about two hundred feet out of a level cultivated plain. On three sides the hill was almost bare granite, a few bushes and boulders being the only cover, and the country was open all round it. On the east face there was a little more cover, and the main jungle was distant five hundred yards. But between it and the hill was open ground, so that the tigress was in an isolated position.

I ordered a pad-elephant at once, whilst I thought over the best plan for hunting her. Such a chance as getting her into a detached hill could hardly be hoped for again, and the present situation offered a fine opportunity. The only alternatives were to drive her out or to watch for her return to the carcass. The first I saw could not do, as all the Morlay men (the only ones amongst the villagers who would have been useful for this service as the others were too terrified), were at their fields, and time would be lost in collecting them. Though possibly the tigress might have been driven out, as there was no doubt she would flee readily from a hunting-party, it would be impossible for one rifle to command the entire east side of the hill, at any point of which she might break. I therefore decided to watch for her return to the carcass and, hastily securing a bottle of water and some bread, and an overcoat in case of night-watching, I started out. On the way the tracker told me how the party had met the tigress. They were going across open fields and saw an object moving over the bare ground which they could not at first make out, but presently discovered to be a tiger on the far side of, and partly hidden by, a bullock, which it was half dragging, half carrying towards the hill. They immediately realised it was the man-eater, and ran shouting towards her, forcing her to drop the bullock at the foot of the hill, up which she then trotted. One tracker then hastened to camp; the others remaining to prevent her returning to the bullock before I arrived.

When we got near the hill we left the elephant and joined the trackers. The only cover near the carcass was a large rock, but the wind was wrong for watching from that quarter. About seventy yards away in the plain was one solitary bush, not sufficiently large to hide a man. Otherwise there was neither tree nor other cover within a couple of hundred yards. The situation certainly presented difficulties and it was not easy to decide what to do. Eventually I sent the men to bring leafy branches and creepers which we walked past the bush in a body, onto which the branches were thrown to make it larger. At the same time Bommay Gouda and I hid behind it, the others going on in full view from the hill. By this manoeuvre, should the tigress be watching, she would not perceive that we had concealed ourselves.

We sat till evening. The sinking sun threw a long light from behind us upon the granite hill, whilst in the distance the Billiga-runguns were bathed in purple light, deepening to blue in the gorges. The smoke of evening fires began to ascend from the small hamlet of Hebsur away to our left, and a thick white cloud of dust moving slowly along the riverbank towards the village marked the return homewards of the village herds. There would only be sufficient light to shoot at so long a range as seventy yards for half an hour or more, and I was beginning to fear the tigress might not return during daylight.

The afternoon had been hot and I had drunk all the water in the bottle, whilst patient Bommay Gouda, who being of good caste could not drink from my bottle, had sat with his bare back exposed to the grilling sun, watching without a movement. In January at this time of the year the change in temperature in Mysore and, in fact, the whole of India, is very considerable between day and night, sometimes upwards of thirty degrees, and as the sun neared the horizon the evening quickly became chilly. A couple of hares appeared from somewhere and gambolled in the space between us and the hill. A peacock perched himself upon a rock, and with his spreading fan of purple and gold opened to the full, turned slowly round and round, courting the admiration of a group of hens who pecked about more intent upon their evening meal.

We had been whispering quietly, as we were out of earshot of the cover, and after a glance at the sinking sun, Bommay Gouda had just said that it was the time, par excellence, for a tiger's return to its prey, when a peahen which had been hidden amongst boulders on the hillside to our right, rose with a startling clamour. This unmistakable signal made us glance through the leafy screen. There we saw the man-eater. She was a handsome but small tigress, her colour doubly rich in the light of the sinking sun. She walked from behind a rock across the side of the hill, here a bare sheet of blue granite, and came downwards towards the carcass. She halted now and again to look far out into the plain behind us.

I followed her with my rifle so eagerly that Bommay Gouda whispered to me to let her get to the carcass before I fired. When she reached the bullock she stopped. At the same instant I fired at her shoulder, broadside on, with my express. Bommay Gouda could contain himself no longer and jumped up before I could stop him; I did so also, but could see no tigress! It was extraordinary, but we looked up the hillside and she was not there. She had vanished seemingly into thin air. Just then up went a tail on the far side of the bullock in a convulsive quiver; she had fallen exactly behind the carcass.

I ran along the hillside to intercept her should she gain her feet, but it was all right. She was only opening her mouth in spasmodic gasps, and I settled her. The trackers came up in great glee. They had seen the tigress come over the summit of the hill and enter the rocks on our side half an hour before we saw her: they were in a large tamarind tree away in the plain. On examining her we found that she was in milk, which was the first intimation we had that she had a cub; she was in the prime of life and condition, and had no lameness or apparent injury to account for her having taken to man-killing.

We soon had the tigress padded (after the trackers had beaten her with their slippers and abused her in dreadful terms). As our way to Morlay lay through Hebsur, a messenger started off in advance with the news. Before we had gone far we were met by almost the whole community of Hebsur, with torches and tomtoms, who begged us to parade the tigress through the village. The women and children were delighted, though half terrified, at the sight of her. They had never seen a tiger before, there being no Zoological Gardens handy in India. The creature was only known as a fearful beast which had eaten papa or mamma or sons or daughters. Soondargowry, the elephant, was fed with cakes, balls of sugar, rice and plantains by the pleased housewives. She seemed to enjoy herself, though at first the torches and shouts made her rather nervous, especially as this was the first tiger she had carried and she had been a wild animal herself not long before.

On the way to Morlay beyond Hebsur we entered an extensive stretch of rice fields, then dry and the crops cut on the ground, below the Ramasamudrum lake. Ordinarily fires were kept up at the threshing floors and much merriment went on all night; but the dread of the tigress latterly had been so great that all was quiet and apparently deserted. Not a fire was to be seen nor a voice heard. Dotted about the plain were large trees which we knew sheltered the anxious watchers of the threshing floors below. We had brought torches and men from Hebsur and, after much calling that the tigress had been shot, voices were at last heard from different trees, lights began to appear, and watchers came from all directions, some shouting to us from the distance to let them come up and see the 'dog'.

I was struck at the quick return of everything to its old groove after this. Instead of small bodies of people hurrying fearfully homewards early in the afternoon and not a villager visible after five o'clock, as had lately been the case, odd villagers now used the path past camp after dusk, and the rice fields were again the scene of work and harvest merry-making. There was little doubt that the tigress was the man-eater, though we could not be positive of this, as there were several tigers about. I was relieved, therefore, as time progressed, to find that all killing ceased.

It will be years before the recollection of the Iyenpur tigress is lost in that part of the country.

III. An Uninvited Guest

Not every attempt to end a man-eater's activities is successful. All involve danger and require knowledge and skill if the quarry is not to escape or even turn the tables on its pursuers. An unsuccessful and ultimately tragic attempt by inexperienced hunters to kill a man-eating lion, which had succeeded in bringing all construction work to a halt on the Uganda railway in 1898, was related by the railway's supervising engineer, J H Patterson, and two of the hunters involved.

Towards the end of my stay in British East Africa [included modern-day Kenya], I dined one evening with Mr Ryall, the superintendent of police, in his inspection carriage on the railway. As we dined I little thought then what a terrible fate was to overtake Ryall only a few months later in that very carriage.

A man-eating lion had taken up his quarters at a little roadside station called Kimaa, and had developed an extraordinary taste for the members of the railway staff. He was a most daring brute, quite indifferent as to whether he carried off the station master, the signalman, or the pointsman. One night, in his efforts to obtain a meal, he actually climbed up onto the roof of the station buildings and tried to tear off the corrugated iron sheets. At this the terrified Indian in charge of the telegraph instrument below sent the following laconic message to the traffic manager: 'Lion fighting with station. Send urgent succour.'

Fortunately the lion was not victorious in his fight with the station, but he tried so hard to get in that he cut his feet badly on the iron sheeting, leaving large bloodstains on the roof. Another night, however, he succeeded in carrying off the native driver of the pumping engine, and soon afterwards added several other victims to his list. On one occasion an engine-driver arranged to sit up all night in a large iron water-tank in the hope of getting a shot at him, and had a loop-hole cut in the side of the tank from which to fire. But as so often happens, the hunter became the hunted: the lion turned up in the middle of the night, overthrew the tank and actually tried to drag the driver out through the narrow circular hole in the top through which he had squeezed in. Fortunately the tank was just too deep for the brute to be able to reach the man at the bottom, but the latter was naturally half paralysed with fear and had to crouch so low down as to be unable to take anything like proper aim. He fired, however, and succeeded in frightening the lion away for the time being.

It was in a vain attempt to destroy this pest that Ryall met his tragic and untimely end. On June 6, 1900, he was travelling up in his inspection carriage from Makindu to Nairobi, accompanied by two friends, Mr Huebner and Mr Parenti. When they reached Kimaa, which is about two hundred and fifty miles from Mombasa, they were told that the man-eater had been seen close to the station only a short time before their train arrived, so they at once made up their minds to remain there for the night and endeavour to shoot him.

Ryall's carriage was accordingly detached from the train and shunted into a siding close to the station where, owing to the unfinished state of the line, it did not stand perfectly level, but had a pronounced list to one side. In the afternoon the three friends went out to look for the lion, but finding no traces of him whatever, they returned to the carriage for dinner. Afterwards they all sat up on guard for some time. The one noticeable thing they saw was what they took to be two very bright and steady glow-worms. Later events proved that these could have been nothing else than the eyes of the man-eater steadily watching them all the time and studying their every movement.

The hour now growing late, and there being apparently no sign of the lion, Ryall persuaded his two friends to lie down, while he kept the first watch. Huebner occupied the high berth over the table on the one side of the carriage, the only other berth being on the opposite side of the compartment and lower down. This Ryall offered to Parenti, who declined it, saying that he would be quite comfortable on the floor and he accordingly lay down to sleep, with his feet towards the sliding door which gave admission to the carriage.

It is supposed that Ryall, after watching for some considerable time, must have come to the conclusion that the lion was not going to make its appearance that night, for he lay down on the lower berth and dozed off. No sooner had he retired than the man-eater began cautiously to stalk the three sleepers. In order to reach the little platform at the end of the carriage, he had to mount two very high steps from the railway line, but these he managed to negotiate successfully and in silence. The door from this platform into the carriage was a sliding one on wheels, which ran very easily on a brass runner; and as it was probably not quite shut, or at any rate not secured in any way, it was an easy matter for the lion to thrust in a paw and shove it open. But owing to the tilt of the carriage and to his great extra weight on the one side, the door slid to and snapped into the lock the moment he got his body right in, thus leaving him shut up with the three sleeping men in the compartment.

He sprang at once at Ryall, but in order to reach him had actually to plant his feet on Parenti who, it will be remembered, was sleeping on the floor. Parenti later vividly recalled this moment: 'I was awakened from a sound sleep by the sensation of a weight holding me down on the floor, and for a moment was unable to move. Then the weight was taken off me and I raised my head with a jerk. My face immediately came in contact with a soft hairy body, and I became conscious of a disagreeable smell. In an instant I realised that there was a lion in the railway carriage, and that at that moment it was killing poor Mr Ryall, as I heard a sort of gurgling noise, the only sound he ever made.'

At this moment Huebner was suddenly awakened, and on looking down from his berth was horrified to see an enormous lion standing with his hind feet on Parenti's body, while his forepaws rested on poor Ryall. Small wonder that he was panic-stricken at the sight. 'The situation was terrible' Huebner related later. 'I saw the brute at arm's length on Ryall's bed. Violently he grabbed the sleeping man - a cry - and this was the end of my friend! The right paw hit the left side of the head; the teeth sank deep into the chest, near the left armpit. Everything was deadly quiet for the next few seconds. The lion then dragged the body off the bed and deposited it on the floor of the carriage.'

There was only one possible way of escape and that was through the second sliding door communicating with the servants' quarters, which was opposite to that by which the lion had entered. In order to reach this door Huebner had literally to jump onto the man-eater's back, for its great bulk filled up all the space beneath his berth. It sounds scarcely credible, but it appears that in the excitement and horror of the moment he actually did this, and fortunately the lion was too busily engaged with his victim to pay any attention to him.

Huebner managed to reach the door in safety but there, to his dismay, he found that it was held fast on the other side by the terrified Indians, who had been aroused by the disturbance caused by the lion's entrance. In utter desperation he made frantic efforts to open it, and exerting all his strength at last managed to pull it back sufficiently far to allow him to squeeze through, when the trembling Indians instantly tied it up again with their turbans. A moment afterwards a great crash was heard, and the whole carriage lurched violently to one side; the lion had broken through one of the windows, carrying off poor Ryall with him.

Being now released, Parenti lost no time in jumping through the window on the opposite side of the carriage and fled for refuge to one of the station buildings. His escape was little short of miraculous, having had the lion actually standing on him as he lay on the floor. The carriage itself was badly shattered, and the woodwork of the window had been broken to pieces by the passage of the lion as he sprang through with his victim in his mouth.

All that can be hoped is that poor Ryall's death was instantaneous. His remains were found next morning about a quarter of a mile away in the bush and were taken to Nairobi for burial. I am glad to be able to add that very shortly afterwards the animal which was responsible for this awful tragedy was caught in an ingenious trap constructed by one of the railway staff and then shot.

CHAPTER TWO

Machans and a Boa Constrictor

IMMEDIATELY AFTER A KILL, a man-eater will usually consume only part of its victim, returning again to the scene later to resume feeding. This pattern of behaviour affords a hunter an opportunity to meet up with the animal. In the jungle a platform or machan is then built in a tree conveniently close to the remains, from where the hunter hopes to get an opportunity of a shot at the man-eater on its return.

This is the theory.

I. The Jerangau Man-eater

The habitat of the Indian tiger includes the countries of south-east Asia bordering on the Bay of Bengal. This account of a man-eater in the Malaysian jungle, by a government officer in 1951, illustrates how even the most painstaking care and patience needed for the pursuit of the man-eater is often thwarted by the concern of the relatives for the human victim's remains and their misguided attempts to help.

Jerangau is the name of a small riverside village, fifteen miles inland from Dungun. On the opposite bank of the Dungun river, but three miles downstream from Jerangau, lies Kampong Wau, *kampong* being the Malay word for village. Yet a further three miles towards the river's mouth is Kampong Manchis on the same side of the river as Jerangau. It was over the area bounded by these three small Malay villages, which are all dependent for their livelihood on the surrounding rubber plantations, that the Jerangau man-eater ranged during the latter part of 1950 and the first half of 1951.

There are three ways of reaching Jerangau from Dungun. The first is to go by river. In a reliable motor boat this takes three-and-a-half hours if you do not strike a sandbank or sunken log and so damage the propeller of your craft. By taking the second or third way a saving of half an hour can be effected, if luck is on your side. In both cases you start the journey by making use of the light railway which follows the course of the river to the local iron mine, but descend from the train at a halt called Padang Pulut. From Padang Pulut, which is almost opposite Kampong Manchis, there are two alternatives - to go upstream in a dugout canoe, or to cross the river and walk the six miles to Jerangau through rubber and jungle. I am quite certain which of these two is quicker: it is always the one which you decide not to take on that particular day.

My house at Kemaman was three hours by road south of Dungun, so that I could not possibly get to Jerangau until at least six hours after the news of a death from a man-eater had reached me. Add the time taken for the kill to be reported at Jerangau, for a man from Jerangau to go to the nearest telephone (at Padang Pulut six miles away) and for the message to be transmitted to me in Kemaman, and it will be appreciated that a delay of eight hours, at the very least, must elapse before I could be on the man-eater's trail. Luckily, I was visiting Dungun on duty when some of the kills took place. On these occasions a considerable part of the delay was avoided. Communist terrorists, reported at irregular intervals as having been in the Jerangau district, constituted a threat which had to be ignored, although we did what we could to be on our guard against them.

The death of the man-eater's first victim was not reported to me. Nor did I hear of the second death until it was too late to do anything about it. This second victim was a Malay killed on the bank of the Dungun river between Jerangau and Kampong Wau on the 12th July 1950. Local Malays asserted that two tigers fed from the body. So few of them understand that a tiger's front paws are much larger than the hind paws, however, that they frequently believe that two tigers have left the pugs, although these have actually been made by the same animal. Two tigers may have been at work on that occasion; that I cannot say, but I do know that the Jerangau man-eater killed his remaining victims, and fed from them, alone.

The Malay in question had walked from Kampong Wau to Jerangau to visit relatives. His failure to complete the return journey at first caused no alarm, as his wife thought that he was still at Jerangau, while the relatives whom he had visited knew that he had gone back to Kampong Wau. Consequently his disappearance was not discovered until the third day. The search-party which then set out soon found his knife lying on the river bank. Approaching this spot were the man's footprints; following them, and superimposed on them in places, were the pugs of a large tiger. A blood-stained sarong was found inside the jungle at right angles to the river at a spot two hundred yards from the knife. The remains, bearing little likeness to the man as he had been known, were discovered some four hundred yards further on.

That night the tiger, following the path along which the search party had returned with their burden, approached close to Kampong Wau before giving up his search for that which he had left lying in the jungle. This habit of trying to find out where their kill has been taken is, I think, one of the most ghoulish things about man-eating tigers.

From the details given me by the acting Penghulu of Jerangau, it was evident that this was not an attack resulting from a chance encounter, but a deliberate stalk and kill. I therefore instructed him to warn his people to be on their guard and to go about in groups of not less than three people. This advice, heeded at first, was soon forgotten. Another Malay, this time a rubber tapper, was killed on the 27th January 1951. In this case the body was recovered with only one leg eaten. Again I learnt of the death too late to reach the spot in time to attempt to follow up the tiger.

The man-eater soon struck again, on the morning of the 1st February 1951, and this time there occurred the first of the series of exasperating incidents which were to dog my efforts to kill this tiger. Work connected with the activities of communist terrorists had taken me far up the Dungun river. While returning by boat

I passed Kampong Wau, in which the fourth victim had lived, just before noon on the 1st February 1951. I noticed a number of people gathered on the river bank. Concluding that, as it was a Friday, they were going to the mosque, and having much on my mind, I overcame my inclination to stop and went on downstream. Had I halted, as I intended to do when I first saw those Malays, I would have had my first real opportunity to go after the tiger. When I saw them they were actually awaiting the return of the party of men which had gone off to look for the body.

It became clear at this stage that not only would this tiger almost certainly kill again, but that unless I could obtain early news of the next death and, preferably, arrive at the spot before the body was moved, I would have little chance to deal with him. As a result, instructions were issued to the acting Penghulu to impress upon the local Malays and Chinese the need to report the next death at once. The officer-in-charge of the Dungun police district, H K Batchelor, made similar arrangements with the Malay police officer in charge at Jerangau.

Nothing more was heard of the man-eater for over a month until, on the 7th March 1951, he killed his fifth man, another Malay rubber tapper. I happened to be in Dungun when the news was received there and set off at once by motor boat for Jerangau with great hopes of arriving at the spot before the body was moved. Half-way up the river, however, we met another motor boat towing a smaller craft. In this was the body of the dead man. Whilst changing the clothes on the body – I needed the blood-stained ones for a scheme that I had in mind – I saw that the tiger had killed in the usual manner, seizing the unfortunate Malay from behind by the face and shoulder and sinking his teeth into the neck. I also noticed from the wounds that the man-eater's lower right canine tooth was either missing or broken.

From enquiries which I made on arriving at Jerangau, I learnt that I would have little chance of finding any clear pugs, as at least sixty men had joined in the search for the body. At this stage, it should be realized, I did not know whether the man-eater was a tiger or a tigress, or anything else about it. I could learn a great deal from an examination of its footprints. It was for this reason that I asked first to be shown where the man had been killed. From this spot a great newly-trampled track went off into the jungle where the villagers had followed the drag. I began to cast round for the place from which the tiger had launched its attack. I had to exercise a great deal of patience while innumerable people pointed to the huge trampled track (as though I could not see it) and repeatedly said, 'He went that way, Tuan, and not where you are looking'.

At last my search was rewarded and I was able to piece together what had happened. The tiger had been coming down through the jungle where it bordered the rubber estate, when it had heard or caught sight of the Malay. The man had finished his tapping and was engaged in collecting the liquid rubber from the cups fastened to the trees. After watching him for a while, the tiger crept out among the rubber trees, belly to ground, as a cat will stalk a bird, until it gained a position behind a rotting fallen tree. There it crouched hidden from view. It waited a while in the hope that the unsuspecting man would come closer. Then, as it saw its victim turn back from the last tree of a row, it launched its attack.

A tiger depends on surprise and his terrific initial speed when making a kill in such circumstances. In the soft ground just behind the fallen tree, I found the two deep impressions made by the tiger's hind paws as they thrust it forward at its prey. The man-eater had covered the ground between it and the man in two great bounds. A companion working a short distance away had heard a terrible cry of fear followed by a snarling roar from the tiger – then silence. Try as I might I could find no pugs sufficiently clear to tell me what I wanted to know about the tiger.

Following the wide track made by the searchers, I saw that the man-eater had taken the body into the jungle at the edge of the estate and had then dragged it about three-quarters of a mile before entering a swamp. This was a gloomy place, through which one walked in half-light, in six inches to two feet of water. Visibility was limited to a bare five yards in the clearer parts of this swamp. On my way I noticed, embedded in a small mound of mud which protruded from the water, a small white chip of what I took to be wood. Picking this up on my return journey, I found it to be a portion of human shin bone, indicating that the man-eater had paused to feed at that spot. The point where the body had been found had little to distinguish it from the rest of the swamp, except that a great deal of the surrounding undergrowth had been cut down as a precautionary measure. Apart from being thoroughly uninviting, it was a poor place in which to try to set the stage for the tiger's destruction.

Going on a little alone into the swamp, where the search-party had not penetrated, I found three clear pugs on a piece of firm soil. These told me that the tiger was a fully-grown male, with exceptionally large fore paws. The individual toes of the hind paws were unusually pointed, being almost triangular in shape. I knew that I would recognise them again anywhere. Leaving the swamp, I followed the path along which the body had been carried back to Jerangau, searching for a suitable tree in which to place the small portable seat which I used for shooting tigers at night.

Rubber trees, with their sparse foliage, are never satisfactory places in which to attempt to conceal oneself. In this case I was forced to select a large tree the overhanging boughs of which were likely to obstruct my view when it came to quick shooting in the dark. When Pa Mat had climbed the tree and I had passed my seat up for him to fasten in position as a machan, I turned to the dead man's bloodstained clothes. With the aid of some dry leaves and grass, I constructed from them an imitation corpse which I arranged on the ground in front of the tree. I hoped that, if the man-eater did decide to follow the body back to the kampong, he must come across this dummy. If he paused to smell at it he should give me a chance to get a shot at him.

I took my place in the tree a good two hours before sunset, sending Pa Mat back to Jerangau with the police escort which had come with us. The police were told to make a good deal of noise as they moved off so that the tiger, if he were within hearing, would think that we had all returned. Then I settled down to wait. As the slightest movement might give my position away to the man-eater if he was watching from cover, I sat completely motionless until nearly nine o'clock without hearing a sound from him. Then I heard him coming towards me in the darkness. He approached, not from the swamp on my left as I had expected, but from directly behind me. Moving very slowly and carefully, he passed directly beneath me, went forward a short distance and then stopped. I already had my rifle held to my shoulder, so that it could be fired without further movement. Immediately the tiger halted, I pressed forward the switch of the torch secured to the rifle.

I found that the tiger was not standing over the dummy corpse as I had imagined. Instead he had his back to me and was slightly to my left. The result was that all but half his head and right shoulder were hidden from me by a bough of the tree in which I was sitting. I took quick but careful aim high on the shoulder and fired. At the exact moment that I did so, the tiger turned sharply on his hind legs and swung off to the left. For an agonising split second I was conscious that the animal was turning away. The realization came to me too late to prevent the completion of the act of squeezing the trigger. The man-eater's movement and the shot seemed to coincide exactly.

I was mystified by the complete silence which followed. Had I missed the tiger completely or wounded him slightly, I would have expected to hear him bound off. Had I killed him outright, I would still have heard the sound of his last convulsions. As it was, I heard nothing. After waiting for ten minutes, I descended from my perch. As both hands were needed in order to reach the ground, I had no option but to sling the rifle over one shoulder with the lighted torch pointed downwards. This climb down into the darkness, with the possibility that the man-eater was waiting below, was not the most pleasant thing that I have done.

I examined the place where the tiger had been standing when I fired at him. I found his pugs and the hole in the ground made by the bullet. There was no hair near this hole, nor was there any blood or fragments of bone. I followed the pugs far enough into the swamp to make sure that no blood had dropped afterwards. Then, feeling that I was permitting the tiger too great an advantage, I returned to my tree. I sat smoking with my back to it, not intending to climb to my seat again, but I began imagining that I could hear rustlings and the sound of movements behind me. Feeling rather cowardly, I eventually returned to my safe perch.

It was some time before Pa Mat and the escort returned, the roar of the Mannlicher having been heard at Jerangau. They came through the rubber in a compact body, torches flashing, with four local Malays bearing two strong poles on which to carry out the dead tiger. Pa Mat had made them bring these, telling them that the tiger was certainly dead. What could I say in the face of such confidence? I had no excuses to make. I had missed a first-rate chance to get the man-eater and that's all there was to it. I have rarely felt more depressed. Our journey next morning back to Dungun and then on to Kemaman was a gloomy one. Quite apart from the fact that the man-eater lived to kill again, I knew that next time he would think twice before returning to a kill in the dark. It was almost certain that the trick with a dummy corpse would not succeed in attracting him again.

Following my unsuccessful attempt to kill the man-eater, written instructions were issued to the village headmen that the body of the next person killed by the tiger was not to be moved until I arrived at the spot. These instructions, written in Jawi, were handed out by a Malay officer who visited the kampongs concerned and explained to the villagers why this step was necessary.

I also obtained a fat cow from Dungun and sent it to Jerangau by motor boat. This beast was tied out in the rubber every night and was rested and fed in the village during the daytime. The tiger took not the slightest interest in it. Because most of the villagers were now frightened to go out to work, there was a local move to put out some spring guns. This proposal was overruled. These dangerous contrivances are easily set off by domestic animals. The shot, passing over a small animal such as a dog, may hit anybody who happens to be in line with the gun. Frequently they only wound the tiger which sets them off, thus making him a greater menace.

After an interval of twenty days, the man-eater killed a Chinese rubber tapper not far from the scene of my previous attempt to shoot the brute. The information that I received late in the afternoon was that the body had been left lying where it had been found. When I arrived early the next morning I was dismayed to discover that the body had been moved to a small clearing to make it easier for me to shoot the tiger. It had also been swathed in cloth like an Egyptian mummy and a big platform had been built in a nearby tree in which parties of men had been guarding the body in relays to prevent the tiger from approaching it.

These misguided attempts to help, all of which were contrary to the instructions which had been issued, had almost certainly frightened the tiger away from the kill for good. However, the local people thought he would return and, more to convince them of my determination to help them than anything else, I waited there alone for fourteen hours. For reasons which must be obvious, since the man had been dead for some time, it was not a very pleasant vigil. I was not sorry when the tetabu birds began to greet the dawn. During my wait I heard nothing of the tiger.

It seemed to me that every time I had a chance to kill the man-eater, it was inevitable that something or another would go wrong. A Malay bomoh, or witch-doctor, at Jerangau and another at Dungun both told me, quite independently, that it would be impossible for me to shoot the tiger until it had killed its eighth man. One was encouraging enough to add the proviso 'If he does not kill you first, Tuan'.

The seventh victim of the man-eater died on the 6th April, south of Kampong Manchis. He was a Malay who had gone fishing in the Dungun river. His body was recovered the same evening. I was away on tour when this kill occurred and learnt about it two days later. The next kill would be the eighth and would prove whether the Malay bomohs were right or not!

Not long after he killed his seventh man, the man-eater attacked and slew a fully-grown male buffalo barely half a mile from the Jerangau police station. Misfortune continued to dog my efforts for the carcass was not discovered until three days later. Until then the tiger had been feeding from the buffalo in the open, offering an excellent opportunity for a clear shot. When the villagers found the dead beast, the man-eater dragged what was left of it into a swamp near at hand.

I was having lunch at Dungun when the news came through but, although I made use of the mine railway, I was unable to reach Padang Pulut until four o'clock. Although we almost certainly broke the record for the walk from Kampong Manchis to Jerangau, we were not at the kill until six o'clock. We immediately began to erect my machan. The pugs round the spot from which the kill had been moved were clearly those of the man-eater. None of the trees near the kill was strong enough to bear the weight of a man, so we chose the biggest that we could find, which was about three inches thick, and erected beside it three other poles which we stuck into the mud. To these four uprights we attached my machan and there camouflaged it. The whole affair was very shaky, working as we were against time, knee-deep in mud and water and pestered by mosquitoes.

It was nearly dark when Pa Mat and the two Malays I had persuaded to help us went off and left me to myself. I had a strong but unaccountable feeling that the tiger had approached while we were at work and had gone off again on hearing the noise that we could not avoid making. Because of this I did not expect him to come to the kill early, if he came at all. Just before 9.30 p.m. he walked towards the back of my machan, moving with even greater caution than on the last occasion on which I had heard him. He stopped when a few yards away from me, stood there for a full minute, then turned and went away again. My machan was well concealed with foliage. I knew from experience that this would make it impossible for me to try turning in order to shoot. The noise that I would make, moving among the leaves, would have sent the tiger off for good.

The man-eater's actions confirmed my impression that he had heard us putting up the machan and was suspicious. I doubted very much whether he would return to the dead buffalo, although I was prepared to wait for him until dawn if necessary. I therefore rested my rifle on the stout stick which I always fastened across the front of the machan for that purpose and adopted a more relaxed position, with my hands resting on my knees. The rifle, the butt of which was in my lap, was so placed that I could return it to the firing position without noise.

I had sat in silence listening to the night noises of the jungle for over two hours – a glance at my wrist-watch later showed that it was nearly midnight – when I suddenly became aware that the man-eater, walking with an almost complete absence of noise which was uncanny in view of the water in which he trod, had come up behind me again. He stood there for a moment or two, then, moving forward again, came in directly beneath my feet – and stopped.

It is difficult to describe the period of suspense which followed. My feet, supported by the foot-rest of my machan, were less than eight feet from the ground. My rifle was not in my hands. Even if it had been, it would have been impossible to fire it at the tiger with any real hope of hitting him, although the noise of it would almost certainly have frightened him away if necessary. Alarmed though I was, this was the last thing that I wished to do.

So there we remained, in complete silence. I was not sure whether the tiger was interested in me or in his dead buffalo. I did know that, if he had a hankering for human flesh, he had only to stand on his hind legs to reach my feet with his forepaws. After a wait of at least three minutes, which to me seemed very much more like fifteen minutes at the time, the man-eater began to creep cautiously towards the dead buffalo, which lay in front of me. With equal care my hands gently found the rifle. Very slowly, I began to raise it to my shoulder. My hopes ran high. I decided that, directly the tiger had moved forward far enough, I would switch on my torch and try a snap shot. He was so close to me that I could hardly miss him. My main difficulty was to make certain of his exact position from the sound of his movements. Until I switched on my torch I would see nothing in the darkness.

Slowly the man-eater crept forward. Slowly the Mannlicher came to my shoulder. Stare as I might, I could see nothing. Suddenly the tiger did something which I have never known one of his kind do before or since. He drew in his breath clearly and sharply in a distinct hiss. The noise was made in much the same way in which people will catch their breath when something unpleasant, which has been half-expected, suddenly happens. Thinking over the incident afterwards, I came to the conclusion that, looking back over his shoulder, the tiger had suddenly made out the bulk of my machan against the sky. I was convinced that I had made no sound to warn him.

As he made this noise the man-eater leapt into crashing movement - not forward, as I had hoped, but backwards and to my right. My torch went on at once, but although I scrambled to my feet immediately and swept the light round the undergrowth behind me, I could discern no movement. It is not easy to rise suddenly from a sitting position in a small seat suspended in mid-air. It was the time taken to do so which helped the tiger to escape. Even had he gone forward, I would have been very fortunate to have hit him because of the rapidity of his movements.

Another chance missed. I put my head in my hands and very nearly wept. Inevitably on such occasions there is ample room for recrimination. Should I have done this and not that? I asked myself a hundred such questions and mentally kicked myself all round the extensive rubber estates of Jerangau while waiting for the dawn to come. Then, miserable and stiff, wondering how I had ever succeeded in shooting any tigers at all, I splashed down into the swamp and walked dejectedly back to the village.

No further news of the man-eater was received and, during the days that followed, the local people began to hope that the two scares that I had given him had driven him away for good. Then, on the 23rd April 1951, he killed another Malay rubber tapper, six miles away from Jerangau at Kampong Manchis. This man was killed at ten o'clock in the morning. I heard later that the man-eater had been seen some time earlier the same morning as he crossed the Dungun river below Kampong Wau.

This was his most daring attack to date. Previously he had attacked people only when they were alone. This time he pulled down his victim while he was standing beside another Malay, again near the extreme edge of the rubber where it met the jungle. The dead man's companion suffered so badly from shock that he was incapable of speech for seven hours afterwards. I, for one, do not blame him. To hear the breath-taking roar of a charging tiger close behind you and to have your companion killed at your very side must be a truly terrifying experience. Some weeks later I had another man-eater threaten me at close range in thick under-growth. That was almost enough to make my heart stop beating momentarily, armed as I was with a good rifle.

For some reason which subsequent enquiries failed to make clear, the people of Kampong Manchis did not report the death of this, the man-eater's eighth victim, until nearly four o'clock in the afternoon. Batchelor rang me up at once and I left Kemaman for Dungun as soon as I had collected my rifle from my quarters. All my other gear, including spare clothing, was already in the car, as it had been every day since my first attempt to shoot this tiger. By the time that we reached Dungun it was obvious that I could not possibly arrive at Kampong Manchis before dark. Batchelor came to my help by arranging that the police escort, which would come down from the iron mine, would meet me at Padang Pulut early the next morning.

We had crossed the river and were in Kampong Manchis before 9 a.m. the following day. There was then some slight bother about the anti-terrorist police escort. The sergeant-in-charge, whom I happened to know personally, had instructions to escort me wher-ever I went. It was clear that I would have no hope of shooting the tiger if I was accompanied by a dozen policemen. We compro-mised. One Malay constable, who volunteered for the job, came along to act as my escort. His real function, although I did not mention this, was to give moral support to Pa Mat, who would have to return by himself if I remained in the jungle alone.

We prepared to start, but a further complication arose. Pa Mat, burdened as he was with the portable machan and with a number of ropes, could not possibly make effective use of the shotgun with which I had armed him in the event of an emergency. Seeing that this was one of the occasions on which he was really uneasy, I agreed that an elderly Malay should accompany us to carry the load. Four people make a party which is exactly three too many when the quarry is a man-eater. In this case it could not be helped. Even as it was I could see that the sergeant was far from happy about the arrangements I had made. We left Kampong Manchis to proceed first to the spot where the man had been killed. We took with us two local rubber tappers to point out the place but they took to their heels as we neared it and I did not see them again.

The rubber small-holding across which we now made our way was roughly rectangular in shape. It lay at an angle to the river Manchis, with the tree in question located at its northern corner only five yards from the riverbank. The dead man had been collecting latex here with his companion. The two of them must either have been seen or heard by the tiger from the further bank of the river, which was there only about fifteen feet wide. Crossing the river, he entered the bushes to their left as they approached this corner tree. Both men were facing the tree and the river. The scrub enabled the man-eater to get within eight feet of their backs before he made his spring. I doubt very much whether the Malay he killed had much time to realize what was happening to him.

Having secured his victim, the tiger took the body across the river and made off with it into the jungle from whence he had come. It was through this rather forbidding-looking jungle that we now began to follow the drag. I went ahead, followed at a distance of some fifteen yards by Pa Mat. The constable and the other Malay walked together, further back still.

A follow-up of this nature is an exacting and tiring business. It is always oppressively hot working in jungle to which no breeze can penetrate. Noise must be kept to an absolute minimum in the hope that the tiger may be surprised feeding, or at rest. A guard must be kept against a surprise attack. Added to these causes of stress is the knowledge that your search will eventually bring you to a most unpleasant sight. On this occasion I was handicapped by having three people with me, a heavy responsibility. Furthermore, the sound of their footsteps, no matter how quietly they tried to walk, made it difficult for me to hear the sound of any movement that there might be ahead of us.

It was one-and-a-half hours before I found the place for which I had been searching. It was then about 11.30 a.m. and the body had been at the man-eater's mercy since 10.00 a.m. the previous day. What struck me most forcibly was that the face of the victim, a young Malay with a particularly fair skin, was as peaceful in death as it might have been if he had merely been sleeping quietly. Many writers would have their readers believe that persons who die in horrible circumstances have on their faces afterwards a look of extreme terror. This is not always true and was certainly not so in this case.

My examination of the remains showed that the tiger had been feeding from them very recently. From what I saw I decided that he had not left the spot because of our approach, but had gone off for a drink, as tigers frequently do when feeding. Pa Mat and I wasted little time over the body but began to look round for a suitable place in which I could await the man-eater's return. No trees near at hand appeared suitable. It looked as if I would have to conceal myself on the ground near the body. I did not relish this idea for several reasons, among which was the possibility that the tiger would not return until after dark.

Whilst we were trying to find an answer to this problem, a squirrel called sharply several times off to my left. I knew that he was scolding to give warning that the tiger was on the move. I gently tapped twice on a tree with my big hunting-knife. The squirrel stopped almost immediately. It was safe to assume that the tiger had heard the noise, as I had intended he should and had stopped, probably lying down, to await developments. It was at this moment that I noticed that a stout sapling, ignored previously because of its slender girth, branched into two about seven feet from the ground. This small tree was about eight yards from the kill. Mounting to this fork I found myself looking down onto the bushes beneath which lay the remains of the corpse.

It took but a moment or two to jam and rope the machan into place. While Pa Mat carefully removed sufficient foliage for me to be able to make out the body, I fastened a cord in front of me and over this hung several wild banana leaves, thus hiding myself behind a complete screen. In the centre leaf I tore a small hole and through this thrust the barrel of my rifle. Directly these hasty preparations were completed, Pa Mat, following the instructions that I had been whispering to him while we worked, ran noisily to where the two other men were standing. The three of them made off at some speed through the jungle back towards the rubber estate. I had hopes that the man-eater, hearing them go, would think that they were frightened and that the jungle, and the body, were his again. I glanced at my watch as the sounds of their departure receded. It was then 11.43 a.m. I sat with my rifle held ready to my shoulder, the sweat running down my face, chest and arms. I vividly remember even now how thirsty I was.

Not many minutes had passed before the squirrel called again twice. Shortly afterwards, to my intense satisfaction, I heard the faint sounds made by his great feet as the man-eater advanced towards me. Slowly these sounds came closer. Then the head of the tiger came into view as he neared the body. The manner in which he had approached suggested that he intended to move the remains to a new hiding place. When the head appeared I was sorely tempted to send a bullet into it, but head shots are not as certain as one would think. So I waited with all the patience at my command until the tiger, reaching out to seize the body, exposed the side of his neck to me. It was at the centre of this mark that I took aim and fired. The whole jungle seemed to explode with noise.

After the shot the tiger fell on his belly, with his forepaws doubled beneath him. A final convulsion brought one big forepaw flopping out to fall, as though protectingly, across the human remains that lay close by. When all movement had ceased, I swung my rifle skywards in the direction in which I knew Pa Mat would be standing, having heard the report of the rifle, and fired a second shot to tell him that all was over. It was then 11.57 a.m.

Pa Mat returned with the constable, having sent off the other Malay to fetch the remainder of the escort and some men from Kampong Manchis to carry out the remains of the dead man and the dead tiger. We photographed the two of them as they lay to provide positive proof that it was the man-eater which had been killed. Then we tied the legs of the dead tiger together to facilitate its removal. The man-eater, as I had believed, had outsized front paws. He was in splendid condition, apart from one upper canine which was broken. Measured later he went eight feet six inches between pegs.

When the dead tiger had been carried out of the jungle into the sunlight, I took a less gruesome photograph of him which was sent to the Penghulu of Jerangau. He affixed it to the wall of the most popular coffee-shop there, so that it could be seen by the Malays and Chinese who lived in the area which had been terrorized by the man-eater.

So far as I was concerned, this was the end of the Jerangau man-eater. Six weeks after I shot him, however, a minor Malay official living at Dungun began trying to make trouble. Without bothering to learn the facts of the man-eater's career, or of his death, this man sent a petition to the state government. In it he complained that I had used a dead Malay 'as bait, in order to enjoy the sport of tiger shooting'. Anybody reading the petition, a copy of which came into my hands, would have imagined that I had taken corpses away from protesting relatives and had left them lying about in the jungle in the hope that stray tigers would be attracted to them. No mention was made of the fact that the delay of six hours in reporting the death of the man-eater's last victim had been the main reason why it had been impossible to recover the body the same day.

The petition annoyed me immensely, but I took no action on it until the head of the state religious department wrote to me. In his letter he asked me not to make use of dead Malays if I wished to shoot tigers. I replied in carefully-worded Malay, asking whether it was really believed that I had done this. Was it thought better, I asked, to allow more people to be killed than to permit a dead body to remain unburied for a few hours? I pointed out the delay in reporting the death of the last victim and emphasised the respect that I had always shown for the religious beliefs of the people of my area.

The matter created something of a stir locally until the mufti of Trengganu, supreme in religious matters within the state, intervened. He issued a letter deprecating the action of the petitioner in making use of the word 'bait' and reproving him in no uncertain terms for writing the petition at all.

'It appears,' said the mufti's letter, 'that the body was allowed to remain in its original position solely for the purpose of killing a tiger which was interfering with the peaceful lives of the kampong people. This is a praiseworthy undertaking and one that is esteemed under Islamic law'.

II. A Unique Embrace

An engineer, F Pollock, working in Burma in the 1890's took his family for leave one year to the hill station of Ootacamund, southern India, to avoid the worst of the seasonal heat. There he heard of a man-eating tiger which was causing havoc near the town of Coimbatore, some miles to the south, and offered his assistance in dealing with the animal in the two weeks remaining of his leave.

The Corumbirs, who inhabit the jungle in those parts, much as the Karens do in Burma, and wear nothing but an apology for clothing, appeared one day mentioning that a tiger had been killing a good many people, but while there were reports of a kill here and a kill there, when I got to the place the replies were indefinite or nobody visible.

On the sixth day of my remaining leave a man rushed into my camp saying his daughter had been killed that morning at daybreak, and if I would come at once they would beat the jungle for the animal, and that people had surrounded it. I hurried there, but the victim's remains had been removed and were being cremated. Also, the circle formed round the man-eater had been so defective that he or she had got away. I was very angry, and swore they might all be decimated before I trudged a mile to save them. These people are very superstitious, and believe that if the body of a person killed by a tiger is not recovered and burnt, the deceased will arise and destroy all his relatives who have failed to give him the rights of burial, which in most cases means being burnt.

I then removed my camp further inland about ten miles. Hearing of a human being killed here and there, notwithstanding what I had stated, I did go frequently to try and get a shot at the man-eater, but it was all in vain; the people would not leave the victims alone before I could get to the scene of the tragedies.

On the eleventh day I was accompanied by my shikari, a local man, and a Corumbir. We were far from the haunts of man, and all was solitude, when we heard a piercing cry, which was unmistakably the death shriek of some miserable creature struck down by a beast of prey. I rushed forward, followed most reluctantly by my two attendants, and found a poor wood-cutter. He was a small, wiry, man probably about forty years of age, all but naked, and the breath was scarcely out of his body. As I stooped over him to ascertain whether there was the least hope of recovery, I found that the back of his skull had been beaten in, as with a sledge hammer.

When I turned round the Corumbir was making tracks, evidently with a view of giving notice of the misfortune to some villagers. As I knew if he once got away we should have a posse of men with torches coming for the body, I caught him and told him if he attempted to leave I would break every bone in his body. Now that I had a corpse I meant to utilise it, so I forcibly detained him and made him and the shikari collect wood and erect a machan. The body lay with the face uppermost, and had fallen amid some brushwood close to a stout sapling, while a fair-sized tree commanded the position from a distance of about fifteen yards.

There was fortunately a good moon, so soon before dusk we climbed into our perch, the villager muttering that we were guilty of sacrilege and that surely the corpse would arise and slay us. Finally I procured silence by telling the men, if they made the least noise, I would tie them up as living bait. It was a gruesome sight, watching that dead body as the moon shone on its face, exaggerating every feature. I must own, were it not that I considered it a duty to try and rid the country of that man-eater, I would even at the last moment have gone back to camp.

The time went by but slowly. Eleven o'clock arrived; no appearance of the tiger. Some tall trees cast a shadow over the corpse, but I could not take my eyes off that poor, thin, ghastly upturned face, when, oh, horror! one eye opened, then the other; soon after an arm moved, succeeded by a shiver of the body. Was it going to rise and kill us as the men asserted? It was too absurd. The sight was too much for my companions. They dropped forward in a swoon. Even I, too, felt as if icy cold water was being poured down the back of my neck.

Demoralised I was certainly getting, and I do not think that I could have borne the gruesome sight much longer, when there was a roar, and a mass sprang at something which was invisible to me. Instantaneously there was a struggle, bones seemed to be crunched to bits, there was a feeble roar or two, and then all was still except an occasional convulsive heaving.

In that fearful effort, the corpse had been shifted so that its wide and sightless orbs no longer stared upwards. That alone was a relief but what had occurred I could not conjecture on account of the brushwood and debris.

The men, when they recovered from their faint, still lay prone with their hands over their faces, muttering that we were now as good as dead. I asked one what he was afraid of. 'The corpse will kill us,' he muttered. 'The dead cannot come to life again,' I said. 'The woodcutter is dead, and something has killed his destroyer. We shall know all about it in the morning. I am going to sleep; you had better do so too.'

I knew the men were in too great a fright to descend from the machan and seek a village at that time of night, so making myself as comfortable as I could, I turned over on my side and dozed off, giving a convulsive start now and then as I dreamt that the woodcutter was threatening me. But everything has an end. That long, long night at length terminated and thankful I was to see the dawn of day and hear the jungle fowls proclaim the sunrise.

Losing no time I descended to solve last night's mystery. The sight that met my eyes was marvellous. A huge boa constrictor, just over twenty-one feet in length, lay coiled round the body of the tiger, whose fangs in turn were imbedded in the back of the snake's head, while the reptile's folds, after enveloping the tiger, had got a purchase by lashing its tail round the adjoining sapling, and so assisted the vast muscular power it possessed in crushing the tiger to death.

On examining the corpse of the man, we found saliva or slime over the face and the upper part of the body, and so I have no doubt the snake had thus prepared the human prize for swallowing when the tiger sprang upon it, resulting in the two meeting their deaths. The movements of the man's body were doubtless caused by the snake's pressure and by its progress round and about the carcass.

The boa constrictor, though dead some hours, had still sufficient muscular power left to make it appear dangerous. These reptiles' power of contraction when they have a purchase to aid them is immense, and I have heard the natives tell wonderful tales about their strength, even to their making buffaloes their victims. Having procured villagers, we unwound the snake from its hold on the tree, with the united strength of twenty men, aided with coils of strong rope. A cart being procured, the two, lying dead in each other's embrace, were conveyed to the village.

The dead woodcutter was duly cremated. I remained a week longer, but heard no more of anybody being killed. There is little doubt therefore that it was the man-eater that was destroyed by the snake. The tiger was in perfect condition as to skin, but very emaciated, for so vigilant were these people that they never gave the depredator time to make a square meal off her numerous victims. But for my chance of having witnessed the woodcutter's death, and so prevented the men removing the corpse, the probabilities are the man-eater would have lived many a day longer and continued its ravages upon the Corumbir community.

CHAPTER THREE

African Tales

EARLY SETTLERS AND OTHERS travelling through central and east Africa were the first to report of the perpetual threat which lions posed, particularly at night, for camps, villages or any isolated settlement in the bush. Precautions like lighting fires, building thorn fences or barricading huts proved of little protection.

I. Poor Hendrick

An early explorer and hunter, R G Gordon-Cumming, experienced a man-eater night attack on his camp in the 1840's while journeying through the bush of south-east Africa near the Limpopo river.

On the 29th we arrived at a small village of Bakalahari. These natives told me that elephants were abundant on the opposite side of the river. I accordingly resolved to halt here and hunt, and drew my waggons up on the river's bank, within thirty yards of the water and about one hundred yards from the native village. Having outspanned, we at once set about making a kraal for the cattle of the worst description of thorn trees. Of this I had now become very particular since my severe loss by lions on the first of the month; and my cattle were secured by a strong kraal at night which enclosed my two waggons, the horses being made fast to a trektow stretched between the hind-wheels of the waggons.

I had yet, however, a fearful lesson to learn as to the nature and character of the lion, of which I had at one time entertained so little fear; and on this night a horrible tragedy was to be acted in my little lonely camp of so very awful and appalling a nature as to make the blood curdle in our veins.

I worked till near sundown at one side of the kraal with Hendrick, my first waggon-driver - I cutting down the trees with my axe, and he dragging them to the kraal. When the kraal for the cattle was finished, I turned my attention to making a pot of barley broth, and lit a fire between the waggons and the water, close on the river's bank and under a dense grove of shady trees, making no sort of kraal around our sitting-place for the evening.

The Hottentots, without any reason, made their fire about fifty yards from mine; they, according to their usual custom, being satisfied with the shelter of a large dense bush. The evening passed away cheerfully. Soon after it was dark we heard elephants breaking the trees in the forest across the river and once or twice I strode away into the darkness some distance from the fireside to stand and listen to them. I little realised at that moment the imminent peril to which I was exposing my life, nor thought that a man-eater lion was crouching near, and only watching his opportunity to spring into the kraal and consign one of us to a most horrible death.

About three hours after the sun went down I called to my men to come and take their coffee and supper, which was ready for them at my fire. After supper three of them returned before their comrades to their own fireside and lay down; these were John Stofolus, Hendrick, and Ruyter. At one point an ox got out by the gate of the kraal and walked round the back of it. Hendrick got up and drove him in again and then went back to his fireside and lay down. Hendrick and Ruyter lay on one side of the fire under one blanket and John Stofolus lay on the other. At this moment I was sitting taking some barley broth; our fire was very small, and the night was pitch dark and windy. Owing to our proximity to the native village wood was very scarce, the Bakalahari having burnt it all in their fires.

Suddenly the appalling voice of an angry lion burst upon my ear within a few yards of us, followed by the shrieking of the Hottentots. Again and again the roar of attack was repeated. We heard John and Ruyter shriek 'The lion! the lion!' but for a few moments we thought he was but chasing one of the dogs round the kraal. But next instant John Stofolus rushed into the midst of us almost speechless with fear and terror, his eyes bursting from their sockets, and shrieked out, 'The lion! the lion! It's got Hendrick. It dragged him away from the fire beside me. I struck it with burning brands on its head, but it would'nt let go its hold. Hendrick's dead! Oh, God! Hendrick's dead! Take lights and look for him.'

The rest of my people rushed about, shrieking and yelling as if they were mad. I was at once angry with them for their folly and told them that if they did not stand still and keep quiet the lion would have another of us, and that very likely there was a troop of them. I ordered the dogs, which were nearly all tied up, to be made loose and the fire to be increased as far as could be. I then shouted Hendrick's name, but all was still. I told my men that Hendrick was dead and that a regiment of soldiers could not now help him. Then, hunting my dogs forward, I had everything brought within the cattle kraal, when we lit our fire and closed the entrance as well as we could.

My terrified people sat round the fire with guns in their hands till the day broke, still fancying that every moment the lion would return and spring again into the midst of us. When the dogs were first let go, the stupid brutes, as dogs often prove when most required, instead of going at the lion, rushed fiercely on one another and fought desperately for some minutes. After this they got his wind and, going at him, disclosed to us his position; they kept up a continued barking until the day dawned, the lion occasionally springing after them and driving them in upon the kraal. The animal lay all night within forty yards of us, consuming the wretched man whom he had chosen for his prey. It dragged him into a little hollow at the back of the thick bush, beside which the fire was kindled, and there it remained till the day dawned, careless of our proximity.

It appeared that when the unfortunate Hendrick rose to drive in the ox, the lion had watched him go to the fireside, and he had scarcely lain down when the animal sprang upon him and Ruyter (both were lying under one blanket). With its appalling roar, it grappled Hendrick with its claws and kept biting him on the breast and shoulder, all the while feeling for his neck; having got hold of which, it at once dragged him away backwards round the bush into the dense shade.

As the lion lay upon the unfortunate Hendrick he faintly cried 'Help me, help me! Oh, God! men, help me!' After which the animal got a hold of his neck, and then all was still, except that his comrades heard the bones of his neck cracking between the teeth of the lion. John Stofolus had lain with his back to the fire on the opposite side, and on hearing the lion he had sprung up and, seizing a large flaming piece of wood, he had beaten the lion on the head with it; but the animal did not take any notice of him. The bushman had a narrow escape and was not altogether unscathed, the lion having inflicted two gashes in his seat with its claws.

The next morning, just as the day began to dawn, we heard the lion dragging something up the riverside under cover of the bank. We drove the cattle out of the kraal and then proceeded to inspect the scene of the night's awful tragedy. In the hollow, where the lion had lain consuming his prey, we found one leg of the unfortunate Hendrick, bitten off below the knee, the shoe still on his foot. The grass and bushes were all stained with his blood, and fragments of his pea-coat lay around.

Poor Hendrick! I knew the fragments of that old coat so well. Hendrick was by far the best man I had about my waggons. He was of a most cheerful disposition, a first-rate waggon-driver, fearless in the field, ever active, willing, and obliging. His loss to us all was very serious. I felt confounded and utterly sick in my heart; I could not remain at the waggons, so I decided to go after elephants to divert my mind. My followers were not a little gratified to see me return later in the day, for terror had taken hold of their minds. They expected that the lion would return and, emboldened by the success of the preceding night, would prove still more daring in his attack.

The lion would most certainly have returned, but fate had otherwise ordained. My health had been better in the last three days; my fever was leaving me, but I was, of course, still very weak. It would still be two hours before the sun would set and, feeling refreshed by a little rest, and able for further work, I ordered the horses to be saddled and went in search of the lion.

I took John and Carey as after-riders, armed, and a party of the natives followed up the spoor and led the dogs. The lion had dragged the remains of poor Hendrick along a native footpath that led up the riverside. We found fragments of his coat all along the spoor, and at last the mangled coat itself. About six hundred yards from our camp a dry river course joined the Limpopo. At this spot was much shade, cover, and heaps of dry reeds and trees deposited by the Limpopo in some great flood.

Here the lion had left the footpath and entered this secluded spot. I at once felt convinced that we were upon him and ordered the natives to loose the dogs. These walked suspiciously forward on the spoor, but next minute began to spring about, barking angrily, with all their hair bristling on their backs. A crash upon the dry reeds immediately followed – it was the lion bounding away.

Several of the dogs were extremely afraid of the animal and kept rushing continually backwards and springing aloft to obtain a view. I now pressed forward and urged them on; old Argyll and Bles took up his spoor in gallant style and led on the other dogs. Then commenced a short but lively and glorious chase, whose conclusion was the only small satisfaction that I could claim for the horrors of the preceding evening. The lion disappeared up the river's bank for a short distance and took away through some wait-a-bit thorn cover, the best he could find, but nevertheless open.

Here, in two minutes, the dogs were up with him and he turned and stood at bay. As I approached he stood, his head right to me, with open jaws growling fiercely, his tail twitching from side to side. I sent a bullet through his shoulder and dropped him on the spot, dead.

II. Tragedy on the Umfuli

The panic induced by a lion attack could lead to other tragedies as the noted African explorer, F C Selous, relates in this account of a night attack on his camp near modern-day Lake Kariba, east Africa, in 1880.

Having formed a camp on the banks of a small stream, a tributary of the Umfuli river, Messrs Jameson, Collison and myself went away on the 30th of June to the north-east in search of elephants. We left Dr Crook, a gentleman who had accompanied Mr Jameson from the diamond fields and who was not a very ardent sportsman, in charge of the encampment. Besides Dr Crook, there remained at the waggons a young colonist, Ruthven by name, in Mr Jameson's employ, a lot of colonial coloured drivers who were going away hunting in the 'fly' country on the following day, plus at least twenty Matabele Kafirs.

The camp was arranged thus: in the centre stood our four waggons, parallel with one another, enough space being allowed for the horses to be tied between them. In front of the waggons was our cattle kraal, containing nearly sixty oxen, made very high and strong. Surrounding both the kraal and the waggons, and leaving the latter standing in an open space about sixty yards in diameter, was a second strong, high fence. At intervals round the inside of this fence the different parties of Kafirs had made their sleeping places, each party keeping up one or two fires, so that the whole camp presented a very animated appearance.

On the evening of the 8th July we returned home and were surprised to find our camp deserted. Riding into the enclosure we found a cross, the letters R R deeply cut on the stem of a tree that grew on one side of the kraal and, at its foot, a newly-made grave. Full of conjecture as to what this evidence of disaster might signify, we at once galloped along the broad track left by our four waggons and half an hour later found them standing on the bank of the Umfuli itself, where Dr Crook had made a new encampment.

We learned the following story. In the dead of night of the very day on which we left the waggons, every one was awakened by the shrieking of Mr Jameson's pet baboon, 'Susan,' that was fastened just in front of one of the waggons. At the same time a horse was heard struggling between the waggons. Ruthven and a Bamangwato boy named Buckram rushed forwards to see what was the matter and found old Jordan, one of Mr Jameson's horses, struggling in the

clutches of a lioness.   Upon their shouting and waving their
blankets, the lioness left the horse and retreated into the darkness.
After this the fires were kept up, and nothing further occurred to
disturb the peace. Jordan, though badly bitten on the back of the
neck just behind the head, and scratched about the throat, had not
sustained any very material injury. The wounds did not heal up,
however, and eight months afterwards they were still sloughing.

The following morning Dr Crook found the hole in the fence
through which the lioness had crept. Here he set two guns with
strings tied on their triggers, brought across the gap in the fence in
such a way that if the lioness were to return by the same path
during the coming night she would in all probability shoot herself.
When evening came, Ruthven and two colonial boys (waggon
drivers) did not turn in, but sat up round a fire, hoping to get a shot
at the lioness should she return and make an attack from another
quarter.

It was ten o'clock by the doctor's watch when old Umzobo, a
Matabele man who was in charge of my property whilst I was away
hunting, and who was at that moment sitting by a fire alongside my
waggon, said to a young Kafir near him, 'Blow up the fire, I hear
something moving outside the fence.' The boy was in the act of
doing as he had been told, and the fire was just blazing up, when
the lioness suddenly appeared in their midst and seized old Umzobo
from in front by the leg, making her teeth meet behind the shin-
bones. With great presence of mind, the old fellow forced his
hands into her mouth one on each side, when she let go and then
seized Impewan, another Kafir of mine, by the fleshy part of the
buttock, just as he was preparing to make tracks. Feeling the
sensation behind, he instinctively put his hand there, when the
lioness, quitting her first hold, instantly seized it, and was dragging
him away into the darkness, the poor fellow all the while shrieking
with terror and agony, when Ruthven fired. The shot frightened
the lioness, and she released Impewan and disappeared in the
darkness. Immediately after Ruthven fired two other shots rang out
in quick succession.

Dr Crook, awakened by the growling of the lioness, the shrieking of the Kafirs, and the reports of the rifles, jumped out of the waggon and ran to see what had happened. At the fire where Ruthven had been sitting he found Norris, one of the coloured drivers, crying over a prostrate figure, which upon turning over he found to be poor young Ruthven with half his head blown off. How this untoward accident happened will never be exactly known, but there is no doubt that it was owing to one or other of the drivers losing their wits at the sudden and alarming nature of the disturbance and firing off their guns at random. I think myself that Ruthven must have been sitting down when he fired, and that he then stood up suddenly, bringing his head close to the muzzle of one of their guns. He fell dead, poor fellow, with his head in the fire.

Having restored some sort of order amongst the panic-stricken Kafirs, dressed the wounds of those that had been bitten, and covered poor Ruthven's body with a blanket, Dr Crook again turned in. At twelve o'clock one of the set guns went off, but no other sound broke the stillness of the night. At 2 a.m. the other gun went off and the Kafirs all said they heard a low groan at the same time. As may be imagined, no one slept during the remainder of this eventful night.

At daylight the doctor, hearing cries of 'Gwasa! Gwasa! ' (Stab her! Stab her!), went out and found that the lioness, which had returned to the attack three more times, had met her fate at last. She lay dead before the muzzle of the second gun and just at the gap in the fence through which she had entered the encampment on the first night. The bullet had passed right through her heart. The first gun had not injured her and could not have been properly set.

This lioness was apparently in the prime of life, with a good coat and fine long teeth; she was, however, very thin, and had nothing in her stomach, and no doubt desperate from hunger.   The following day Dr Crook buried poor Ruthven and then moved the camp to the Umfuli where, as I have related, we found him.

III. A Doctor's Rounds

During the 1890's a medical officer, W J Ansorge, was in the habit of making caravan journeys with porters from Mombasa inland as part of his professional duties. Among the less conventional responsibilites on his rounds was attempting to rid a village of a man-eating lion.

On my fourth journey, I was warned by the missionaries at Kibwezi not to camp at Ngomeni because a man-eating lion was haunting the neighbourhood. I had at the time amongst my porters a man who had camped at Ngomeni a few weeks before with another caravan. According to his story, he must have had a wonderful escape, for the lion pounced on him and carried off his blanket and the tiny tent under which he lay sheltered. The porter however escaped unhurt. From Kinani to Ngomeni is twelve miles, but my caravan were in such a dread of spending the night at Ngomeni that they begged me to push on to the next camp on the Tsavo river, nine miles farther. We therefore marched the twenty-one miles, crossed the Tsavo river, and camped.

It was a hot still night, and most of the porters slept in the open air by their camp-fires. No one dreamt there could be any danger; we all thought that the man-eating lion had been left nine miles behind us at Ngomeni. I felt unaccountably restless, tossing on my camp-bed and could not sleep. I sauntered out of my tent, saw that the night-watchman was awake, looked at the sleeping figures around the glowing camp-fires and then strolled into the silent darkness beyond the camp.

It was providential that I was not seized by the man-eater, for he was close at hand at that very moment. He had followed us from Ngomeni, having swum across the Tsavo river. My dog had followed me and at one point he growled angrily at some bush, so near that I could see some of the leaves stirring. I was so completely unconscious of any danger that I remember saying to the dog: 'You silly! to growl when the wind stirs a few leaves.' Since this night I never like to venture outside the circle of camp-fires on a dark night, however safe others may consider the surrounding uninhabited country.

Leisurely returning to my tent, I lay down on my camp-bed, when I heard a horrid growling sound a few yards from my tent-door. The next moment there were shrieks and cries. In a second every man was awake and shouting, 'Simba! simba!' Dashing out with a loaded rifle, I found that the man-eater had carried off one of my porters. Every one seized a firebrand and we rushed in pursuit. Astonishingly, we rescued the man: about two hundred yards from the camp we found him lying on the ground severely lacerated where the lion had dropped him and fled.

The wounded man was carried to my tent. He had dreadful wounds in the upper part of the thigh where the lion's jaws had seized him. As I had every surgical requisite at hand, he was soon bandaged up and he remained that night under my tent. No one ventured to go to sleep, as we fully expected the baffled man-eater would make another attempt before dawn. The injured man was in great pain and his moans were distressing. He told us a remarkable story: though the lion had seized him and was carrying him off, he was still asleep. Our shouts woke him up and to his horror he found that he himself was the one being carried off by the lion. Then he clasped his arms round the lion's neck and screamed.

We were all wondering why the lion did not pay us another visit, but it was explained the next morning. A number of Wakamba natives on their way to Mombasa to barter their sheep and goats for cloth, beads and brass wire, had passed us. They camped for the night about half an hour farther on. The man-eater had visited them instead and had carried off a native and devoured him. The others had fled. The road next day bore plain evidence of their headlong flight, being littered with beans, broken provision bags and some leather garments.

With early dawn we left Tsavo, carrying the injured porter in a hammock. We saw the footprints of the lion along the dusty road apparently following the Wakamba. Two of my men declared that they saw the animal about midday, standing panting under a shady bush by the roadside, tongue hanging out of its mouth. I hurried up to them with a loaded rifle, but saw nothing except the footprints, which here turned off the road. We made a double march, reaching the camp at Ndi in safety and seeing nothing further of the lion for the rest of the journey. The wounded man progressed favourably and, on our reaching Mombasa, insisted on walking in the procession, supporting himself with a stick. He refused to be carried or to be assisted by others. The safe home-coming of a caravan to Mombasa is generally a day of rejoicing with the porters.

On my second visit to Fajao, our farthest military station towards the north, there was another lion incident. It was on the 25th November 1897. I had arrived in the early morning and, having attended to my medical duties, went in the afternoon for a walk to a narrow rocky gully which winds through the wood. Suddenly I observed the fresh footprints of a lion in the moist sandy patches between the rocks. The footprints of a young one by its side showed it to be a lioness with her cub. The tracks were so fresh that it was evident the beasts had been disturbed by my approach and had just passed ahead.

I had never heard of any lions being in this immediate neighbour-hood and it was not pleasant to find myself unarmed and in such proximity to them. I retraced my steps pretty sharp, beating a hurried retreat and thanking Providence for bringing me safely back to the station. I told the men what I had seen and I inquired if they knew that there were lions so near to us. I received the disturbing news that a man-eating lion had harassed the neighbour-ing Wanyoro village for the past month and that it had carried off four of the villagers. The inhabitants had deserted their homes en masse, fleeing for safety to another village. Hitherto the man-eater had not visited this Sudanese settlement.

Darkness sets in about 6 p.m. and though I ventured by myself only sixty yards from my hut, I found next morning that for the second time I must have been pretty close to the man-eater, as his track was but six inches from mine. I realised how the merciful God had twice that day preserved me from death. Soon afterwards, news was brought me that the man-eater had just attempted to carry off a woman at the nearest Wanyoro village, but was driven off, presumably with firebrands, by men who happened to sit near her. This alarming news was shortly followed by my cow stampeding. She was tied to a peg, close to the Sudanese watch-fire and tearing herself loose, had bolted like mad. She never stopped until she reached a distant village, from where she was returned to me next day. The Sudanese on guard declared that he saw the lion crouching and trying to spring upon the cow when, fortunately, she just tore herself loose in time and escaped. It was too dark for the guard to aim or he would have fired his rifle.

Through the evening the general excitement was increasing. At one point terrific screams of pain suddenly arose from the Sudanese village, followed by soldiers firing off their rifles in every direction under the belief that they had seen the man-eater here, there, and everywhere. The animal seemed ubiquitous. At the thought that the bullets might knock some of us over, we put a stop to this haphazard shooting with the help of the native officers, which was endangering our lives more than the man-eater's. On hurrying to the scene of the screams, I found that the man-eater had entered a hut, the door having foolishly been left open, and had tried to carry off one of our Sudanese soldiers.

The huts are crowded together, with a reed fence round each and narrow paths and winding entrances lead to each separate enclosure. It was therefore no easy matter, even for a lion, to carry off its prey. Owing to the general hubbub the lion had dropped the man. As in the Tsavo case, I was fortunately at hand to dress the wounds. There were ten of them. A scratch, about two inches long, had splintered the heel-bone from where I removed a piece of bone about the size of a shilling. This was one of the minor wounds, the worst were in the thigh. The man ultimately made a good recovery, as did the woman who was injured earlier.

To allay the excitement and to calm the people, I told them I would kill the lion next day. The natives were not surprised at this claim, for they are very superstitious, and with them 'medicine-man' and wizard are synonymous terms. I advised the men to retire to their huts and to see that their doors were firmly secured. As regards my own hut, this was easier said than done as the door was only a reed screen leaning against the aperture, which it failed to close. But natives usually take the precaution of fixing two vertical poles inside the hut, so that the reed screen slides between them and is retained in position; the door is then firmly closed by some faggots placed transversely. Having dispersed the crowd, I determined to put out a bait for the man-eater and to sit up and watch for him.

We tied a young goat to a tree a few feet from my door. The night was very dark and I was obliged to kindle a fire to enable me to see the foresight of my rifle. Then the silent and dreary watch began. As the hours crept on, the stillness and the darkness told on me. I had had a fatiguing day: in the early morning I had marched from Wakibara to Fajao, afterwards I had attended to patients, and then came the lively doings of the evening. By-and-by I caught myself nodding. If the man-eater had chosen to pass my hut once more, it could have had me, notwithstanding the loaded rifle on my knees. At 3.30 a.m. I gave up the struggle to keep awake and, resolving to set a trap for the lion, I went to bed.

At 8 a.m. next morning I began to build the trap. Everybody helped willingly although it was Friday, equivalent to Sunday for the Mohammedan Sudanese. First of all we made a firm stockade of stout perpendicular poles; to these we lashed tree stems laid out horizontally one on top of the other; finally we planted an outer row of poles, perpendicular like the first row, firmly and deeply into the ground. This gave us the sides of the cage. The top we closed in with horizontally laid tree-trunks, onto which we piled large heavy stones till we felt satisfied that the fiercest lion could not possibly break out of this cage. The trapdoor consisted of seven heavy blocks of wood fastened together horizontally on top of each other and held in position by short perpendicular pieces on both sides. So far all went smoothly. But never having constructed a wild-beast trap before, I was seriously puzzled how to make the trapdoor act.

There is something in this Robinson Crusoe life which stimulates the most uninventive intellect. Unless I found some solution the cage would very shortly be ready and I placed in the ridiculous position of not knowing how to make the trap work. I had asked the native officers, the Sudanese soldiers, the Swahili porters, my Arab servant, and the Wanyoro onlookers, to find out if anyone could help me. They calmly assured me that they had never built a trap; in vain I told them – nor had I. But inspiration came at last and I hit on the following plan. I constructed a sort of picture frame, the trapdoor resting in the forked ends of the two perpendicular pieces. Attaching a rope to the middle of the lower horizontal stick, even a slight tug withdrew the supporting framework, causing the heavy trapdoor to fall down into the required position and thereby to shut the cage most effectively. The rope went to the farthest end of the cage and there, passing over a horizontal pole and returning in the direction of the door, had its end securely tied to a goat placed as a bait inside the trap.

The goat had previously had its legs tied, so as to render it quite helpless. The principle I went upon was that the lion would not stop to devour its prey, but would seize it and try to carry it off and therefore would pull at the rope to which the goat was tied, and thus close the trapdoor. As the lion had refused to accept the goat we had placed for it as a bait out in the open air on the previous night, we built a native hut over the trap and the lion trap was completed.

Just before dark we baited the trap and awaited the result. Everybody in the village was warned to stay inside his own hut before dusk and to see that his door was securely fastened. Though a tiger man-eater, having once tasted human flesh, is said ever after to prefer it to all other flesh, I do not know if the lion man-eater resembles it in this predilection but it would seem it does, for this particular lion refused to take the goat twice offered him as a bait on two successive nights.

The same evening the Sudanese lieutenant, Said Jabara, was eating his meal at the door of his hut when the man-eater suddenly entered his enclosure and bounded into the adjoining hut. With great presence of mind, the lieutenant at once flung burning brands in front of this hut and thus promptly made a prisoner of the man-eater. Soon a blazing fire was roaring, fed by many willing hands, the occupant of the hut luckily being absent.

When I arrived on the scene and heard how matters stood, I climbed on to the anterior shed, followed by my Arab servant carrying my rifle and a lantern. The Sudanese lieutenant also joined me. The lion had taken refuge in the inner hut. Cautiously the Sudanese officer removed some of the thatch. I pushed the rifle through the opening and peered into the dark interior of the hut, whilst my Arab endeavoured to throw the light of the lantern into it. It was very doubtful whether the weak framework of the roof would bear our united weight much longer; there were ominous crackings and we were in danger of being precipitated into the hut right in front of the man-eater. There was also the possibility that the lion, in endeavouring to escape by this new opening, might spring at us. We had some trouble too in pushing aside, with sticks, a mosquito curtain intercepting our view of the interior.

It seemed a long while, though probably only a minute or two, before I succeeded in distinguishing the outline of the lion. I fired, but as I could not see the foresight of my rifle very clearly, I probably missed. The lion gave an ominous growl which was heard and received with mad shouts by the crowd surging around us at a safe distance. The brute bounded to the other end of the hut but, as it did so, it left the hind part of its body exposed and I was able this time to take a better aim and fired. As the lion turned to escape by the door I had time to re-load - I was using a Martini-Henri rifle - and to give it a good shoulder-shot. It staggered and then fell in the outer shed, dead.

The men guarding the entrance, of course, did not know that it was all over with the man-eater and they fired off their rifles. There was not much aiming, for one of these bad shots passed close to the Sudanese lieutenant and me. We slid off the roof and got the men to stop firing.

The man-eater turned out to be a lioness. It was gaunt and old, with five other wounds, in addition to the subsequent fusillade and the two inflicted by me. It required seven men to carry the lioness to where I camped. There was a feeling of joy and relief that the man-eater was slain and I had to remain close to the body to prevent its being torn to pieces by the frenzied mob. The women joined in the uproar with their shrill tremulo-scream of 'he-he-he-he-he' ad infinitum, a sort of truimphal chant, only stopping when quite out of breath.

It was a strange scene: a pitch-dark night in the heart of Africa, scores of blazing torches lighting up the gloom of the tall forest trees around us, a surging crowd of black faces, half-naked women uttering their shrill cry, in the distance the incessant boom of the Victoria Nile where it foams down the Murchison Falls, and the dead lioness!

I had left my hut at 7.30 p.m. and at 7.45 p.m. I was back with the dead man-eater, and yet so much was crowded into this quarter of an hour. It took a long time before everybody quietened down and went off to sleep. The goat was released from its unenviable position of serving as live bait for a lion, and then I too thought it high time to prepare for rest. Just then terrific screams from the Sudanese village once more caused me to hurry with loaded rifle to the rescue. Guided by the shrieks, we - the native lieutenant and others having joined me promptly on the way - reached a hut with the door fast closed. We burst the door open and rushed in. The torches lit up the interior and showed us two women clinging to each other. One of them had had a nightmare and dreamt the dead lioness had come to life again and entered her hut, her shrieks causing the other woman to scream in terror-stricken sympathy. This incident closed the evening; we calmed and reassured the women and then returned to our respective huts.

IV. The Majili Man-eater

On another journey, F C Selous recorded the activities of a man-eater which terrorised local villages and a camp of his situated along a tributary of the Zambesi.

In the early part of 1886 two half-caste elephant hunters, Henry

Wall and Black Jantje – the latter for several years a trusted servant of my own – crossed the Zambesi at its junction with the Quito or Chobi, in order to hunt in the country to the north between the Majili and Ungwesi rivers.

They soon heard from the natives that there was a man-eating lion in the district which had already killed several people, and they were therefore careful to see that a strong fence was made every night behind their camp, and sufficient dry wood collected to keep up good fires during the hours of darkness. The two hunters were accustomed to sleep by themselves within a strong semicircular fence, the open end of which was protected by a large fire. All but one of their native boys – wild Batonas and Masubias – slept together, lying in a row with a strong fence behind them and a succession of fires near their feet. One boy, who would not sleep with the others, always lay by one or other of the fires by himself.

One night, Henry Wall, who was a very light sleeper, was awakened, as he afterwards declared, by the sound of a low growl or purr close to him. Springing to his feet, he shouted out, 'The lion's here! Wake up, Jantje!' But Jantje and all the blacks were fast asleep, and it was not until they had been woken up and questioned that it was discovered that the man who had been lying by one of the fires all alone was gone. Where he had gone and why was not left long in doubt, for almost immediately a lion was heard eating his remains close behind the encampment. Henry Wall and Jantje at once fired in the direction of the sound, at which the lion retired to a safer distance with its prey.

As soon as it was broad daylight, the hunters took up the spoor of the lion which was, they told me, quite easy to follow through the dewy grass. It was not long before they saw it walking slowly along with its head half-turned, holding the dead man by one shoulder, so that his legs dragged at its side. As soon as it became aware that it was being followed it dropped its prey and, wheeling round, stood looking at its pursuers, twitching its tail and growling angrily.

Henry Wall, who was a very good shot and a cool and courageous man, now tried to fire, but the old, clumsy muzzle-loading elephant gun he was using only snapped the cap. At this juncture Jantje, who was a little to one side, was unable to fire because there was a bush in his way. Before Henry Wall could get another cap on the nipple of his gun, the black who carried his second weapon fired at and missed the lion which instantly turned and, running into a patch of bush, made good its escape.

On examination, it was found that the dead man had been seized by the head. He must have been killed instantaneously, as the two upper canine teeth had been driven through the top of the skull, whilst one of the lower ones had entered beneath the jaw and broken the bone. During the night the corpse had been disembowelled and all the flesh eaten off the thighs and buttocks.

A few days later, a native family was attacked not far from the scene of this episode and almost certainly by the same lion.

All over Africa, wherever game is plentiful, it is customary for the natives to build huts in their fields for use during the season when their crops are ripening, in which they spend the night and endeavour to keep buffaloes, elephants, and all kinds of antelopes out of their corn by shouting and beating tom-toms. The huts are often built on the top of platforms raised ten or twelve feet above the ground and reached by a ladder. The native family in question occupied two huts: a large one built on the ground which was occupied by a woman and her two children, and a small open one on the top of a platform in which her husband kept watch alone.

One night the man-eater of the Majili came prowling round and, scenting the native on the platform, either sprang up and seized him with its teeth or, more probably, half clambered up by the help of the ladder, and dragged him from his shelter with its claws. At any rate, it bore him to the ground and speedily killed him, but not before he had made a good deal of noise, as reported afterwards by his children. His wife, woken by the cries of her husband, opened the door of her hut and rushed out, leaving the two children inside. The lion at once left the man, who was then dead, and seizing the woman quickly killed her. It never returned to the body of the man at all, but ate all the fleshy parts of the woman, retiring into the bush before daylight and never revisiting the corpses.

All through the dry season this lion kept the natives in the neighbourhood of the Majili river in a constant state of alarm, and whilst adding steadily to the number of its victims, baffled every attempt made to hunt it down and destroy it. After having been away for some months, hunting in the country farther north, Henry Wall and Black Jantje once again camped on the Majili river on their way back to the Zambesi, and for the second time the man-eater paid them a visit. This time Jantje was awake, and hearing, as he told me, a low purring growl, jumped up, calling out, 'That's the lion again!'.

He then checked to see if everyone was there and it soon appeared that one of the natives was missing. The lion must have crept or sprung in amongst the sleepers and, seizing one of them by the head, must have killed him instantly and carried him off. The body of the man who had been carried off was not recovered because the rest of the blacks would give Henry Wall and Jantje no assistance in following up the lion the next day.

This dangerous man-eater was at last mortally wounded by the spears of two young men whom it attacked in broad daylight close to a small native village. One of these youths died the same evening from the mauling he received in the encounter, but he had driven his spear into the lion's chest when it attacked him, and his companion had also struck it in the side with a light throwing spear.

The next day, all the men from the two or three little villages in the neighbourhood turned out and followed up the bloody tracks of the wounded lion. They had not far to go, for the grim animal lay dead, with the two spears still sticking in it, within a short distance from the spot where it had attacked the two young men the previous day. As is the custom when man-eating lions are killed in the interior of Africa, a great quantity of dry wood was then collected, and a huge fire lit on which the carcass was thrown and utterly consumed.

V. Village Incidents

With no direct access to firearms, and only spears to rely on, Africans were effectively helpless in face of lion attacks on their villages. James Sutherland saw how vulnerable they were during his years as a hunter in central and east Africa at the turn of the century.

In nearly all cases, the man-eater is an animal well on in years. He has lost his youthful strength and agility and the capture of wild game for food has become for him a difficult task. He therefore adds man to his diet because the latter is easier to procure. He also appears to be well aware that the natives fear him and are comparatively helpless against his attack for he will, if pressed by hunger, force his way into their huts at night.

All over east and central Africa the idea is firmly imbedded in the native mind that man-eating lions are simply reincarnations of chiefs and medicine men who prowl about taking vengeance on those who wronged them during their lives in human shape.

Some years ago, I was in the neighbourhood of the Luhanyando stream, a tributary of the Luwegu. The country is mountainous, full of dense bush and grassy ravines and affords excellent cover for lions who were constantly killing natives in these parts. The details of a particularly sad occurrence that happened in a village in this district are still vividly fresh in my mind and give some idea of the determination, ferocity and daring of the king of beasts when he has acquired a taste for human flesh.

On the day previous to our arrival one of the villagers had buried her husband and she and her daughter, having passed the night in her mother-in-law's hut, rose at early dawn to return to their own dwelling which was not more than a couple of hundred yards distant. The homeward path lay through dense grass and as they sauntered back the girl, who walked a little in advance of her mother, all of a sudden heard a terrified shriek and a fierce growl. Turning round, she saw a lion seize her mother by the thigh, fling her to the ground and bite her through the neck. Yelling, '*Simba mama wae!* ' (Lion, my mother!) she immediately rushed to her hut, only about a score of yards away. The villagers living close by, hearing her piteous cries, snatched up their spears and quickly appeared on the scene. By this time the lion had dragged the unfortunate woman into the long grass and could be heard devouring the body some twenty or thirty yards from the path, but to penetrate such a bush after a man-eating lion was an undertaking upon which they would not venture.

Knowing that I was encamped near the village, they decided to appeal to me for assistance and without further delay came running to my tent and excitedly explained to me what had occurred. Picking up my double 577, and taking particular care to insert cartridges with capped, expanding bullets, I hastened to the spot where the native woman had been killed. Holding my rifle in front of me ready for instant action, I stealthily entered the long grass, my tracker, Simba, armed with a spear following me as if he were my shadow. After making our way for about forty yards through the thicket we were brought to a standstill by an ominous growl and, shortly afterwards, heard the long jungle grass rustling as the lion slunk away on our approach.

Cautiously following up the spoor, we came to the spot where he had stopped to devour his victim, the grass in the immediate neighbourhood being all trampled down and covered with blood; determined not to be cheated of his horrible meal the brute had dragged the body away with him. By this time not a sound was to be heard, and knowing that the animal could not be far off I advanced with utmost care, ready, should I get a chance, instantly to place a bullet in him. A little further on, we came across the gruesome sight of the woman's half-eaten body and could see that death must have been almost instantaneous, for the animal had bitten her right through the back of the neck.

Leaving the remains where they were, we continued our pursuit, moving a few yards at a time and expecting at any moment to come upon the beast. Suddenly, our progress was arrested by a fierce growl a few yards ahead of us and, next instant, I caught a fleeting glimpse of the animal slinking away, but it was much too brief to risk a shot. Before advancing further, I told Simba to climb a tree some yards to our right and spy out the nature of the country. Returning a few seconds later, he informed me that about thirty yards ahead of us there was a clearing where the natives had been preparing the ground for a garden, beyond which space lay an extensive patch of bush. Feeling certain that the lion had left the long grass and made for the bush, we were hastening along, when Simba suddenly whispered: 'Bwana, I heard the grass rustling ahead and maybe the lion has just left this cover and is making for the bush on the other side of the clearing. If we hurry, you may be able to get a shot at him before he has crossed the open space.'

Making speedy progress we emerged from the long grass, just in time to see the brute on the point of entering the thicket on the other side of the open space. Taking hasty aim, I fired, the bullet striking him and rolling him over. In an instant, he was up again, and was about to disappear when I fired my second barrel, unfortunately missing him. Crossing the clearing, we approached to within a score of yards of the spot at which he had vanished into the jungle, there to be met with a growling challenge. Imagining that he was severely wounded and would before long succumb to the effect of the bullet he had received, I thought it advisable that we should retrace our steps for about thirty yards and await developments.

After the lapse of about an hour I decided to explore the bush, fully expecting to find the brute dead. Listening for some moments and hearing no sounds, we cautiously entered the dense growth and began once more to follow up his spoor; this revealed that he had lost a considerable quantity of blood and appeared to be trailing one of his hind legs. We had not made more than thirty yards of wary progress when Simba, who was following closely behind me, touched me on the shoulder and pointed out a spot to my left front. Straining my eyes for a few seconds I could just discern the lion's tawny form, crouching absolutely motionless about twelve yards away, his head between his paws, his eyes gleaming in the shade and gazing steadily in our direction.

I raised my rifle quickly to my shoulder, but without giving me

time to aim the brute charged me, roaring. I promptly fired, the
bullet striking him on the right side of the head and smashing his
shoulder. My third shot knocked him down, but he was up again
in an instant and came on as quickly as ever. When within five
yards of me, I gave him the contents of the second barrel. The
impact brought him down and Simba, instantly raising his spear,
drove it with all his might into the brute's shoulder. Another bullet
from my rifle finished him.

The villagers were overjoyed at the news of the lion's death, and
to commemorate the occasion indulged in a prodigious beer-
drink, later fashioning amulets from the animal's bones.

The tragic incidents which follow happened in 1902 on the
eastern shores of Lake Nyasa where some natives, having left their
old homes with the intention of settling down anew, had erected
temporary grass huts and were tilling their shambas for the coming
rains. Arriving on the day following the unhappy affair I gathered
an account of it from the askaris, or native police, who had
participated in the occurrence.

On the night in question, five of these askaris were sleeping in one hut
when, about three o'clock in the morning, one of them was woken up
by a low growl and the noise of a sudden crash, which he realised
meant the presence of a man-eating lion. He immediately woke his
comrades who, picking up their rifles, went outside the hut and listened
intently for any noise that might confirm their comrade's suspicions. A
low moan broke the stillness of the night, and discovering that the
sound came from a hut some fifty yards away in which a woman and
her child were sleeping, they crept closer and distinctly heard the sound
of bones being crunched inside.

Convinced that a lion had broken into the hut and was making
a meal of the woman, whom he had killed, they promptly emptied
their rifles into the dwelling, trusting that a lucky bullet might find
the animal. They then waited to see if the man-eater would come
out, but as he made no appearance and silence reigned in the hut,
they came to the conclusion that he had either been killed or was
crouching ready to spring on the first man who dared venture too
close. Deciding to take no risks, they made torches of dry grass and,

setting them alight, flung them from a distance on to the dry inflammable thatch roof of the hut, which was soon ablaze.

Before the conflagration had died down, the dawn had broken in the east and with the light of day they learned the truth. Going over to the still glowing embers – all that was left of the hut – they discovered the charred remains of a lion, a woman, and a child. Only one bullet had struck the lion, but that one had gone right through his heart probably killing him instantly; the woman's body had received three bullets, though she had probably died long before being hit by them because her right shoulder and breast had been terribly bitten and chewed. The child's head had been crushed in, evidently by one blow of the man-eater's paw.

Some years later, while hunting in the Sultan Leanduka's country, I noticed that the natives always went about together in twos and threes fully armed. On my asking the reason of this behaviour Leanduka told me that his people were living in terror of man-eating lions, one of which monsters had accounted for no less than fifteen individuals during the rainy season. The beast, he said, never visited the same village on successive nights, but came one night here, next night there, another night several miles away.

One day, as I was returning after an elephant hunt to my camp near this village, I was met some miles from home by a native. In great distress he informed me that on the afternoon of the previous day lions had killed his brother and his brother's two wives while they were on their way from one village to another. On returning to camp, I immediately set out on the tracks of the beasts. I followed the spoor for two days but, owing to the grassy nature of the country, I failed to come up with them at all, the cunning brutes seeming to know that they were being hunted and making off at once on our approach.

In July, 1905, I had occasion to send a couple of my men from my camp on the banks of the Rovuma river to Songea, about eight days' journey away. Some thirty miles on their way they decided to put up for the night at Gwia's village where, so the inhabitants informed them, lions had recently accounted for nine lives. They slept by themselves in a hut, in the centre of which they had

kindled a large fire, Majemba lying on one side of the fire and
Hyiah on the opposite side, nearest the door. Paying heed to the
warning they had received about man-eaters, they took particular
care before retiring to secure the door as strongly as possible.

About three o'clock in the morning the door was violently burst
in and, before my men exactly knew what had happened, a lion
seized Hyiah by the thigh and proceeded to drag him out of the
hut. Immediately Majemba, who had been woken up by the
commotion, seized his rifle and fired at the brute luckily putting a
bullet in the region of his heart, whereupon the animal instantly
dropped Hyiah and cleared into the surrounding bush. At break of
day the villagers discovered the animal's dead body, some seventy
yards from the hut, and it proved to be that of a mangy old lioness.

After cleansing Hyiah's thigh with hot water the natives fashioned
a maschilla and carried him into my camp, where I immediately
bathed and syringed the poor fellow's wounds with disinfectants to
prevent blood-poisoning setting in. These precautions proved
effective and within six weeks Hyiah was able to get about again.

Two years after this occurrence, I chanced to meet the headman
of the village where the events had taken place, and he informed
me that his kraal had not been disturbed by lions during the
interval; a fact which seems to prove that the lioness shot by
Majemba had accounted for the three men and six women that had
been carried off previous to the arrival of my men.

Some years ago I was on the Upper Shire river in British Central
Africa. I was sitting in my tent when one of my men, whom I had
paid off two days before, came running up in a state of great
excitement, shouting 'Incango a mio, incango a mio!' (Lion, my
mother, lion, my mother!) and informed me that a number of lions
had taken possession of his home. Picking up my rifle I at once set
out for his hut, which was about a mile distant, and on arriving
there found several natives in a state of great perturbation, gathered
about the door of the dwelling.

From them I learned that my man's wife, carrying her youngest
child on her back as is the custom with native women even when
working, had been grinding flour for the evening meal just outside

her hut. Her mother and other child were resting inside when, all of a sudden, without a warning sound, a lion appeared on the scene and snatched the babe from her mother's back. Dropping the child almost immediately, the brute sprang on the mother, bit her through the neck, and having dragged her into the shamba where the matama corn lay cut, began to devour the body. Shortly afterwards, another lion appeared on the scene and joined in the ghastly meal, the whole tragedy being enacted before the eyes of those in the hut. They were too terrified to run or cry for help to the woman's husband who was fishing from the riverbank, not more than a couple of hundred yards away.

When the husband returned to his hut an awful sight met his eyes: his youngest child, bitten through the skull, lay dead at the door, while in the distance two lions were growling over and gorging themselves on his wife's body. Remembering that I was in the neighbourhood the distracted fellow then ran to my camp and begged me to come to his assistance.

In his absence some natives, who had heard his terrified yells, at once made their way to his hut and the lions, on seeing them, left their victim's body and vanished into the bush. On reaching the spot, I at once went into the shamba and discovered the horribly mangled remains of the unfortunate woman lying among the matama corn, but as nothing more could be done as far as she was concerned, accompanied by two of my men, I immediately set out in pursuit of the lions. Though we followed their spoor till sunset, never a glimpse of them did we get. Returning to the village, I made the natives leave the woman's body where we had found it, hoping that under cover of night the brutes would return to finish their meal and give us a chance of avenging the deaths. Making as comfortable a perch as possible in the branches of a convenient tree, rifle in hand, I kept a weary vigil till dawn broke out, throughout the long tropical night, no lion's shape darkened the brightly moonlit shamba.

Strange to relate, the native who had thus lost wife and child in one afternoon was, a few days after his bereavement, himself seized and devoured by a crocodile.

CHAPTER FOUR

The Champawat Man-eater

JIM CORBETT pursued man-eating tigers from 1907 to 1939, a period of thirty seven years. The first man-eater he ever pursued accounted for 436 human deaths before it was shot, nearly one half of these deaths occurring in Nepal followed by a four year reign of terror in the Naini Tal district of northern India.

The tigress had arrived in Kumaon as a full-fledged man-eater from Nepal, from where she had been driven out by a body of armed Nepalese after she had killed two hundred human beings, and during the four years she had been operating in Kumaon had added two hundred and thirty-four to this number. She was causing government a great deal of anxiety: rewards were offered, special shikaris employed, and parties of Gurkhas sent out from the depot in Almora. Yet in spite of these measures, the toll of human victims continued to mount alarmingly.

This is how matters stood when shortly after my arrival in Naini Tal I received a visit from Berthoud. Berthoud, who was deputy commissioner of Naini Tal at that time, and who after his tragic death now lies buried in an obscure grave in Haldwani, was a man who was loved and respected by all who knew him. It is not surprising therefore that when he told me of the trouble the man-eater was giving the people of his district, and the anxiety it was causing him, he took my promise with him that I would start for Champawat immediately on receipt of news of the next human kill.

Two conditions I made, however: one that the government

rewards be cancelled, and the other that the special shikaris and regulars from Almora be withdrawn. My reasons for making these conditions were an aversion to being classed as a reward-hunter and my anxiety to avoid the risk of being accidentally shot. These conditions were agreed to, and a week later Berthoud paid me an early morning visit and informed me that news had been brought in during the night by runners that a woman had been killed by the man-eater at Pali, a village between Dabidhura and Dhunaghat.

In anticipation of a start at short notice, I had engaged six men to carry my camp kit and, leaving after breakfast, we did a march the first day of seventeen miles to Dhari. Breakfasting at Mornaula next morning, we spent the night at Dabidhura, and arrived at Pali the following evening, five days after the woman had been killed.

The people of the village, numbering some fifty men, women, and children, were in a state of abject terror, and though the sun was still up when I arrived I found the entire population inside their homes behind locked doors. It was not until my men had made a fire in the courtyard and I was sitting down to a cup of tea that a door here and there was cautiously opened, and the frightened inmates emerged.

I was informed that for five days no one had gone beyond their own doorsteps - the insanitary condition of the courtyard testified to the truth of this statement - that food was running short, and that the people would starve if the tiger was not killed or driven away.

That the tiger was still in the vicinity was apparent. For three nights it had been heard calling on the road, a hundred yards from the houses, and that very day it had been seen on the cultivated land at the lower end of the village.

The headman of the village very willingly placed a room at my disposal, but as there were eight of us to share it, and the only door it possessed opened onto the insanitary courtyard, I elected to spend the night in the open.

After a scratch meal which had to do duty for dinner, I saw my men safely shut into the room and myself took up a position on the side of the road, with my back to a tree. The villagers said the tiger was in the habit of perambulating along this road, and as soon as the moon was at the full I thought there was a chance of my getting a shot – provided I saw it first.

I had spent many nights in the jungle looking for game, but this was the first time I had ever spent a night looking for a man-eater. The length of road immediately in front of me was brilliantly lit by the moon, but to right and left the overhanging trees cast dark shadows, and when the night wind agitated the branches and the shadows moved, I saw a dozen tigers advancing on me, and bitterly regretted the impulse that had induced me to place myself at the man-eater's mercy.

I lacked the courage to return to the village and admit I was too frightened to carry out my self-imposed task, and with teeth chattering, as much from fear as from cold, I sat out the long night. As the grey dawn was lighting up the snowy range which I was facing, I rested my head on my drawn-up knees and it was in this position my men an hour later found me – fast asleep; of the tiger I had neither heard nor seen anything.

Back in the village I tried to get the men – who I could see were very surprised I had survived the night – to take me to the places where the people of the village had from time to time been killed, but this they were unwilling to do. From the courtyard they pointed out the direction in which the kills had taken place. I was told the last kill – the one that had brought me to the spot – had taken place round the shoulder of the hill to the west of the village. The women and girls, some twenty in number, who had been out collecting oak leaves for the cattle when the unfortunate woman had been killed, were eager to give me details of the occurrence.

It appeared that the party had set out two hours before midday and, after going half a mile, had climbed into trees to cut leaves. The victim and two other women had selected a tree growing on the edge of a ravine, which I subsequently found was about four feet deep and ten to twelve feet wide. Having cut all the leaves she needed, the woman was climbing down from the tree when the tiger, who had approached unseen, stood up on its hind legs and caught her by the foot. Her hold was torn from the branch she was letting herself down by and, pulling her into the ravine, the tiger released her foot and while she was struggling to rise caught her by the throat. After killing her it sprang up the side of the ravine and disappeared with her into some heavy undergrowth.

All this had taken place a few feet from the two women on the tree, and had been witnessed by the entire party. As soon as the tiger and its victim were out of sight, the terror-stricken women and girls ran back to the village. The men had just come in for their midday meal and, when all were assembled and armed with drums, metal cooking-pots - anything in fact that would produce a noise - the rescue party set off, the men leading and the women bringing up the rear. Having arrived at the ravine in which the woman had been killed, the very important question of 'what next?' was being debated when the tiger interrupted the proceedings by emitting a loud roar from the bushes thirty yards away. As one man, the party turned and fled helter-skelter back to the village.

When breath had been regained, accusations were made as to who had been the first to run and cause the stampede. Words ran high until it was suggested that if no one was afraid and all were as brave as they claimed to be, why not go back and rescue the woman without loss of more time? The suggestion was adopted, and three times the party got as far as the ravine. On the third occasion the one man who was armed with a gun fired it off, and brought the tiger roaring out of the bushes. After this the at-tempted rescue was very wisely abandoned. On my asking the gun man why he had not discharged his piece into the bushes instead of up into the air, he said the tiger was already greatly enraged and that if by any mischance he had hit it, the tiger would undoubtedly have killed him.

For three hours that morning I walked round the village looking for tracks and hoping, and at the same time dreading to meet the tiger. At one place in a dark heavily-wooded ravine, while I was skirting some bushes, a covey of kaleege pheasants fluttered scream-ing out of them and I thought my heart had stopped beating for good.

My men had cleared a spot under a walnut tree for my meals, and after breakfast the headman of the village asked me to mount guard while the wheat crop was being cut. He said that if the crop was not harvested in my presence, it would not be harvested at all, for the people were too frightened to leave their homes. Half an hour later the entire population of the village, assisted by my men, were hard at work while I stood on guard with a loaded rifle. By evening the crop from five large fields had been gathered, leaving only two small patches close to the houses, which the headman said he would have no difficulty in dealing with the next day.

The sanitary condition of the village had been much improved, and a second room for my exclusive use placed at my disposal. That night, with thorn bushes securely wedged in the doorway to admit ventilation and exclude the man-eater, I made up for the sleep I had lost the previous night.

My presence was beginning to put new heart into the people and they were moving about more freely, but I had not yet gained sufficient of their confidence to renew my request of being shown round the jungle, to which I attached some importance. These people knew every foot of the ground for miles round and could, if they wished, show me where I was most likely to find the tiger, or in any case where I could see its pug marks. That the man-eater was a tiger was an established fact, but it was not known whether the animal was young or old, a male or a female and this information, which I believed would help me to get in touch with it, I could only ascertain by examining its pug marks.

After an early tea that morning I announced that I wanted meat for my men and asked the villagers if they could direct me to where I could shoot a ghooral or mountain goat. The village was situated on the top of a long ridge running east and west, and just below the road on which I had spent the night the hill fell steeply away to the north in a series of grassy slopes. On these slopes I was told ghooral were plentiful, and several men volunteered to show me over the ground. I was careful not to show my pleasure at this offer and, selecting three men, I set out, telling the headman that if I found the ghooral as plentiful as he said they were, I would shoot two for the village in addition to shooting one for my men.

Crossing the road we went down a very steep ridge, keeping a sharp lookout to right and left, but saw nothing. Half a mile down the hill the ravines converged, and from their junction there was a good view of the rocky and grass-covered slope to the right. I had been sitting with my back to a solitary pine which grew at this spot for some minutes scanning the slope, when a movement high up on the hill caught my eye. When the movement was repeated I saw it was a ghooral flapping its ears; the animal was standing in grass and only its head was visible. The men had not seen the movement, and as the head was now stationary and blended with its surroundings it was not possible to point it out to them. Giving them a general idea of the animal's position, I made them sit down and watch while I took a shot. I was armed with an old Martini Henry rifle, a weapon that atoned for its vicious kick by being dead accurate - up to any range. The distance was as near two hundred yards as made no matter and, lying down and resting the rifle on a convenient pine root, I took careful aim and fired.

The smoke from the black powder cartridge obscured my view and the men said nothing had happened and that I had probably fired at a rock, or a bunch of dead leaves. Retaining my position I reloaded the rifle and presently saw the grass, a little below where I had fired, moving, and the hind quarters of the ghooral appeared. When the whole animal was free of the grass it started to roll over and over, gaining momentum as it came down the steep hill. When it was halfway down it disappeared into heavy grass and disturbed two ghooral that had been lying up there. Sneezing their alarm call, the two animals dashed out of the grass and went bounding up the hill. The range was shorter now and, adjusting the leaf sight, I waited until the bigger of the two slowed down and put a bullet through its back; as the other one turned, and made off diagonally across the hill, I shot it through the shoulder.

On occasions one is privileged to accomplish the seemingly impossible. Lying in an uncomfortable position and shooting up at an angle of sixty degrees at a range of two hundred yards at the small white mark on the ghooral's throat, there did not appear to be one chance in a million of the shot coming off, and yet the heavy lead bullet driven by black powder had not been deflected by a hair's breadth and had gone true to its mark, killing the animal instantaneously. Again, on the steep hillside which was broken up by small ravines and jutting rocks, the dead animal had slipped and rolled straight to the spot where its two companions were lying up; and before it had cleared the patch of grass the two companions in their turn were slipping and rolling down the hill. As the three dead animals landed in the ravine in front of us it was amusing to observe the surprise and delight of the men who never before had seen a rifle in action. All thought of the man-eater was for the time being forgotten as they scrambled down into the ravine to retrieve the bag.

The expedition was a great success in more ways than one, for in addition to providing a ration of meat for everyone, it gained me the confidence of the entire village. Shikar yarns, as everyone knows, never lose anything in repetition, and while the ghooral were being skinned and divided up the three men who had accompanied me gave full reign to their imagination. From where I sat in the open having breakfast I could hear the exclamations of the assembled crowd when they were told that the ghooral had been shot at a range of over a mile, and that the magic bullets used had not only killed the animals - like that - but had also drawn them to the sahib's feet.

After the midday meal the headman asked me where I wanted to go and how many men I wished to take with me. From the eager throng of men who pressed round I selected two of my late companions, and with them to guide me set off to visit the scent of the last human tragedy.

The people of our hills are Hindus and cremate their dead, and when one of their number has been carried off by a man-eater it is incumbent on the relatives to recover some portion of the body for cremation even if it be only a few splinters of bone. In the case of this woman the cremation ceremony was yet to be performed, and as we started out the relatives requested us to bring back any portion of the body we might find.

From early boyhood I have made a hobby of reading and interpreting jungle signs. In the present case I had the account of the eyewitnesses who were present when the woman was killed, but eyewitnesses are not always reliable, whereas jungle signs are a true record of all that has transpired. On arrival at the spot a glance at the ground showed me that the tiger could only have approached the tree one way, without being seen, and that was up the ravine. Entering the ravine a hundred yards below the tree, and working up, I found the pug marks of a tiger in some fine earth that had sifted down between two big rocks; these pug marks showed the animal to be a tigress, a little past her prime. Further up the ravine, and some ten yards from the tree, the tigress had lain down behind a rock, presumably to wait for the woman to climb down the tree. The victim had been the first to cut all the leaves she needed, and as she was letting herself down by a branch some two inches in diameter the tigress had crept forward and, standing up on her hind legs, had caught the woman by the foot and pulled her down into the ravine.

The branch showed the desperation with which the unfortunate woman had clung to it, for adhering to the rough oak bark where the branch, and eventually the leaves, had slipped through her grasp, were strands of skin which had been torn from the palms of her hands and fingers. Where the tigress had killed the woman there were signs of a struggle and a big patch of dried blood; from here the blood trail, now dry but distinctly visible, led across the ravine and up the opposite bank. Following the blood trail from where it left the ravine we found the place in the bushes where the tigress had eaten her kill.

It is a popular belief that man-eaters never eat the head, hands, and feet of their human victims. This is incorrect. Man-eaters, if not disturbed, sometimes eat everything - including the blood-soaked clothes. Thus on the present occasion we found just the woman's clothes, and a few pieces of bone which we wrapped up in the clean cloth we had brought for the purpose. Pitifully little as these remains were, they would suffice for the cremation ceremony which would ensure the ashes of the high caste woman reaching Mother Ganges.

After tea I visited the scene of yet another tragedy. Separated from the main village by the public road was a smallholding of a few acres. The owner of this holding had built himself a hut on the hillside just above the road. The man's wife and the mother of his two children, a boy and a girl aged four and six respectively, was the younger of two sisters. These two sisters were out cutting grass one day on the hill above the hut when the tigress suddenly appeared and carried off the elder sister. For a hundred yards the younger woman ran after the tigress brandishing her sickle and screaming at the tigress to let her sister go, and take her instead. This incredible act of heroism was witnessed by the people in the main village.

After carrying the dead woman for a hundred yards the tigress put her down and turned on her pursuer. With a loud roar it sprang at the brave woman who, turning, raced down the hillside, across the road and into the village, evidently with the intention of telling the people what they, unknown to her, had already witnessed. The woman's incoherent noises were at the time attributed to loss of breath, fear and excitement, and it was not until the rescue party that had set out with all speed had returned, unsuccessful, that it was found the woman had lost her power of speech. I was told this tale in the village, and when I climbed the path to the two-roomed hut where the woman was engaged in washing clothes, she had then been dumb for a year.

Except for a strained look in her eyes the dumb woman appeared to be quite normal and, when I stopped to speak to her and tell her I had come to try and shoot the tiger that had killed her sister, she put her hands together and stooping down touched my feet, making me feel a wretched impostor. True, I had come with the avowed object of shooting the man-eater, but with an animal that had the reputation of never killing twice in the same locality, never returning to a kill, and whose domain extended over an area of many hundred square miles, the chance of my accomplishing my object was about as good as finding a needle in two haystacks.

Plans in plenty I had made way back in Naini Tal; one I had already tried, and wild horses would not induce me to try it again, and the others – now that I was on the ground – were just as unattractive. Further, there was no one I could ask for advice, for this was the first man-eater that had ever been known in Kumaon; and yet something would have to be done. So for the next three days I wandered through the jungles from sunrise to sunset, visiting all the places for miles round where the villagers told me there was a chance of my seeing the tigress.

I would like to interrupt my tale here for a few minutes to refute a rumour current throughout the hills that on this, and on several subsequent occasions, I assumed the dress of a hill woman and, going into the jungle, attracted the man-eaters to myself and killed them with either a sickle or an axe. All I have ever done in the matter of alteration of dress has been to borrow a sari and with it draped round me I cut grass, or climbed into trees and cut leaves. In no case has the ruse proved successful though on two occasions – to my knowledge – man-eaters have stalked the tree I was on, taking cover on one occasion behind a rock and on the other behind a fallen tree, but giving me no opportunity of shooting them.

To continue. As the tigress now appeared to have left this locality I decided, much to the regret of the people of Pali, to move to Champawat, fifteen miles due east of Pali. Making an early start, I breakfasted at Dhunaghat, and completed the journey to Champawat by sunset. The roads in this area were considered very unsafe and men only moved from village to village or to the bazars in large parties. After leaving Dhunaghat, my party of eight was added to by men from villages adjoining the road, and we arrived at Champawat thirty strong. Some of the men who joined me had been in a party of twenty men who had visited Champawat two months earlier and they told me the following very pitiful story.

'The road for a few miles on this side of Champawat runs along the south face of the hill, parallel to, and about fifty yards above, the valley. Two months ago a party of twenty of us men were on our way to the bazaar at Champawat, and as we were going along this length of the road at about midday, we were startled by hearing the agonized cries of a human being coming from the valley below.

Huddled together on the edge of the road we cowered in fright as
these cries drew nearer and nearer, and presently into view came
a tiger, carrying a naked woman. The woman's hair was trailing on
the ground on one side of the tiger, and her feet on the other – the
tiger was holding her by the small of the back – and she was beating
her chest and calling alternately to God and man to help her. Fifty
yards away, and in clear view of us, the tiger passed with its burden,
and when the cries had died away in the distance we continued on
our way.'

'And you twenty men did nothing?'

'No, sahib, we did nothing, for we were afraid, and what can men
do when they are afraid? And, further, even if we had been able
to rescue the woman without angering the tiger and bringing
misfortune on ourselves, it would have availed the woman nothing, for she was covered with blood and would of a surety have
died of her wounds.'

I subsequently learned that the victim belonged to a village near
Champawat and that she had been carried off by the tiger while
collecting dry sticks. Her companions had run back to the village
and raised an alarm, and just as a rescue party was starting the
twenty frightened men arrived. As these men knew the direction
in which the tiger had gone with its victim, they joined the party,
and can best carry on the story.

'We were fifty or sixty strong when we set out to rescue the
woman, and several of the party were armed with guns. A furlong
from where the sticks collected by the woman were lying, and
from where she had been carried off, we found her torn clothes.
Thereafter the men started beating their drums and firing off their
guns, and in this way we proceeded for more than a mile right up
to the head of the valley, where we found the woman, who was
little more than a girl, lying dead on a great slab of rock. Beyond
licking off all the blood and making her body clean the tiger had
not touched her and, there being no woman in our party, we men
averted our faces as we wrapped her body in the loincloths which
one and another gave, for she looked as she lay on her back as one
who sleeps and would waken in shame when touched.'

With experiences such as these to tell and retell through the long night watches behind fast-shut doors, it is little wonder that the character and outlook on life of people living year after year in a man-eater country should change, and that one coming from the outside should feel that he had stepped right into a world of stark realities and the rule of the tooth and claw, which forced man in the reign of the sabre-toothed tiger to shelter in dark caverns. I was young and inexperienced in those far-off Champawat days but, even so, the conviction I came to after a brief sojourn in that stricken land, that there is no more terrible thing than to live and have one's being under the shadow of a man-eater, has been strengthened by thirty-two years' subsequent experience.

The tahsildar of Champawat, to whom I had been given letters of introduction, paid me a visit that night at the Dak bungalow where I was putting up, and suggested I should move next day to a bungalow a few miles away, in the vicinity of which many human beings had been killed.

Early next morning, accompanied by the tahsildar, I set out for the bungalow, and while I was having breakfast on the verandah two men arrived with news that a cow had been killed by a tiger in a village ten miles away. The tahsildar excused himself to attend to some urgent work at Champawat, and said he would return to the bungalow in the evening and stay the night with me. My guides were good walkers, and as the track went downhill most of the way we covered the ten miles in record time. Arrived at the village I was taken to a cattle-shed in which I found a week-old calf, killed and partly eaten by a leopard.

Not having the time or the inclination to shoot the leopard I rewarded my guides and retraced my steps to the bungalow. Here I found the tahsildar had not returned, and as there was still an hour or more of daylight left I went out with the chowkidar of the bungalow to look at a place where, he informed me, a tiger was in the habit of drinking; this place I found to be the head of the spring which supplied the garden with irrigation water. In the soft earth round the spring were tiger pug marks several days old, but these tracks were quite different from the pug marks I had seen, and carefully examined, in the ravine in which the woman of Pali village had been killed.

On returning to the bungalow I found the tahsildar was back, and as we sat on the verandah I told him of my day's experience. Expressing regret at my having had to go so far on a wild-goose chase, he rose, saying that as he had a long way to go he must start at once. This announcement caused me no little surprise, for twice that day he had said he would stay the night with me. It was not the question of his staying the night that concerned me, but the risk he was taking. However, he was deaf to all my arguments and as he stepped off the verandah into the dark night, with only one man following him carrying a smoky lantern which gave a mere glimmer of light, to do a walk of four miles in a locality in which men only moved in large parties in daylight, I took off my hat to a very brave man. Having watched him out of sight I turned and entered the bungalow.

I spent the following morning in going round the very extensive fruit orchard and tea garden and in having a bath at the spring, and at about midday the tahsildar, much to my relief, returned safely from Champawat.

I was standing talking to him while looking down a long sloping hill with a village surrounded by cultivated land in the distance, when I saw a man leave the village and start up the hill in our direction. As the man drew nearer I saw he was alternately running and walking, and was quite evidently the bearer of important news. Telling the tahsildar I would return in a few minutes, I set off at a run down the hill, and when the man saw me coming he sat down to take breath. As soon as I was near enough to hear him he called out, 'Come quickly, sahib, the man-eater has just killed a girl.' 'Sit still,' I called back and, turning, ran up to the bungalow. I passed the news to the tahsildar while I was getting a rifle and some cartridges, and asked him to follow me down to the village.

The man who had come for me was one of those exasperating individuals whose legs and tongue cannot function at the same time. When he opened his mouth he stopped dead, and when he started to run his mouth closed; so telling him to shut his mouth and lead the way, we ran in silence down the hill.

At the village an excited crowd of men, women, and children awaited us and, as usually happens on these occasions, all started to talk at the same time. One man was vainly trying to quieten the babel. I led him aside and asked him to tell me what had happened. Pointing to some scattered oak trees on a gentle slope a furlong or so from the village, he said a dozen people were collecting dry sticks under the trees when a tiger suddenly appeared and caught one of their number, a girl sixteen or seventeen years of age. The rest of the party had run back to the village and as it was known that I was staying at the bungalow a man had immediately been dispatched to inform me.

The wife of the man I was speaking to had been one of the party and she now pointed out the tree, on the shoulder of the hill, under which the girl had been taken. None of the party had looked back to see if the tiger was carrying away its victim and, if so, in which direction it had gone.

Instructing the crowd not to make a noise and to remain in the village until I returned, I set off in the direction of the tree. The ground here was quite open and it was difficult to conceive how an animal the size of a tiger could have approached twelve people unseen, and its presence not detected, until attention had been attracted by the choking sound made by the girl.

The spot where the girl had been killed was marked by a pool of blood and near it, and in vivid contrast to the crimson pool, was a broken necklace of brightly coloured blue beads which the girl had been wearing. From this spot the track led up and round the shoulder of the hill.

The track of the tigress was clearly visible. On one side of it were great splashes of blood where the girl's head had hung down and on the other side the trail of her feet. Half a mile up the hill I found the girl's sari, and on the brow of the hill her skirt. Once again the tigress was carrying a naked woman, but mercifully on this occasion her burden was dead.

On the brow of the hill the track led through a thicket of blackthorn, on the thorns of which long strands of the girl's raven-black hair had caught. Beyond this was a bed of nettles through which the tigress had gone, and I was looking for a way round this obstruction when I heard footsteps behind me. Turning round I saw a man armed with a rifle coming towards me. I asked him why he had followed me when I had left instructions at the village that no one was to leave it. He said the tahsildar had instructed him to accompany me and that he was afraid to disobey orders. As he appeared determined to carry out his orders, and to argue the point would have meant the loss of valuable time, I told him to remove the heavy pair of boots he was wearing and, when he had hidden them under a bush, I advised him to keep close to me, and to keep a sharp lookout behind.

I was wearing a very thin pair of stockings, shorts, and a pair of rubber-soled shoes, and as there appeared to be no way round the nettles I followed the tigress through them - much to my discomfort.

Beyond the nettles the blood trail turned sharply to the left, and went straight down the very steep hill, which was densely clothed with bracken and bamboos. A hundred yards further down the trail of blood led into a narrow and very steep watercourse, down which the tigress had gone with some difficulty as could be seen from the dislodged stones of earth. I followed this watercourse for five or six hundred yards, my companion getting more and more agitated the further we went. A dozen times he caught my arm and whispered - in a voice full of tears - that he could hear the tiger, either on one side or the other, or behind us. Halfway down the hill we came on a great pinnacle of rock some thirty feet high, and as the man by now had had all the man-eater hunting he could stand, I told him to climb the rock and remain on it until I returned. Very gladly he went up, and when he straddled the top and signalled to me that he was alright I continued on down the watercourse which, after skirting round the rock, went straight down for a hundred yards to where it met a deep ravine coming down from the left. At the junction was a small pool and as I approached it I saw patches of blood on my side of the water.

The tigress had carried the girl straight down to this spot and my approach had disturbed her at her meal. Splinters of bone were scattered round the deep pug marks into which discoloured water was slowly seeping and at the edge of the pool was an object which had puzzled me as I came down the watercourse, and which I now found was part of a human leg. In all the subsequent years I have hunted man-eaters I have not seen anything as pitiful as that young comely leg - bitten off a little below the knee as clean as though severed by the stroke of an axe - out of which the warm blood was trickling.

While looking at the leg I had forgotten all about the tigress until I suddenly felt that I was in great danger. Hurriedly grounding the butt of the rifle I put two fingers on the triggers, raising my head as I did so, and saw a little earth, from the fifteen-foot bank in front of me, come rolling down the steep side and plop into the pool. I was new to this game of man-eater hunting or I should not have exposed myself to an attack in the way I had done. My prompt action in pointing the rifle upwards had possibly saved my life and, in stopping her spring, or in turning to get away, the tigress had dislodged the earth from the top of the bank.

The bank was too steep for scrambling, and the only way of getting up was to take it at a run. Going up the watercourse a short distance I sprinted down, took the pool in my stride, and got far enough up the other side to grasp a bush, and pull myself onto the bank. A bed of strobilanthes, the bent stalks of which were slowly regaining their upright position, showed where and how recently the tigress had passed, and a little further on under an overhanging rock I found where she had left her kill when she came to have a look at me.

Her tracks now - as she carried away the girl - led into a wilderness of rocks, some acres in extent, where the going was both difficult and dangerous. The cracks and chasms between the rocks were masked with ferns and blackberry vines, and a false step, which might easily have resulted in a broken limb, would have been fatal. Progress under these conditions was of necessity slow, and the tigress was taking advantage of it to continue her meal. A dozen times I found where she had rested and after each of these rests the blood trail became more distinct.

This was her four hundred and thirty-sixth human kill and she was quite accustomed to being disturbed at her meals by rescue parties, but this, I think, was the first time she had been followed up so persistently and she now began to show her resentment by growling. To appreciate a tiger's growl to the full it is necessary to be situated as I then was - rocks all round with dense vegetation between, and the imperative necessity of testing each footstep to avoid falling headlong into unseen chasms and caves.

I cannot expect you who read this at your fireside to appreciate my feelings at the time. The sound of the growling and the expectation of an attack terrified me at the same time as it gave me hope. If the tigress lost her temper sufficiently to launch an attack, it would not only give me an opportunity of accomplishing the object for which I had come, but it would enable me to get even with her for all the pain and suffering she had caused.

The growling, however, was only a gesture, and, when the tigress found that instead of shooing me off it was bringing me faster on her heels, she abandoned it. I had now been on her track for over four hours. Though I had repeatedly seen the undergrowth moving I had not seen so much as a hair of her hide, and a glance at the shadows climbing up the opposite hillside warned me it was time to retrace my steps if I was to reach the village before dark. The late owner of the severed leg was a Hindu, and some portion of her would be needed for the cremation, so as I passed the pool I dug a hole in the bank and buried the leg where it would be safe from the tigress and could be found when wanted.

My companion on the rock was very relieved to see me. My long absence, and the growling he had heard, had convinced him that the tigress had secured another kill and his difficulty, as he quite frankly admitted, was how he was going to get back to the village alone. I thought when we were climbing down the watercourse that I knew of no more dangerous proceeding than walking in front of a nervous man carrying a loaded gun, but I changed my opinion when on walking behind him he slipped and fell, and I saw where the muzzle of his gun - a converted 450 without a safety catch - was pointing. Since that day I have made it a hard and fast rule to go alone when hunting man-eaters, for if one's companion is unarmed it is difficult to protect him, and if he is armed, it is even more difficult to protect oneself.

Arrived at the crest of the hill, where the man had hidden his boots, I sat down to have a smoke and think out my plans for the morrow.

The tigress would finish what was left of the kill during the night and would certainly lie up among the rocks next day. On the ground she was on there was very little hope of my being able to stalk her, and if I disturbed her without getting a shot, she would probably leave the locality and I should lose touch with her. A beat therefore was the only thing to do, provided I could raise sufficient men.

I was sitting on the south edge of a great amphitheatre of hills, without a habitation of any kind in sight. A stream entering from the west had fretted its way down, cutting a deep valley right across the amphitheatre. To the east the stream had struck solid rock, and turning north had left the amphitheatre by a narrow gorge.

The hill in front of me, rising to a height of some two thousand feet, was clothed in short grass with a pine tree dotted here and there, and the hill to the east was too precipitous for anything but a ghooral to negotiate. If I could collect sufficient men to man the entire length of the ridge from the stream to the precipitous hill, and get them to stir up the tigress, her most natural line of retreat would be through the narrow gorge. Admittedly a very difficult beat, for the steep hillside facing north, on which I had left the tigress, was densely wooded and roughly three-quarters of a mile long and half a mile wide; however, if I could get the beaters to carry out instructions, there was a reasonable chance of my getting a shot.

The tahsildar was waiting for me at the village. I explained the position to him, and asked him to take immediate steps to collect as many men as he could, and to meet me at the tree where the girl had been killed - at ten o'clock the following morning. Promising to do his best, he left for Champawat, while I climbed the hill to the bungalow.

I was up at crack of dawn next morning, and after a substantial meal told my men to pack up and wait for me at Champawat, and went down to have another look at the ground I intended beating. I could find nothing wrong with the plans I had made, and an hour before my time I was at the spot where I had asked the tahsildar to meet me.

That he would have a hard time in collecting the men I had no doubt, for the fear of the man-eater had sunk deep into the countryside and more than mild persuasion would be needed to make the men leave the shelter of their homes. At ten o'clock the tahsildar and one man turned up, and thereafter the men came in twos, and threes, and tens, until by midday two hundred and ninety-eight had collected. The tahsildar had let it be known that he would turn a blind eye towards all unlicensed firearms, and further that he would provide ammunition where required; and the weapons that were produced that day would have stocked a museum.

When the men were assembled and had received the ammunition they needed I took them to the brow of the hill where the girl's skirt was lying and, pointing to a pine tree on the opposite hill that had been struck by lightning and stripped of bark, I told them to line themselves up along the ridge. When they saw me wave a handkerchief from under the pine those of them who were armed were to fire off their pieces, while the others were to beat drums, shout and roll down rocks, and no one was on any account to leave the ridge until I returned and personally collected him. When I was assured that all present had heard and understood my instructions, I set off with the tahsildar, who said he would be safer with me than with the beaters whose guns would probably burst and cause many casualties.

Making a wide detour I crossed the upper end of the valley, gained the opposite hill, and made my way down to the blasted pine. From here the hill went steeply down and the tahsildar, who had on a thin pair of patent-leather shoes, said it was impossible for him to go any further. While he was removing his inadequate footgear to ease his blisters, the men on the ridge, thinking I had forgotten to give the prearranged signal, fired off their guns and set up a great shout. I was still a hundred and fifty yards from the gorge, and that I did not break my neck a dozen times in covering this distance was due to my having been brought up on the hills and being, in consequence, as sure-footed as a goat.

As I ran down the hill I noticed that there was a patch of green grass near the mouth of the gorge, and as there was no time to look for a better place, I sat down in the grass, with my back to the hill down which I had just come. The grass was about two feet high and hid half my body, and if I kept perfectly still there was a good chance of my not being seen. Facing me was the hill that was being beaten, and the gorge that I hoped the tigress would make for was behind my left shoulder.

Pandemonium had broken loose on the ridge. Added to the fusillade of guns was the wild beating of drums and the shouting of hundreds of men, and when the din was at its worst I caught sight of the tigress bounding down a grassy slope between two ravines to my right front, and about three hundred yards away. She had only gone a short distance when the tahsildar from his position under the pine let off both barrels of his shotgun. On hearing the shots the tigress whipped round and went straight back the way she had come, and as she disappeared into thick cover I threw up my rifle and sent a despairing bullet after her.

The men on the ridge, hearing the three shots, not unnaturally concluded that the tigress had been killed. They emptied all their guns and gave a final yell, and I was holding my breath and listening for the screams that would herald the tigress's arrival on the ridge, when she suddenly broke cover to my left front and, taking the stream at a bound, came straight for the gorge. The 500 modified cordite rifle, sighted at sea level, shoots high at this altitude, and when the tigress stopped dead I thought the bullet had gone over her back, and that she had pulled up on finding her retreat cut off; as a matter of fact I had hit her all right, but a little far back. Lowering her head, she half turned towards me, giving me a shot at the point of her shoulder at a range of less than thirty yards. She flinched at this second shot but continued, with her ears laid flat and bared teeth, to stand her ground, while I sat with rifle to shoulder trying to think what it would be best for me to do when she charged, for the rifle was empty and I had no more cartridges. Three cartridges were all that I had brought with me, for I never thought I should get a chance of firing more than two shots and the third cartridge was for an emergency.

Fortunately the wounded animal most unaccountably decided against a charge. Very slowly she turned, crossed the stream to her right, climbed over some fallen rocks, and found a narrow ledge that went diagonally up and across the face of the precipitous hill to where there was a great flat projecting rock. Where this rock joined the cliff a small bush had found root-hold, and going up to it the tigress started to strip its branches. Throwing caution to the winds I shouted to the tahsildar to bring me his gun. A long reply was shouted back, the only word of which I caught was, 'feet'. Laying down my rifle, I took the hill at a run, grabbed the gun out of the tahsildar's hands and raced back.

As I approached the stream the tigress left the bush and came out on the projecting rock towards me. When I was within twenty feet of her I raised the gun and found to my horror that there was a gap of about three-eighths of an inch between the barrels and the breech-block. The gun had not burst when both barrels had been fired, and would probably not burst now, but there was danger of being blinded by a blow-back. However, the risk would have to be taken and, aligning the great blob of a bead that did duty as a sight on the tigress's open mouth, I fired. Maybe I bobbed, or maybe the gun was not capable of throwing the cylindrical bullet accurately for twenty feet; anyway, the missile missed the tigress's mouth and struck her on the right paw, from where I removed it later with my fingernails. Fortunately she was at her last gasp, and the tap on the foot was sufficient to make her lurch forward. She came to rest with her head projecting over the side of the rock.

From the moment the tigress had broken cover in her attempt to get through the gorge I had forgotten the beaters, until I was suddenly reminded of their existence by hearing a shout, from a short distance up the hill, of 'There it is, on the rock! Pull it down and let's hack it to bits.' I could not believe my ears when I heard 'hack it to bits', and yet I had heard correctly, for others now had caught sight of the tigress and from all over the hillside the shout was being repeated.

The ledge by which the wounded animal had gained the projecting rock was fortunately on the opposite side from the beaters, and was just wide enough to permit my shuffling along it sideways. As I reached the rock and stepped over the tigress - hoping devoutly she was dead for I had not had time to carry out the usual test of pelting her with stones - the men emerged from the forest and came running across the open, brandishing guns, axes, rusty swords and spears.

At the rock, which was twelve to fourteen feet in height, their advance was checked, for the outer face had been worn smooth by the stream when in spate and afforded no foothold even for their bare toes. The rage of the crowd on seeing their dread enemy was quite understandable, for there was not a man among them who had not suffered at her hands. One man, who appeared demented and was acting as ring-leader, was shouting over and over again as he ran to and fro brandishing a sword, 'This is the *shaitan* (devil) that killed my wife and my two sons'.

As happens with crowds, the excitement died down as suddenly as it had flared up, and to the credit of the man who had lost his wife and sons be it said that he was the first to lay down his weapon. He came near to the rock and said, 'We were mad, sahib, when we saw our enemy, but the madness has now passed, and we ask you and the tahsildar sahib to forgive us'. Extracting the unspent cartridge, I laid the gun across the tigress and, hanging down by my hands, was assisted to the ground. When I showed the men how I had gained the rock the dead animal was very gently lowered and carried to an open spot, where all could crowd round and look at her.

When the tigress had stood on the rock looking down at me I had noticed that there was something wrong with her mouth, and on examining her now I found that the upper and lower canine teeth on the right side of her mouth were broken, the upper one in half, and the lower one right down to the bone. This permanent injury to her teeth – the result of a gun-shot wound – had prevented her from killing her natural prey, and had been the cause of her becoming a man-eater.

The men begged me not to skin the tigress there, and asked me to let them have her until nightfall to carry through their villages, saying that if their womenfolk and children did not see her with their own eyes, they would not believe that their dread enemy was dead.

Two saplings were now cut and laid one on either side of the tigress, and with puggrees, waist-bands and loincloths she was carefully and very securely lashed to them. When all was ready the saplings were manned and we moved to the foot of the precipitous hill. The men preferred to take the tigress up this hill, on the far side of which their villages lay, to going up the densely wooded hill which they had just beaten. Two human ropes were made by the simple expedient of the man behind taking a firm grip of the waist-band, or other portion of clothing, of the man in front of him.

When it was considered that the ropes were long and strong enough to stand the strain, they attached themselves to the saplings, and with men on either side to hold the feet of the bearers and give them foothold, the procession moved up hill, looking for all the world like an army of ants carrying a beetle up the face of a wall. Behind the main army was a second and a smaller one – the tahsildar being carried up. Had the ropes broken at any stage of that thousand-foot climb, the casualties would have been appalling, but the rope did not break. The men gained the crest of the hill and set off eastward, singing on their triumphal march, while the tahsildar and I turned west and made for Champawat.

Our way lay along the ridge and once again I stood among the blackthorn bushes on the thorns of which long tresses of the girl's hair had caught, and for the last time looked down into the amphitheatre which had been the scene of our recent exploit.

On the way down the hill the beaters had found the head of the unfortunate girl, and a thin column of smoke rising straight up into the still air from the mouth of the gorge showed where the relations were performing the last rites of the Champawat man-eater's final victim on the very spot on which the man-eater had been shot.

After dinner, while I was standing in the courtyard of the tahsil, I saw a long procession of pine torches winding its way down the opposite hillside, and presently the chanting of a hill song by a great concourse of men was borne up on the still night air. An hour later, the tigress was laid down at my feet.

It was difficult to skin the animal with so many people crowding round, and to curtail the job I cut the head and paws from the trunk and left them adhering to the skin, to be dealt with later. A police guard was then mounted over the carcass and next day, when all the people of the countryside were assembled, the trunk, legs and tail of the tigress were cut up into small pieces and distributed. These pieces of flesh and bone were required for the lockets which hill children wear round their necks, and the addition of a piece of tiger to the other potent charms is credited with giving the wearer courage, as well as immunity from the attacks of wild animals. The fingers of the girl which the tigress had swallowed whole were sent to me by the tahsildar pickled in spirits, and were buried by me at the Naini Tal lake close to the Nandadevi temples.

While I had been skinning the tigress, the tahsildar and his staff, assisted by the headman and greybeards of the surrounding villages and merchants of the Champawat bazaar, had been busy drawing up a programme for a great feast and dance for the morrow at which I was to preside. Round about midnight, when the last of the great throng of men had left with shouts of delight at being able to use roads and village paths that the man-eater had closed for four years, I had a final smoke with the tahsildar, and telling him that I could not stay any longer and that he would have to take my place at the festivities, my men and I set off on our seventy-five-mile journey, with two days in hand to do it in.

At sunrise I left my men and, with the tigress's skin strapped to the saddle of my horse, rode on ahead to put in a few hours in cleaning the skin at Dabidhura, where I intended spending the night. When passing the hut on the hill at Pali it occurred to me that it would be some little satisfaction to the dumb woman to know that her sister had been avenged so, leaving the horse to browse – he had been bred near the snow-line and could eat anything from oak trees to nettles – I climbed the hill to the hut, and spread out the skin with the head supported on a stone facing the door. The children of the house had been round-eyed spectators of these proceedings and, hearing me talking to them, their mother, who was inside cooking, came to the door.

I am not going to hazard any theories about shock, and counter-shock, for I know nothing of these matters. All I know is that this woman, who was alleged to have been dumb for twelve months and who four days previously had made no attempt to answer my questions, was now running backwards and forwards from the hut to the road calling to her husband and the people in the village to come quickly and see what the sahib had brought. This sudden return of speech appeared greatly to mystify the children, who could not take their eyes off their mother's face.

I rested in the village while a dish of tea was being prepared for me and told the people who thronged round how the man-eater had been killed. An hour later I continued my journey and for half a mile along my way I could hear the shouts of goodwill of the men of Pali.

I had a very thrilling encounter with a leopard the following morning, which I only mention because it delayed my start from Dabidhura and put an extra strain on my small mount and myself. Fortunately the little pony was as strong on his legs as he was tough inside, and by holding his tail on the up-grades, riding him on the flat, and running behind him on the down-grades, we covered the forty-five miles to Naini Tal between 9 a.m. and 6 p.m.

At a durbar held in Naini Tal a few months later Sir John Hewett, Lieutenant-Governor of the United Provinces, presented the tahsildar of Champawat with a gun, and the man who accompanied me when I was looking for the girl, with a beautiful hunting-knife, for the help they had given me. Both weapons were suitably engraved and will be handed down as heirlooms in the respective families.

CHAPTER FIVE

The Ultimate Live Bait

THERE ARE SEVERAL alternative strategies that can be tried to lure a man-eating tiger out into the open, but the animal's predilection for human beings means that using cattle as bait, over which a hunter can wait in a machan, may not always have the effect of attracting the man-eater.

If the human remains from the last victim have been disturbed, or moved, or not even made available for use as bait by the grieving relatives, then another means by which a confirmed man-eater can be lured into the open is also denied.

In these circumstances, in order to draw out the man-eater, there is a last option remaining for the hunter to consider: using himself as a live bait.

It is a course of action usually spawned of desperation and offering a high chance of an unfavourable outcome for the hunter.

I. Duet with a Tiger

In Assam, north-central India, a tea-plantation was under siege from a man-eater at the turn of the century. The estate manager and his assistant had lost, besides a number of other employees, two Indian watchmen within a few days of each other, both from off the verandah of the manager's own bungalow.

After fruitless other efforts to rid the area of this tiger, the two planters eventually concluded that the only option open to them was to see if they could induce the man-eater to return to the verandah from which the animal had already taken two victims. The planters therefore decided to sit up at night on the bungalow verandah, armed, and dressed as Indian estate workers, in the hope they might attract the man-eater close enough to get a shot at it.

On the same evening the two men sat up until 3 a.m., but without anything happening. The manager then decided the animal was not going to pay the bungalow a visit that night and announced to his colleague he was going to bed. The second planter said he would remain perhaps another half-an-hour outside before he came in also. As a contemporary was later to relate, it turned out to be a rash decision.

There were large windows opening down to the floor of the verandah and through one of these the estate manager retired. After entering his room, he had just closed the window and was gazing out for an instant, when he saw a dark mass land on the verandah, right onto his friend, and then heard sounds of a scuffle and a cry for help.

Seizing his rifle, to which a sword-bayonet was attached, and flinging up the window, he rushed out, in time to see his assistant walking down the steps that led up to the verandah from the garden alongside the tiger and with his hand in the latter's mouth.

The manager was afraid to fire lest he should hit his colleague, so running after him and with admirable presence of mind, he went up to the tiger apparently undetected and plunging his bayonet into the animal's body, at the same instant fired.

There was a roar and a scuffle, and the assistant took advantage of the moment to release his hand. The tiger, after tumbling about for a moment or two, died. The hand was terribly mauled and the assistant subsequently, I believe, had to have it amputated; but the loss of a hand was a comparatively cheap price to pay for his life, which was mainly owing to the wonderful coolness of himself and his friend.

It appears that as soon as the manager had closed the window, the tiger (who must have been all the time lying close by them) landed on the verandah with a mighty spring, and seized the estate assistant by the hand. He, with wonderful coolness on being seized, made no effort to extricate the limb, though the pain must have been excruciating, but quietly rising, followed the tiger's movements, and walked alongside the man-eater with his hand in the tiger's mouth, until his colleague by his prompt and determined action released him.

II. The Man-eater of Botta Singarum

A hunter, H A Leveson, acted as his own bait when on the trail of a man-eater which was reputedly responsible for some one hundred human deaths in the Deccan, south-central India, in the 1870's.

I was in the neighbourhood of Mulkapore when I heard that a man-eating tiger, which I had been after for some days, had been seen near the outskirts of the village of Botta Singarum. I had on an earlier occasion tracked this animal to one of his lairs, where the remains of several of his victims were discovered and had also twice used beaters through all his usual haunts in the jungle, but up to this time had never been able to get a shot at him. Sending my gang of trackers on before I mounted my horse, and guided by the villager who brought the news, I made my way to the place where the tiger had been seen the evening before, and where I found unmistakable signs of his fresh pugs.

I sent my horse back to the village and, accompanied by the gang, followed the tiger's track through a narrow ravine which was densely wooded. Here the trail became exceedingly difficult to follow, as the tiger had evidently been walking about backwards and forwards in the bed and along the banks of a dry nullah and we could not distinguish his last trail. I caused the trackers to separate, and for half an hour or so we were wandering about as if in a maze, for the animal had been describing circles and often, by following the trail, we arrived at the place we started from.

Whilst we were all at a loss, suddenly I heard a low 'coo' twice repeated and I knew that my tracker, Googulu, who was seldom at fault, was now on warm scent; from his call I was as certain that the game was afoot as any master of hounds would have been, while breaking cover, hearing his favourite dog give tongue. The gang closed up and, guided by the sound, we made our way through thick bush to where Googulu was standing by a pool of water in the bed of the nullah.

Here were unmistakable marks of the tiger having quenched his thirst quite lately, as the water was still flowing into the deeply-imprinted pugs of his forefeet, which were close to the edge of the pool, and I noticed that the water had still the appearance of having been disturbed. After having drunk, the tiger made his way to some very thick jungle, much overgrown with creepers, through which we could not follow without the aid of our axes. Stalking with any hope of success was out of the question, so I held a solemn consultation with Kistimah, Chineah, Googulu and the dhoby as to the best means of proceeding.

I felt convinced that the man-eater was still lurking somewhere near at hand in the jungle for, besides the very recent trail we were on, I fancied I heard the yelling of a swarm of monkeys, which I attributed to their having been frightened by his appearance. This was also just the kind of place that a tiger would be likely to remain during the heat of the day, as it afforded water and cool shade from the sun.

All the gang were of my opinion and Kistimah observed that, on two different occasions after a post-runner had been carried off, he had noticed that the trail of the tiger led from this part of the jungle to a bend in the road where the animal had been known frequently to lie in wait for his prey. He added that 'these man-eaters were very cunning, and I should not at all wonder if even now he was watching us from some dark thicket.' As he said this I carefully examined the caps of my rifle, and I noticed some of the gang give a strange shudder, for this tiger had inspired them all with a wholesome fear which prevented their straggling. Two or three spoke almost in whispers, as if they were afraid of his being so near as to hear them conspiring for his destruction.

At length Kistimah said that he had been thinking of a plan which, though dangerous, might yield success. It was for me to go, with a man dressed as a runner, down the main road at sunset, being the time the tiger generally carried off his victims, and to run the chance of getting a shot. However, from the exclamation of 'Abah!' 'Arrez!' 'Toba!' 'Toba!' from the by-standers, and their shaking of heads and other unmistakable signs, I could see that the suggestion had not found much favour in their eyes. Only Chineah, the dhoby and one or two of the gang approved of the plan, Kistimah offering to accompany me as the post-runner. This, however, I objected to, for I thought that I should have a better chance of meeting the tiger if I went alone than in company; besides, I preferred having only myself to look after.

The plan of action once settled, I returned to the village and obtained from the patel the bamboo on which the tappal-runners sling the mailbags over their shoulders. To the end of this is an iron ring with a number of small pieces of metal attached, making a jingling noise as the man runs; this gives warning of the coming of the post to any crowd that might be obstructing the path, allowing them time to get out of his way. Having broken off the ring, I fastened it to my belt, so as to allow it to jingle as I walked. Arming myself with a short double rifle by Westley Richards, a brace of pistols and a huge shikar knife, I then made Kistimah lead the way down the road towards the place where the man-eater was said to be.

About a mile from the village I made the gang and the villagers who accompanied me halt, and went on with Kistimah, Chineah, and Googulu to reconnoitre the ground. The road was intersected by a narrow valley or ravine, along the bottom of which was a dry, sandy watercourse and the banks of which were overgrown with high rank grass and reeds, intermixed with low scrubby thorn bushes. To the left was a low, rocky hill, in some places bare and in others covered with thick jungle, with wild date or custard-apple clumps here and there. Kistimah pointed out to me a clump of rather thick jungle to the right of the road where, he said, the tiger often lurked whilst on the lookout for his prey, and here we saw two or three old trails. He also showed me a rock from behind which the animal had sprung upon a post-runner some weeks before but we saw no signs of his having been there lately. It was, however, quite a likely place for a tiger: bold, scarped rocks and naked, fantastic peaks rose in every direction from amongst the dense foliage of the surrounding jungle, whilst here and there noble forest trees lowered above the vegetation of every shade and colour. Not a breath of air was stirring, nor a leaf moving. The sun was still high up, without a cloud, the heat being most oppressive. Breathing was even becoming difficult on account of a closeness arising from the decayed vegetation under foot, and the overpowering perfume of the blossoms of jungle plants.

Having reconnoitred the ground, I felt rather overcome with lassitude and returned to the gang whom I found sleeping in a clump of deep jungle a little off the roadside.

Here I lay down to rest, protected from the sun by the shade of a natural bower formed by two trees weighed down with the weight of an immense mass of parasitical plants.

I must have slept several hours, for when I awoke I found the sun sinking low in the horizon. I got up considerably refreshed by my nap and prepared for my task. I carefully examined my firearms and ascertained that nothing had been seen by any of my gang. While keeping a lookout, I told my people to listen for the sound of my gun which, if they heard, they might come up, otherwise they were to remain quiet where they were until my return. I ordered Chineah, Kistimah, Googulu and the dhoby to accompany me down the road with spare guns in case I might want them. When I arrived at a spot which commanded a view of the ravine which was supposed to be the haunt of the man-eater, I sent them to climb different trees.

Kistimah begged hard to be allowed to accompany me, as he said this tiger never attacked a man in front, but always from behind;

but I would not permit him, as I thought that two people would perhaps scare the animal and his footsteps might prevent me from hearing any sound intimating his approach.

The sun had almost set as I proceeded slowly down the road and, although I was perfectly cool and as steady as possible, I felt cold drops of perspiration start from my forehead as I approached the spot where so many victims had been sacrificed. I passed the rock, keeping well on the lookout, listening carefully for the slightest sound, and I remember feeling considerably annoyed by the chirping made by a couple of little Indian nightingales that were fighting in a bush close to the roadside. Partridges were calling loudly all around, and as I passed the watercourse I saw a jackal skulking along its bed. I stopped, shook my jingling affair, and listened several times as I went along, but to no purpose.

Whilst ascending the opposite side of the ravine I suddenly heard a slight noise like the crackling of a dry leaf. I paused and, turning to the left, looked at the spot from where I thought the noise came. I distinctly saw a movement or waving in the high grass, as if something was making its way towards me. Then I heard a loud purring sound and saw something twitching backwards and forwards behind a clump of low bush and long grass, about eight or ten paces from me, and a little in the rear. It was a ticklish moment, but I felt prepared.

I stepped back a couple of paces in order to get a better view. This action probably saved my life, for immediately a tiger sprang into the middle of the road landing about six feet from the place where I was standing. I fired a hurried shot before he could gather himself up for another spring. When the smoke cleared away I saw him rolling over and over in the dusty road. My shot had entered the tiger's neck and into his chest. A slight tremor passed over all his limbs. The man-eater was dead.

My gang, attracted by the sound of my shots, came rushing up almost breathless, and long and loud were the rejoicings when the tiger was recognised by Kistimah as the man-eater who had been the scourge of the surrounding country for months. He was supposed to have carried off more than a hundred individuals. On the spot where the tiger was killed a large mausoleum now stands, caused by the passers-by each throwing a stone until a large heap is formed. Since that day many a traveller passing that way has been entertained by the old pensioned sepoy, who is in charge of the travellers' bungalow, with an account of the man-eater of Botta Singarum.

III. Mr Duff's Stratagem

Roads along the edge of jungle have often offered a man-eater a ready source of potential victims. S W Baker, a government officer, encountered a man-eater in the Mandla area of north-central India which succeeded in bringing all traffic to a halt on such a highway in the 1890's. An ingenious attempt to bait a trap for this man-eater using a dummy, rather than a human being, had its farcical aspects.

A few years ago in the Mandla district a tiger took possession of a road to the extent that it permanently stopped the traffic. This was not the generally accepted specimen of a man-eater, old and incapacitated, but an exceedingly powerful beast of unexampled ferocity and audacity. The animal was a merciless highwayman who infested a well-known portion of the road, levying a toll upon the drivers of the native carts not by an attack upon their bullocks, but by seizing the driver himself and carrying him off to be devoured in the neighbouring jungle.

The tiger had killed a number of people, and nothing would induce a native to venture upon that fatal road with a single cart. It had therefore become the custom to travel in company with several carts together, as numbers were supposed to afford additional security. This proved to be a vain expectation as the tiger was in no way perplexed by the arrangement. It bounded from the jungle where it had lain in wait and having allowed the train of carts to pass in single file, it seized the driver of the last one, and as usual carried the man away in spite of the cries of his terrified companions.

Such terrible attacks had been enacted on several occasions and the traffic was entirely stopped. A large reward was offered by the government, but without effect, as the man–eater never could be found by any of the shikaris.

At length the superintendent of police, Mr Duff, who unfortunately had lost one arm in a gun accident, determined to make an effort at the animal's destruction, and he adroitly arranged a plan that would be a fatal trap catching the tiger in its own snare. He obtained two covered carts, each drawn as usual by two bullocks. The leading cart was fitted in front and behind with strong bars of lashed bamboo forming an impervious cage. In this the driver was seated together with Mr Duff himself who sat with his face towards the rear, prepared to fire through the bars should the tiger, according to its custom, attack the driver of the rearmost cart.

This would have been an exciting moment for the driver, but Mr Duff had carefully prepared a dummy dressed exactly to impersonate the usual native carter. The bullocks, being well trained, would follow closely in the rear of the leading cart, from which a splendid shot would be obtained should the tiger choose to attack.

All went well; the road was desolate, bordered by jungle upon one side, and wild grassland upon the other. Eventually the carts reached the locality where the danger lay and they slowly moved along the road in their usual apathetic manner. This must have been an exciting moment and Mr Duff was no doubt thoroughly on the lookout. Suddenly there was a roar. A large tiger bounded from the jungle and with extraordinary quickness seized the dummy driver from his seat upon the rearmost cart, dragging the unresisting victim towards the jungle.

Nothing could have been better planned, but one chance had been forgotten which was necessary to success. No sooner had the tiger roared and bounded upon the cart than the bullocks, terrified by the dreadful sound, at once stampeded off the road, going full gallop across country followed by Mr Duff's bullocks in the wildest panic. It was impossible to fire and, after a few seconds of desperate chariot race, both carts capsized among the numerous small nullahs of the broken ground, where bullocks and vehicles lay in superlative confusion.

The victorious man-eater was left to enjoy rather a dry meal of a straw-stuffed carter, instead of a juicy Indian which he had expected. This was a disappointment to all parties concerned, except the dummy driver, who was of course unmoved by the failure of the arrangement. The tiger was subsequently killed by a native shikari when watching from a tree over a tied buffalo.

IV. The Marauder of Kempekarai

To act as live bait in order to be able to get at close quarters with a man-eater involves terrifying personal risk. Kenneth Anderson, a volunteer hunter of man-eaters for many years in India until retirement in the 1960's, found himself in this unenviable predicament on several occasions.

If you try to imagine two parallel ranges of lofty hills, averaging 4000 feet and more above the sea, with a valley between them about five miles across, covered with dense forest except for the craggy summits, you will have in your mind's eye the background of my story. It is set in the north Salem district of the Presidency of Madras in southern India.

The hills run from north to south, and the easterly range is the more lofty of the two, culminating at its southern point in the peak of Gutherayan, which is over 4,500 feet high. On its slopes stands a lovely little forest lodge, known as Kodekarai bungalow, amidst some of the finest scenery in the world. Rolling hills and jutting cliffs are to be seen in every direction. The sun rises in shades of rose-pink above the clouds of morning mist, to set eventually in orange-bronze reflections behind the western range. The pallid moon is then silent witness to many a jungle tragedy in the dark forests below. The scream of a dying sambar or the shrill shriek of a spotted stag have often been raised in vain to that same full moon as they spilled their life-blood beneath the paws of a hungry tiger.

Kempekarai is a small hamlet standing on the lower slopes of the western range. Around it lie a few fields and beyond the fields the forest of dense bamboo, intersected by a rocky stream that flows down the centre of the valley. This valley, which I call Spider Valley because of the immense spiders that spin their webs across the narrow footpath that runs beside the stream, broadens out towards the south into a larger tract known as the Morappur Valley, where the rocky stream finally joins the Chinar river at a spot called Sopathy, some ten miles from the Cauvery river.

I have described the area so that the reader may, with a little imagination, savour for a few minutes its lavish beauty: the dank smell of rotting vegetation, the twilight of a dense jungle, the distant half-roar, half-moan of a man-eating tiger searching for its prey, the eerie and deathly silence that follows those thrilling calls, and finally that faint rustle in the undergrowth, the indefinable creeping something that is the man-eater, watching as he becomes aware of your presence and pits the age-long hunting skill of his kind against the civilised intellect of man.

But let me begin my story.

Kempekarai was in a state of great fear, for a man-eating tiger had appeared and three of its few inhabitants had already gone to fill his bill of fare.

One month ago the first victim, an old Poojaree, had left Muttur eleven miles away to come to Kempekarai. He was never seen again. Elephants infest these areas and very occasionally kill men, so when the Poojaree failed to arrive at Kempekarai, a search-party set out towards Muttur. Perhaps the men who composed it expected to come upon the plate-like spoor of an elephant, and to find the squashed remains. But they found neither. Instead, about five miles from Kempekarai they came upon the tracks of a male tiger, a little blood by the pathside, the old man's staff and his loin-cloth – and nothing more.

Some ten days later, a woman went down to the community well near sunset to fill her water-pot for the night. She never returned. At 8 p.m. her husband and some of his friends, carrying lanterns and staves, visited the well to look for her. The brass water-pot, half-filled with water, lay on its side some twenty feet from the well, where it had been dropped by the woman on her return to the village. Of her there was no trace.

Next morning, a search-party was instituted, which duly came across the woman's sari, later a silver anklet, and finally her remains. Her head lay under a bush; her hands and feet were scattered about; of the remainder of her body, a number of gnawed bones showed the tiger had indeed been hungry and had done justice to a succulent repast.

A month dragged by. Kempekarai assumed the air of a fortress besieged. Nobody came in; nobody went out. The immediate precincts, and in some cases interiors, of the few huts stank with human filth. Was there not a killer nearby, waiting for the first victim who was bold enough to even venture outside to answer the call of nature? The matter was particularly perilous at night; human beings, with their cattle and sometimes their dogs, were barricaded together within their cramped huts behind doors that were kept shut with logs of wood or rounded boulders from the stream. The huts became more filthy every day under the force of the terrible circumstances in which the people were placed.

But the very best of precautions sometimes fall short of attaining their desired results. Mara, one of the sons-in-law of my old friend Byra, the Poojaree, had spurned to live in such insanitary conditions. He had told his wife that, man-eating tiger or not, he for one would not soil the inside of his house. Nightly he had gone outside to relieve himself, and nightly he had returned. Then one night he went out as usual for the same purpose, but this time he did not return. His wife, anxiously waiting inside, admits she heard a dull thud, a rasping gurgle, but nothing more.

After fifteen minutes she raised the alarm. Nobody would come to her rescue, for nobody dared. The inhabitants of the barricaded huts heard her shrieks for help. They knew that by this time Mara was beyond human assistance. He was dead, but they were alive. What was the use of going outside? So they remained indoors and listened to her screaming for the remainder of that long night.

Next morning, a half-hearted attempt was made to find out what was left of Mara, and it would have been unsuccessful except that the tiger had boldly eaten his fill among the bushes within two hundred yards of the village. A little more was left of Mara than had been left of the woman who had gone to the well. Perhaps his flesh was tougher, or perhaps the tiger was less hungry because his head and torso, at least, were found still in one piece.

Because of the fate that had befallen his son-in-law, my old friend Byra, who happened to be at Kempekarai at that time, undertook the hazardous eighteen mile journey to the village of Pennagram next day. He came by himself, as nobody would accompany him, and made the journey without catching sight or sound of the man-eater. At Pennagram he sought out his old acquaintance, Ranga, and the two of them came by bus to Bangalore. At 9 p.m. the same night voices called me to the front door and, going outside, I was surprised but delighted to see my old jungle companions once more.

My two visitors, being simple, honest forest folk, enjoyed a shot of good spirits in the form of half a tumbler of neat brandy. Thus refreshed, they began at the beginning, or rather Byra did, and related the brief history of the coming and doings of the man-eater, closing with the flat statement that his son-in-law, Mara, must be avenged and that I was to do it.

In face of his childlike confidence in me, I could find no very convincing reply and three days later I was on the road to Pennagram. We bought supplies at the local market and, within a few hours, the three of us were trudging the last eighteen miles to the little hamlet of Kempekarai where, because of the state of the track, the Studebaker could not go.

A couple of miles before our destination we found fresh pug-marks of a tiger on the footpath. No human travellers had passed along this track for many days and the spoor was clear. I made careful measurements and noted the pugs belonged to a male tiger of average size. This gave no indication whether he was an old animal, or of normal adult age, nor could any of us say at that time whether he was the man-eater or just another passing tiger.

The few inhabitants of Kempekarai were unable to add much material information to that which had already been given to me by Byra. They thought the man-eater was an enormous animal but, of course, all simple folk, when keyed-up to a state of sheer terror as had been the case with these poor people for the past few weeks, are given to attributing superhuman cunning and wholly impossible bodily strength and size to their oppressor.

The problem now was how to proceed? The answer was to wait for a kill, or present a live-bait. This particular tiger had not killed a single cow or other domestic animal belonging to the villagers. So far, at least, it had killed only human beings. The question was: would the tiger kill an animal bait, or should that bait be human?

Byra, Ranga and myself went into close conference, over successive mugs of tea, and eventually an answer began to take shape: I thought we should try animal baits, but they thought a human bait would produce immediate results. In a three-man committee, any two form an overwhelming majority. The odd man must give in but I managed to force my point to the extent of agreeing that, together with the human bait, there would be no harm in tying out a couple of young bullocks at selected spots as an additional attraction.

I bought two bullocks at Kempekarai, one of which we tied at the spot where we had found the pug marks and the other on the bed of the stream that meandered along the bottom of the valley. I sat on the stone parapet wall of the well, my back resting against one of the wooden uprights that supported the pulley-wheel, through which ran a rope for drawing water. I arranged for a metal pot to be tied to the end of this rope, which I kept beside me on the parapet wall; fresh water is always preferable to that from a water-bottle.

The jungle began some fifty yards from the well in all directions except one. Here were planted a dozen or more papaya trees. With the occasional watering from the well that these trees received, an undergrowth, mainly of grass with a few shrubs here and there, had sprung up around them. In daylight this undergrowth appeared negligible, but with twilight and approaching darkness, I began to feel it presented an admirable line of approach for the man-eater, which could easily crawl through it on its belly and come within almost springing distance of where I sat, without my being aware of its presence.

When this thought came to my mind, I changed my position to the other side of the well, using the opposite wooden-upright as a back-rest, so that I now faced the papayas. I had only decided to expose myself because it was just before full moon. Moonrise almost synchronised with sunset, but I had forgotten that the moon still had to top the range of hills to the east before it could cast its brilliance on that benighted well. This would only happen after 8 p.m. and I spent one of the worst ninety minutes of my life awaiting – I cannot hope to express how eagerly and anxiously – the first beams of that longed-for moon.

The darkness was deathly still; not even the familiar nightjar came anywhere near me. A few bats flitted down the well, to sip the limpid water in a series of flying-kisses as they quenched their thirst after the hot day. I strained my eyes, not just towards the papaya trees but in all directions. Imagination created the form of the man-eater, slowly creeping, stealthily stalking me, from just outside my range of vision. I sat glued to the parapet wall, my 405 cocked, my thumb on the torch switch. The thoughts that spring to a man's mind at such times are often strange and unaccountable: the tiger first assumed the role of possible avenging fate; at other times it practically faded from conscious thought.

Shortly after 8 o'clock the sky-line above the eastern range grew more distinct; a pale glow diffused itself against the sky, dimming the stars, and then the moon appeared, lightening both the surroundings and my nervous condition. As the moon rose higher in the heavens, the scene became brighter, until I could see almost clearly between the stems of the papaya trees. Not a sound disturbed the silence of my vigil for practically the first half of the night.

Shortly after 11 p.m. a sambar stag voiced its strident call from the bed of the stream where I had tied one of my bullocks. I recognised the note of alarm and fear in its voice, as the call was repeated over and over again, dying away in the distance as the stag ascended the rampart of the opposing range of hills to safety.

Again silence fell, and the night dragged out its last hours. It then struck me that I might perhaps be able to catch the tiger's acute hearing, if he was anywhere within a mile, by operating the pulley-wheel above the well which, I had noticed earlier in the afternoon, creaked and squealed loudly as it revolved about its unoiled axle. Perhaps he would hear and be attracted, thinking another prospective victim was drawing water from the well.

So I went around the well to where the water-pot rested on the ground. I stood the firearm up against the wall and then let the pot down till it touched the water, drawing it up and letting it down in slow succession thereafter. The pulley screeched loudly in the silence of the night and I continued for nearly an hour, stopping every now and again to survey my surroundings intently, particularly the deep shadows cast by every bush. But none stirred. Not a leaf moved in the breathless air, nothing rustled in the dried debris that carpeted the ground beneath the adjacent papayas. It was as if I were the only living thing present except for the inmates of the huts, secure behind barricaded doors.

After 3 a.m. the moon began to sink behind the western range of hills and, as in the previous evening, it grew darker and darker; soon I could see only a few yards around me by the radiance of the stars that had come to life, twinkling overhead. There were only ninety minutes of darkness left, and I felt terribly sleepy. Now I had to redouble my guard. Had I not been trying to attract the tiger for the past hour? As he had not passed that way all night, it was just possible he might do so now. Moreover, conditions for a surprise attack were all in his favour, as the papaya trees themselves now became ill-defined, except as a darker blur among the other shadows in my line of vision.

I realised that the man-eater now had me completely at his mercy if he chose to attack. Should he roar as he charged, I could at least discharge my rifle at point-blank range, but if he crept silently upon me I would not be aware of his coming until actually struck down. At the same time, all the rats, rabbits and other small animals which had been conspicuous by their absence all night, appeared to select this moment to rendezvous near the well. They scurried hither and thither, rustling the dead leaves, and all the while in my excited state I imagined 'the man-eater is coming'.

Altogether I had a dreadful time. The false dawn came and went, and then at 5.45 p.m. the brightening of the skyline once more, above the eastern range, told me that daylight was at last at hand and that the tedious vigil was nearly over. It was well past seven before the sun peeped over the eastern hills and I rose to drag my weary, sleepy steps to the tent I had pitched at the southern end of the village.

Hot tea and a nap till ten-thirty and then, accompanied by Ranga and Byra, I visited the bait tethered in the stream bed. It was alive and well. Closer inspection showed that a tiger had approached to within fifteen feet of it and had passed on after a cursory inspection. The sambar stag I had heard during the night had doubtless seen or scented this tiger and had voiced his loud alarm. The tiger's pug marks were clearly indicated in the soft, dry sand, but they could not be identified as having been made by the same animal as had those seen while coming along the path on the western range, where the ground was firmer and dimensions not exaggerated. Nevertheless, I had little doubt that this was the real man-eater, for a normal tiger will not readily leave alive a tempting, unguarded bait.

We then went to see the other bullock, where a surprise awaited us. It had been killed by a tiger whose pug marks were identical with those I had carefully measured the previous day, near the very same spot on the pathway. The question now was this: were there two tigers in the vicinity, or had the second bullock been killed by the man-eater? If the latter was the case and there was only one tiger – and that the man-eater – why had he not killed the bullock which had been tied in the stream bed instead of just looking at it and choosing to kill the other?

I formed the definite opinion that there were two tigers in the vicinity and that it had been the man-eater which had ignored the bullock at the stream. Ranga agreed with me, but Byra would not commit himself to either opinion. He suggested that the man-eater might be the only tiger in the area, and that possibly it had not killed the first bullock because it was a white one. The second, being dark brown, had not seemed suspicious to its killer.

On the question of the colour of a live-bait I have a very open mind. In my own experience, colour makes little or no difference to a tiger, and he will kill your bait provided certain other conditions also exist. He must be hungry for a tiger rarely, if ever, kills wantonly. Moreover, he must not suspect a trap of any kind. In these days when tiger-hunting is becoming intensified, tigers are learning their bitter lessons quickly. Thus a bait secured around the neck by a rope stands a very good chance of not being touched by a tiger. He cannot reason, but his instinct, or sense of self-preservation, tells him that it is unnatural for villagers to tie up their cattle for the night in a forest. A bait secured by a rope tied around the horns stands more chance of being killed, for it is possible for an animal to get entangled in the undergrowth by its horns. A bait secured by its hind leg is also readily taken. The main point is that both tigers and panthers attack the throats of their victims, and there should therefore be no visible obstruction to prevent this method of attack, or the attacker becomes suspicious.

Tying up a sickly live bait is also fatal to success. The Badaga tribe, who inhabit the Nilgiri hills, are very averse to selling healthy animals for bait, no matter what price is offered for them. They feel it is a sin to sacrifice the life of a good bullock. Invariably, they will offer only a sickly animal, whose days are numbered anyhow. I well remember tying up a bullock in the last stages of foot-and-mouth disease. For three nights in succession, as tracks in the sand revealed, the tiger came to the spot, walked around the bait, even squatted before it, and then decided it was too diseased to kill. On the fourth night by eight o'clock its allotted span of life was running out. It collapsed and took the whole night to die. That night the tiger did not even appear.

Returning to my story. There was obviously only one thing to do, and that was to fix a machan above the partly eaten brown bullock. Through experience both our baits had been tethered near suitable trees; so while I went back to the tent for a further nap, Ranga and Byra, both highly qualified in such matters, made a good job of slinging up the canvas camp chair I had brought with me. Next to a charpoy, or Indian rope-cot, a folding chair makes a good machan. It is not nearly so comfortable or roomy as the charpoy, but has an advantage in being easily taken to pieces and folded up.

Returning by 5 p.m., I took up my position, prepared for an all-night vigil. The pathway, situated as it was on the western range above the village of Kempekarai, received the light of the rising moon far earlier than did the village or the well where I had spent the previous night. Thus, soon after the sun sank below the western hilltops, the moon peeped over the eastern range and visibility was good all around me.

Nothing happened till shortly after eight. I then suddenly became aware that the tiger stood directly beneath me. How or from where it had come, I never knew. Certainly not along the path which was clearly visible in both directions as it stretched away into the forest. I knew the tiger was below me by the soft noise it made as it rubbed its body against the trunk of the tree in which I was sitting. In doing so it looked up and became aware of my presence.

Things then began to happen quickly. With a snarling growl, the tiger began at once to claw its way up the tree-trunk. Fortunately, we had selected a tree with a fairly straight trunk till the first bough was reached at about fifteen feet above the ground – where I was sitting on the camp chair. I knew that this was the man-eater, for normally a tiger would have decamped at once on becoming aware that a human being sat above him.

Instinctively I drew up both legs as high as possible, while leaning over the chair sideways and to the left, to get in a shot. Unfortunately, I had leant in the wrong direction, for the tiger was trying to climb the tree on my right side. I quickly corrected myself, but now had to hold the rifle to my left shoulder.

It took longer to read the preceding two paragraphs than events actually took that night. As I have said, I was sitting about fifteen feet above the ground. A normal tiger is about nine feet long from nose-tip to tail-tip. Subtracting the length of his tail and adding something in compensation for an outstretched forepaw, we may come by a working figure of almost eight feet to cover the 'stretching range' of a man-eater, or for that matter, of any tiger. Deducting these eight feet from the original height of fifteen feet, we get a difference of about seven feet, which was about the distance that tiger succeeded in climbing the tree-trunk that night. In his eagerness to get hold of me he stretched out a forepaw, and as the sharp claws drove through the canvas of the camp chair seat, and incidentally partially through the seat of my trousers, the tiger lost his balance and fell backwards to earth. Instinctively, in my anxiety to protect my rear, I half-levered myself out of the chair. I was lucky not to drop my rifle and follow in the wake of the tiger.

Now it is a peculiar fact about man-eaters, both tigers and panthers, that they appear to be craven creatures, although they attack and devour human beings. Almost without exception, such attacks are made from behind when the victim is not aware of the presence of his attacker. Very rarely, indeed, has any man-eater been known to carry out a frontal attack or rush a person who is aware of his presence and faces him.

So it was that night, for, as he fell backwards to earth, the man-eater realised his presence had been disclosed and no sooner had he landed on the ground than, with a bound and a snarl, he disappeared in the surrounding lantana. I cannot say to which of our good fortunes it was that he did so, since, although I had now become aware of his presence and was prepared for him, I might easily have overbalanced, or dropped the rifle, in trying to get a downward shot at that very awkward angle directly below me. Be that as it may, he was gone in a flash, and as suddenly and as unexpectedly as he had come.

My presence having been discovered, there was now no point in remaining motionless or silent. Reviewing the damage done, I discovered three claw marks through the canvas of the chair, each about five inches long, where the tiger's forepaw had swept. Of these, two had penetrated the seat of my trousers - and myself inside them to a lesser extent. The flesh certainly smarted, to remind me of the fact.

The claws of all carnivores are full of poisonous bacteria from the decomposed flesh at which they tear, and a man-eater is no exception to this rule, because the flesh happens to be human. The canvas of the chair, and the cloth of my trousers, were not sufficiently thick to absorb all this poisonous material, so that there was some chance of my wound becoming infected.

I had brought with me a variety of first aids, including a good stock of procaine penicillin and my five c.c. hypodermic syringe. But all these were in my tent at Kempekarai, some two miles away. I had therefore to choose between returning immediately and taking medical precautions, or remaining till morning – which was at least ten hours ahead – by which time the poison might have spread in the wounds. In the one case, I had to face the chance of attack by the man-eater, which might be launched anywhere along the path for the distance of the two miles it extended up to Kempekarai. On the other hand, I had to face the perhaps more certain danger of sepsis, and a long period of incapacitation from pursuing the man-eater.

So I chose to risk the tiger, as the lesser of the two evils, and quickly letting my rifle down on the rope brought for the purpose, I as quickly scrambled down myself, praying fervently that the man-eater would not choose that very moment for a second attack. Reaching the ground, I stood with my back to the tree-trunk, while I freed the rifle from the rope by which I had lowered it. All was as silent as the grave, and not a sound came from any part of the forest to give me any indication of the whereabouts of my recent attacker. He might be ten miles away, or behind the nearest bush. The brilliant moonlight bathed the jungle in its ethereal glow, making visible each leaf and grass blade as they gracefully vibrated in the soft night breezes.

After a few moments, I set forth along the path on the two-mile walk to Kempekarai. Now this path varies in width according to the nature of the soil, and the character of the vegetation, from fifteen feet to hardly a yard. At certain spots it is fringed with long grass and at other places by lantana undergrowth. Several small streams have to be crossed, where bamboos grow in profusion, their tall swaying stems creaking to the gentle breeze, while the fronds, in obliterating the moonlight, cast ghostly, chequered patterns on the ground.

In such circumstances your heart thumps in your chest almost audibly, your nerves are frayed to breaking-point and every faint rustle heralds the man-eater's charge. The inclination is to hurry, if not break into a run. Your nerves signal you to look all around, for the tiger may be making an attack from behind or from either side. All these emotions must be held under close restraint, for to give way to them in the least would mean panic and cause you to lose your presence of mind, with ultimate but certain destruction to follow.

The thing is to make certain that the tiger is not in front, lying in ambush till you come abreast of him. To attack from the rear, he has to make at least some noise in the undergrowth in order to catch up with your normal stride as you walk forward. It is wisest, therefore, to look in front, your eyes searching every shadow before you come abreast of it, rather than keep turning the head from side to side. Keep your rifle cocked and held in the crook of your arm, for you will have to fire from your hip and make certain of your shot. There will be no time to raise the rifle to your shoulder and aim, for the tiger is a killer, and it is not the habit of killers, either animal or human, to go about advertising their presence.

If your quarry is wounded, you may perhaps hear a snarl or growl, but most likely that unnervingly awful, earth-shaking cough as he charges. If he is not wounded, and is a man-eater, he will utter no sound and will be upon you in the twinkling of an eye.

Hardly a quarter-of-a-mile before Kempekarai there is a low outcrop of boulders on both sides of the path. This is the most dangerous spot in the journey home, as the tiger could be behind any one of those boulders. However, seeing him head the other way when he made off, I felt he had not had enough time to retrace his steps. With this mental assurance, I negotiated the rocks and soon came to Kempekarai and my tent.

Ranga and Byra were awake, as they always remained when I went out alone, in case I should require their sudden assistance.

Telling them to make a fire and heat some water, I drank some coffee that had been kept ready, and got out my hypodermic, which I sterilized in the hot water. Thereafter, mixing two phials of 8-lakh units of procaine penicillin, I gave myself a shot with the syringe. I got Ranga and Byra to wash the wounds with a strong solution of potassium permanganate dissolved in the rest of the hot water, followed by a dressing of sulphonamide ointment. The spot was one that could not be bandaged, or plastered, so I went to sleep hoping that no ill effects would develop with my wounds.

I was tired after my sleepless nights and it was nearly nine before I awoke next morning. This is a very late hour for rising in any jungle, where one is usually up and out before sunrise. The wounds, I was glad to note, were not unduly painful and I took another four lakhs of penicillin and redressed the wounds. After breakfasting I set off to visit my bait on the stream bed, which I found as alive and well as on the previous morning. Returning the two miles up the path to where I had sat the previous night, I found the tiger had not come back nor touched the bullock he had killed two nights before. His pug marks, as he had approached the tree, identified him as the tiger whose prints I had seen first.

The forests of Salem, unlike those of the Nilgiris, Coimbatore and Chittoor districts, are mostly thorny in nature, lantana and wait-a-bit thorn predominating. Along the valleys and stream beds these give way to clumps of bamboo, massed in close array. In either case, the effect is the same, namely, to make roaming or stalking unprofitable, if not impossible.

A carnivore moves silently, and the secret of its success as a hunter lies in the animal instinctively watching where it places its front paw in order to make no sound. Next it places its rear paw in exactly the same spot, as the front paw moves forward again to take the next step. The human stalker must move silently, too. He must watch carefully where he places each step, for the smallest dry leaf will crackle when trodden upon; the smallest twig will snap. Wait-a-bit thorns must be avoided, too, for a single thorn is strong enough to halt your progress if it catches in any part of your clothing, while it will rip your flesh if you are foolish enough not to have your arms and legs properly covered.

The jungle at this spot was extremely thorny, so we returned to Kempekarai to hold a council of war with the grey-beards of the village. The facts, as far as we now knew them, showed that the man-eater was a male of average size; that he particularly frequented the path on the western range; and he did not care for bullock meat. We were all uncertain whether or not there was a second tiger in the vicinity.

The conclusion reached after this discussion was the same as that reached by Ranga, Byra and myself on the first day we had come to Kempekarai: either to await the next human kill, or offer a human live bait, preferably somewhere along the pathway to Kempekarai as it descends the western ridge. A couple of bullocks could also be tied out elsewhere in the jungle to tempt the man-eater, but more to find out if there was another tiger operating in the same area.

The scratches which the tiger had inflicted, being located where they were, made it impossible for me to sit still for more than fifteen minutes at a stretch. This fact precluded all chances of sitting-up, in the literal meaning of the word. True, if I was to act as a bait there would be no necessity for me to sit still. In fact, movement would be a necessary factor in helping to attract the tiger. On the other hand, the very act of sitting would not only be agonising, but would also retard the healing of the wounds, which I was naturally anxious to avoid. The alternatives left were either to stand or lie down. The former course was naturally inadvisable for a night-long vigil, so the only practical method under the circumstances was to lie down.

We did a lot of thinking that day and eventually came by what we all thought to be a very ingenious plan. How ingenious it actually turned out - or rather did not turn out to be - we soon found out. I have already explained that the footpath down the western range to Kempekarai was crossed at several places by streamlets, bordered by dense undergrowth and clumps of bamboo. The beds of these small rivulets were rocky and admirably suited the purpose I had in mind.

It so happened that the first of these small streams to be crossed on the way down to Kempekarai, near the tree on which I had sat the night before, was the broadest of the lot and, moreover, contained rounded boulders of all sizes. My plan was to detach a cartwheel from one of the only two bullock carts in the village of Kempekarai, dig a pit in the stream bed, get inside it, place the wheel above, and anchor it securely around the circumference with big boulders. Smaller boulders, and a camouflage of dry leaves, would help to conceal the cartwheel. I would also make a human dummy and seat it somewhere on the footpath, where it crossed the stream. The cartwheel would be raised off the ground at one end, facing the dummy, to allow me a range of fire in that direction.

This was my general plan. For the benefit of those who have not been to India, I would explain that the wheel of an Indian bullock-cart – I am referring to the large type of cart – averages five feet in diameter. The circumference is of wood, some six inches wide by three inches thick, shod with hoop iron to serve as a tyre. There are a dozen stout wooden spokes, all converging on a massive central wooden hub. The central hole in the wooden hub rotates around an iron axle, some one-and-a-half inches thick. The wheel is kept from falling off by a cotter-pin in the form of a flat iron nail, passing through the axle at its outer extremity. Similarly, the wheel is prevented from moving towards the frame of the cart by the axle itself, which is made suddenly thicker immediately beyond the bearing surface of the axle on the hub, which is perhaps a little over a foot in width. In what may be called de luxe models, a better bearing surface is provided by lining the hole in the wooden hub with a piece of iron or galvanised piping. High-grade lubrication, from the village viewpoint, is provided by applying old motor oil, perhaps once a fortnight, on the ends of the axle, after removing the cotter-pin and the wheel to do so. The oil is carried perma-nently on the cart in the shell of an old bullock-horn, suspended somewhere beneath the cart, and is applied to the axle at the end of any piece of stick that may happen to be lying handy when servicing time comes up.

It was too late to set the cartwheel that day, so we busied ourselves gathering old clothing from the villagers. Trousers are unknown in such parts, so I contributed a pair of mine, into which we stuffed two 'legs', made of bamboo and wound around with straw. In case the trousers might strike the tiger as being unfamiliar, we draped a dhoty (which is a cross between a sarong and a loin-cloth) over the trousers. The body of the dummy consisted of straw rammed into an old gunny sack, over which we draped a couple of torn shirts and a very ragged coat. The head of the dummy was a work of art; it was made from a large-sized mature coconut, complete with its coir fibre.

On dress occasions Indian women sometimes augment their natural hair with false hair, which they twist into a bun or coonday behind their heads, into which they stick flowers, particularly jasmine. Fortunately there was a belle in Kempekarai who was vain enough to be the owner of a coil of such hair. This we borrowed, combed out, and fixed around the coconut, to emulate the long hair of a villager. An untidily-tied, yokel-pattern turban was then wound around the nut and a pair of chappals or sandals were put on the dummy's feet. Tigers, as I have said, have no sense of smell, so the dummy looked realistic enough to attract a man-eater, if only he did not watch it long enough to begin wondering at its uncanny stillness.

By 8 a.m. half-a-dozen willing helpers and myself had trundled the cartwheel to the crossing I had in mind. Here we busied ourselves excavating a hole nearly four feet across by about four feet deep. This was easily done, for we were digging in the soft sand of a stream bed. Some grass was then cut and thrown into the hole to absorb, to some degree, the dampness of the sand which naturally increased with the digging of the hole. Once inside, I found I could adopt only a semi-crouched position, which was going to be very uncomfortable indeed, the only recommendation it offered being that it saved me from a sitting position which, as I have said, would have been most uncomfortable in view of my recent wounds.

The dummy we placed with its back to a tamarind tree, some fifteen feet away, which stood on the western bank of the stream where it was crossed by the track to Kempekarai; it was so arranged that its legs stuck out on the track at an angle of forty-five degrees. Thus, it would at once be visible to the tiger from any point along the stream bed or on either section of the track, if he happened to pass in any of those directions. Lastly, we collected some of the larger boulders and, as I stood guard with my rifle, Ranga and Byra gathered brushwood and debris for camouflaging the wheel.

When eventually I got into the hole, the wheel was just a couple of inches above the top of my head. There was a space of six inches between the ground level and the wheel through which I could fire in the direction of the dummy; it was made by placing two stones of that size about three feet apart under the circumference of the wheel. The rest of the wheel was anchored to the ground by large boulders heaped up around the circumference, leaving the central portion open to the sky for purpose of ventilation. Brushwood and debris were scattered and intertwined among the boulders and behind me, to give a natural appearance to things, so that the tiger would not become suspicious of the heaped-up boulders; it would also give me warning if he came up from behind, when the debris would crackle as he brushed against it or trod on it.

For safety's sake, I had arranged that the men should return to Kempekarai in a body, and only come back next morning, again in a body. I would be imprisoned all night in the hole, as the weight of the cartwheel with the boulders above it was too great for me to lift unaided from inside.

It was 4.30 p.m. when I entered my voluntary prison. It had taken nearly another half-hour to position the boulders on the wheel and arrange the camouflage, so that it was almost five when I found myself alone. The heat inside the hole, despite the opening above, was stifling. I removed my coat and shirt, and would have removed the remainder of my clothes but for the fact that I did not want the sand to get into my wounds.

Peeping above the level of the ground, I could clearly distinguish the dummy and quite a wide extent of the background. A clump of henna bushes grew half-way down the sloping bank behind the dummy. A slight movement in that direction caught my eye, which I found was due to the twitching, outstretched ear of a beautiful spotted stag that gazed in curiosity at the motionless dummy. The value of sitting still in a forest was then made apparent to me, for the stag gazed a full ten minutes at that still dummy. Then it appeared to lose interest in the curious object, and came out onto the open track, which it eventually crossed, vanishing into the jungle on the other side. The distance between the dummy and the stag could have not been much more than twenty feet, and yet the latter was quite unalarmed. Had a human been seated in place of the dummy, he would surely have moved, even if it was an eyelid that flickered, and this would have sent the stag crashing away in alarm.

A pair of peafowl then came strutting along the track. The cockbird stopped, fanned out his tail and rustled the quills in display to his admiring spouse. Female-like, she kept one eye on him and the other elsewhere: she saw the dummy, took a short run, and sailed into the air. The cock lowered his tail and saw the dummy too. A much heavier bird than the hen, he flapped wildly and desperately in an effort to take off, his wings beating loudly on the still evening air, before he finally managed to rise just clear of the surrounding bushes and follow his more wary partner to apparent safety.

'Kuck-kaya-kaya-khuck'm' crowed the grey jungle-cocks in all directions, as they came out along the stream bed to peck a few morsels before darkness fell. 'Kukurruka-wack-kukurruka-wack' cackled the smaller spurfowl, belligerent little birds, as male fought male in little duels throughout the jungle for the favour of an accompanying hen. Drab and uninteresting as she looks, to gain her favour was for them the only interest in the world that evening.

Darkness fell, to the farewell call of the pair of peafowl, as they roosted for the night on some tall tree in the forest, perhaps a quarter-of-a-mile away. 'Mia-a-oo-aaow' they cried, as the sun sank behind the western range. Those of you who have been in an Indian forest will remember the almost miraculous switch-over that takes place at sunset, as the birds of the daylight hours cease their calls, and the birds of the night take their place. *'Chuk-chuk-chuk-chuckoo'*, cried the nightjars, as with wide-spread wings they sailed overhead in search of insect morsels, or settled on the ground, resembling stones against a background of sand.

It was pitch-dark where I sat and even the dummy was hidden under the shadows of the tamarind tree beneath which it was propped. I reckoned the moonlight would not reach that spot till after ten. At nine I heard the noisy snuffing and deep-throated gurgle of a sloth bear, as it wended its clumsy way down the stream in my direction. It almost fell over the outlying debris we had placed on the stream bed to give me warning of the tiger's approach, and then saw the newly-heaped boulders placed upon the cartwheel. I could have read the thoughts that crossed the little brain beneath the shaggy black hair. 'Here's a chance to find some luscious fat grubs, or a beetle or two; perhaps a nest of white ants or, most hopeful of all, a beehive built by the small yellow bees that can hardly sting a big bear like me.' With those thoughts, the bear fell to work on the task of clearing away the boulders that so carefully anchored my cartwheel.

'Shoo!' I whispered in an undertone. 'Get away, you interfering...!' The bear heard my voice, and stopped. 'Where did that come from?' he was thinking. A few minutes silence followed, and then he started at the stones again. 'Out! Shoo!' I whispered. The bear stopped, climbed over the boulders, and looked down between the spokes at me. *'Aa-rr, Wr-rr!'* he growled. 'Get out, you idiot!' I growled. *'Wr-oof! Wr-oof! Wr-oof!'* he answered, as he scrambled, helter-skelter, over the boulders, stumbled over the debris, scampered up the bank and crashed away between the dried bamboos.

Hardly ten minutes had passed after the bear's noisy departure when I heard the most infinitesimal of noises, the soft tread of the padded foot of some heavy animal. The tiger had come and in his silent way was negotiating the fringe of the debris we had scattered on the stream bed behind me. He was picking his way carefully across it. Would he attack the dummy? Would he pass in front of me? These were the questions that raced through my mind as I awaited developments. My nerves were taut with anticipation. The moon had already risen, but its beams had not yet reached the shadows cast by the heavy foliage of the tamarind tree. The dummy was not visible to me, but I knew that the tiger could clearly see it.

There was silence for a time – how long I could not say. Then came the clink of a stone as it rolled above my head. Nobody had anticipated an attack in that direction; but my recent visitor, the bear, had already shown that the unexpected could happen. Now the unexpected was being repeated by the presence of the tiger above me. What had caused it to ignore the dummy and come straight to the spot where I lay was a mystery. Very likely, the tiger had been watching the bear, had seen its strange behaviour, had noted its hurried departure and had come to investigate. Even more likely, the behaviour of the bear had caused the tiger to suspect human agency, which he had come over to find out for himself. Or perhaps the wheel just happened to be situated on the shortest line of approach which the tiger was following to get at the dummy.

Whatever the reason, the tiger was now barely two yards away, and above me. As these thoughts raced through my mind, I heard the vague sound caused by the tiger's breathing. Then he stepped gracefully over one of the big boulders that held down the wheel, and peered down at me.

In the meantime I had not been idle. Screwing myself around, as best I could, I now lay half on my back, gazing up at the tiger. The rifle I had drawn inwards and backwards till the butt came up against the side of the hole. It will be recalled that this hole was about four feet across, and about the same in depth. Hence it was impossible to get the rifle to point completely upwards. The most I could manage was an angle of little more than sixty degrees with the bottom of the hole. Unfortunately, the tiger was not in the direction in which the muzzle was pointing, but was standing behind it, and directly above the spot where the butt of my rifle was stuck against the side of the hole.

Then events moved quickly. The tiger did not react quite as the bear had done. His features, dimly visible above me, contorted into a snarl. A succession of deep-throated growls issued from his cavernous chest and, lying down upon the cartwheel, he attempted to rake me with the claws of a foreleg, which he inserted between the spokes of the wheel.

I knew those talons would rip my face and head to ribbons if they only made contact, so, sinking as low into the hole as possible, I struggled desperately to turn the muzzle of the rifle towards the tiger. All this took only seconds to happen. The tiger growled and came a little farther onto the wheel. The muzzle of my rifle contacted his shoulder and I squeezed the trigger.

The explosion, within that confined space, was deafening. The tiger roared hideously as he catapulted backwards. During the next thirty seconds he bit the boulders, the wheel and even the sand, as he gave forth roar after roar of agony. Then I heard him fall amidst the debris, pick himself up, fall again, get up and finally crash into the bushes that bordered the little stream. He was still roaring, and continued to do so for quite fifteen minutes more as he staggered away into the jungle.

Finally silence, total and abysmal, fell over the forest. After the pandemonium that had just reigned, every creature, including the insects, seemed to decide to hide. The hours passed. At one in the morning a stiff breeze began to blow over the hills, dark storm clouds scudded across the sky, completely hiding the moon, and soon the distant sound of falling rain across the western range fell upon my listening ears. Not long afterwards, large raindrops penetrated between the spokes and splashed down upon me.

Then the deluge began, such as can only be experienced in tropical countries, and particularly forest regions with dense vegetation. I was soaked to the skin, and the water began to trickle down the sides of the hole. With that came the sudden realisation that the stream, which had been dry, would soon be flowing with the spate of rainwater that was running into it from all directions along a hundred tributaries. I would be drowned like a rat in a hole.

Jerked into a frenzied action, I got on my hands and knees, placed my back to the wheel and pressed upwards with all my might. The wheel did not budge an inch! My helpers had done their work of protecting me from the tiger only too well. They had placed the heaviest boulders they could find around the circumference of the wheel and I was unable to move them unaided.

There was but one chance left, and that was to dig myself out through the six-inch wide gap we had made for me to fire through. Desperately, with both hands I scooped the earth downwards into the hole, which was already half filled with water and sand; the damp sides were collapsing, making it very obvious that within the next few minutes, unless I got out quickly, cartwheel and boulders would all come down together on top of me.

When I judged there was sufficient room for my body to pass through, I pushed the rifle between the spokes of the wheel and then rested it across them. Next I started squeezing myself through the opening I had just dug, wriggling in the sand and water like a stranded eel, till I finally struggled free onto the stream bed.

The rain continued to fall in torrents. I had no idea how far the tiger had gone, or in which direction, so, picking up the rifle, I first carried the dummy off the stream bed and placed it high up on the western bank. Then I started to recross the stream on the return journey to Kempekarai, and as I did so, I heard the dull roar of the spate of rainwater descending the stream bed from the direction of the hills.

Within a few minutes it arrived, a wall of foaming water over three feet high, carrying all before it. Logs of wood, uprooted trees, dead bamboos and flotsam and jetsam of every description mingled with the crested, frothing waters. They reached the cartwheel and covered it; then cartwheel and boulders were swept away down-stream along with the torrent. In less than five minutes the stream had become a raging river, over four feet deep.

Thankfully, I began the return journey to Kempekarai. No other sound could possibly be heard above the patter and swish of the rain. The darkness was intense, my torch throwing a circle of light before me. Moreover, the ground was extremely slippery to the soft rubber shoes that I was wearing. I had to cross three other streams, slightly smaller than the one where I had sat, but all were raging torrents of water. Half-way to Kempekarai, I saw the flicker of an approaching light. A little later, I met the party of men that were carrying it – Ranga, Byra and a few stalwarts from the village. They had realised the danger I was in when the waters rose and had risked encounter with the man-eater to come to my rescue.

Next morning the sun shone brightly on the saturated forest. We returned to the site of my adventure the night before. All streams were flowing briskly, although they were now no more than two feet deep. There was no trace of the cartwheel anywhere near the crossing. Evidently it had been borne downstream by the spate and probably smashed to bits. We combed both banks thereafter, without finding any signs of the tiger. The torrential rain had only too effectively obliterated any blood trail or pug marks.

Two hours later, a depressed and disappointed group, we returned to Kempekarai. There I remained for three more days, hoping to hear news of the tiger, only to be doomed to disappointment. Both Byra and Ranga felt it had died of its wounds, but I doubted this very much, as I knew I had not been able to aim sufficiently well to score more than a mere raking shot.

My period of leave, taken for the purpose of shooting this animal, had now elapsed, so I left Kempekarai on the morning of the fourth day, instructing Ranga to remain behind to assist Byra in reconnoitring. They were then to come to Pennagram, and thence to Dharmapuri, where there was a telegraph office from which they could send me a message. They were to await my reply there.

Ten days after returning to Bangalore, the hoped-for telegram arrived, stating that a pack-pony belonging to a forest guard of the Kodekarai forest lodge had been killed. Calculating from the telegram that the kill would be four days old by the time I reached it, I sent a reply, telling my henchmen to return to Kempekarai and wait there for any further events, which were to be reported by telegram in the same way.

Six more days passed, when I received a second telegram, stating that a tiger had attacked the driver of a bullock cart that was the last of a convoy travelling from the small hamlet of Morappur towards Sopathy on the Chinar river.

This, no doubt, was the man-eater again. Within an hour I was on my way by car to Dharmapuri, where I picked up my two henchmen. We continued to Pennagram, where we left the car and made a cross-country trip of about twelve miles to Morappur, passing the Chinar river and Sopathy on the way.

I had meanwhile learned that the cartman, who had been attacked by the tiger, had saved his life by jumping from the cart in which he was travelling onto the yoke and then between the two bulls that were hauling his cart. He had yelled vociferously and his yells were taken up by the other cartmen in the convoy. The tiger had then made off.

I spoke to this cartman at Morappur. He said that the tiger had suddenly appeared behind his cart, which was the last in the line, and had attempted to leap into it from the rear, when he had dived between his bulls for protection. Asking him why the tiger had not succeeded in the comparatively easy task of getting into the cart, the man said that as soon as it had jumped half in, he had not waited to see any more.

Meanwhile, a party of travellers who had followed us from Sopathy brought the news that they had come across fresh tiger pug marks, made the previous night, leading down the Chinar river. Hearing this we hurried back to Sopathy and it did not take us long to find the pug marks. The water was running in the Chinar as a silvery stream, meandering from bank to bank, and in the soft, wet sand we clearly noticed that the tiger which had make the marks must have been limping badly. The weight of the body fell almost entirely on the left forefoot, the right being placed very lightly on the sand at each step.

I have said that Spider Valley met the Chinar river at this spot. A half-mile downstream, and in the direction in which the tiger had gone, was a small, longish rock in mid-stream. It rose some four feet above the bed of the river and was about forty feet long by eight feet wide. I decided to sit on top of that rock that night, in the hope the tiger might make his way back up the Chinar and see me in my elevated position.

Borrowing Ranga's turban, old brown coat and dhoty, I donned all three, the two latter above my own clothing, and seated myself on the rock by 5.30 p.m. As Ranga and Byra were afraid to return to Morappur alone, they elected to spend the night high up in the huge muthee trees that border the Chinar in this locality.

The nights were dark at this time, but from my position on the rock I relied upon the white sand to reflect the starlight and to reveal the form of the tiger from whatever direction it might come. The Chinar is about one hundred yards wide at this spot. Apart from being handicapped by its lameness, I knew the tiger would not try to charge its prey over a distance as great as fifty yards, but would try to stalk as close to me as possible before launching the final attack.

After testing my lighting equipment, I carefully loaded and cocked the 405, which I laid on the rock to my right where it could not be seen by the tiger and create suspicion. I had also taken the precaution of bringing my 12-bore double-barrel Jeffries with me as a spare weapon. With LG slugs in the choke barrel, and lethal-ball in the right, I laid the Jeffries on the rock to my left. My flask of tea, some chappaties to satisfy my hunger towards morning and my pipe completed my creature wants for the night. I sat on my great-coat for the cushion it provided against the hard rock; I could also wear it if the night should become too cold.

The usual animal and bird calls from the forest bade farewell to the day, while the creatures of the night welcomed their turn for activity with their less melodious, and more eerie, cries. At seven-thirty it was dark; in the reflected whiteness of the sands of the Chinar my rock looked as if it were an island. Then just after nine there was a loud bustling and crashing, and a tusker came down the bank, walked along the sands, passed the rock where I sat motion-less, and continued beyond. There he met the current of breeze blowing down the river and caught scent of me. Banging the end of his trunk against the ground, and emitting a peculiar sound as if a sheet of zinc were being rapidly bent in half, he turned around, smelled more of me and hurried up the bank into the cover of the thick undergrowth that grew there. Such is the behaviour of an elephant when it is not a rogue.

At eleven I was still keeping my watch in all directions as I had been doing since sunset. Then, half to the rear and my left, I sensed rather than saw a movement. Looking more intently, I could see nothing. No, wait! Was that not a blur against the faint greyish-white carpet of river sand? I looked away and then back again at the spot where I had just noticed the blur. It was not there.

'Are my eyes playing tricks, or are they just becoming tired?'

Staring hard, I saw it again. Only it was much closer to me this time than when I had seen it first. Indeed, it was half-way between the further bank and the rock on which I sat. I could not now risk looking in any other direction until I succeeded in defining this strange object. And as I looked it seemed to stretch, to float towards me, growing longer and shorter at intervals, but making no sound whatever.

Then in a flash I realised what it was. The tiger was crawling towards me on his belly, silently, in quick, short motions, till he judged he was within range to make his final assault.

Perspiration poured down my face and neck; I trembled with terror and excitement. But this would not do; so taking a deep breath and holding it, to allay the trembling, I offered a silent prayer to my Maker and drew the rifle onto my lap, raising it to my shoulder.

The tiger, now some twenty yards away, saw my movement and seemed to guess that his presence had been discovered. A thin black streak - his tail - moved behind him. The blur became compact as he gathered himself for the charge. My torch-beam fell full on his snarling, flattened head. Then the rifle spoke, a split-second before he sprang.

With my bullet he rose and bounded forward. I owe my life to the fact that the torch did not go out, and I was able to fire a second shot. Then he reached the rock.

Because of his earlier wound, or my recent shots, he failed to climb up. My third bullet, fired at point-blank range, stopped the charge that had all but succeeded in reaching me, and he rolled back onto the sands of the Chinar, his career at an end.

On my way back to Sopathy I gathered Ranga and Byra from the muthee trees on which they were sitting. Next morning we found the tiger to be an average-sized, somewhat thin, male. My shot from beneath the cartwheel, fired seventeen days earlier, had done more damage than I had thought, passing through his right shoulder, splintering the bone, and out again. But the wound was in good condition and I have little doubt would eventually have healed, although the tiger would have remained a cripple. My first shot of the night before had passed through his open mouth, and out through the neck. Still he had come on. The second shot had gone high, entering behind the left shoulder, passing downwards through the lungs, and out again. And still he had come on. It was only my last shot, through the crown of his skull, that had overcome his indomitable spirit.

What had made this tiger a man-eater? This is the riddle that every hunter tries to solve. And this beast proved to be no exception to the general rule that it is the human race that often causes a tiger to become a man-eater. It had an old bullet wound in the same leg (the right) as had been injured by me in our first encounter, only lower down: embedded in the elbow joint was a flattened lead ball, fired from some musket or gun a year or more earlier. This had not only caused the tiger to suffer intense agony, but had greatly impeded his movements when it came to killing wild game and cattle, his legitimate food. It had weakened the use of the right leg, which plays an all-important part in gripping and pulling down his normal prey. This was the factor that forced this tiger to turn to human beings as food.

CHAPTER SIX

Man-eater Combat:
Some Survivors' Stories

ONLY ONE IN EVERY HUNDRED victims who ever comes to grips physically with a man-eater escapes with his life. Of the one percent of survivors in Jim Corbett's estimate, most are armed and in pursuit of the man-eater at the time but in a few of the instances the victim is not even aware of the imminent attack before it occurs. The survivors' good fortune, in most instances, is explained by their physical strength together with their remarkable and apparently septic-resistant constitutions.

As in stalking, a man-eater's preferred technique is to surprise his victim from the side or rear, often taking his prey without a sound. Only if the man-eater is himself under attack or being pursued will he resort to a frontal charge. Walking along a jungle path in India with his shikari assistant behind him, a government officer recounts how he 'heard no sound except a sigh, and on turning around saw a tiger with the man's neck in its jaws, standing on its hind legs, its forepaws on his neck and chest or shoulders. In an instant it had gone with its prey.'

But for those who have confronted a man-eater in the act of a full charge, the awesome experience is quite without equal. 'The lion charges with that same coughing roar that the tiger does,' says a witness, 'coming at speed close along the ground. The ears are laid back close to the head, the tail, as with the tiger, held stiff and erect.' The coughing grunts that the animal utters 'make the air quiver and shake' as it presses home the attack.

Harry Wolhuter, a game ranger in south-east Africa earlier this century, engaged in a hand-to-hand encounter with a lion, following such a charge, from which remarkably he survived. He was returning from a two month's patrol in the bush, and was pushing on alone ahead of his bearers and pack donkeys in order to reach the nearest police post before nightfall. Darkness, however, found him still some three miles short of his destination, riding along a path by the side of a reed-bordered stream, accompanied only by his dog 'Bull'. As he rode through the dry river bed where the path crossed it, he saw something move out of the reeds and melt away into the darkness ahead. A few yards further on his dog rushed forward barking, and again the indistinct form moved away.

Taking it to be a buck or game of some kind, Wolhuter rode on without taking any particular notice of the incident, but a few minutes afterwards he saw the shape again, but this time it was approaching him at speed. He hardly had time to reflect that this was an odd action on the part of a reedbuck when he realised it was no antelope, but a lion, attacking.

I had not time to lift my rifle, but simply snatched my horse round to the near side, and drove the spurs in; he gave a bound which, no doubt, caused the lion partially to miss his spring, as his claws slipped on the horse's quarters and, though several ugly wounds were inflicted, he lost hold.

The concussion and the subsequent violent spring of the horse caused me to lose my seat, and simultaneously I saw a second lion rushing up from the opposite direction. I absolutely fell into his jaws, and believe that he had me before I ever touched the ground.

The next thing I recollect was being dragged along the path on my back, my right arm and shoulder in the lion's mouth, my body and legs underneath his belly, while his forepaws kept trampling on me as he trotted along, lacerating the fronts of my thighs considerably and tearing my trousers to shreds. All the time the lion was dragging me along he kept up a sort of growling purr, something like a hungry cat does when she catches a bird or a mouse and is anticipating a welcome meal.

My spurs kept dragging and catching in the ground till at last the leather broke. I cannot say what my feelings at this time were at all except I hope I may never again have to undergo such agony as I then experienced; it seemed hard to die like that, and yet I could see no part of a chance, not the slightest loophole of escape.

As Wolhuter was dragged along he tried to think all the time of what to do to save himself. Suddenly he remembered his six-inch sheath knife, which he carried in a leather case on his belt. Reaching under himself with his left hand, he discovered that mercifully it had not been lost while he was being dragged along. Pulling the knife out, he held onto it firmly, awaiting some opportunity to use it.

After some two hundred yards of dragging his victim along, the lion stopped under a large tree, laying Wolhuter down, either for the purpose of shifting his grip or starting to eat his victim. Wolhuter now had his chance. Feeling very carefully for what he judged to be a vital spot, Wolhuter stabbed the lion twice behind the shoulder.

He dropped me at the first stab, but still stood above me growling, and I then struck him a third time in the throat with all the force of which I was capable, severing some large vein or artery, as the blood deluged me.

At this the lion sprang back several yards, allowing Wolhuter then to scramble to his feet while simultaneously shouting at the lion which stood motionless, facing him. After an interval that must have seemed interminable but was only a few seconds, the man-eater then walked slowly away, turning to growl all the time in Wolhuter's direction.

With great difficulty because of his mangled arm, Wolhuter then had the presence of mind to climb the tree under which the event took place, reaching a branch some ten feet above the ground. It was well he had, because sometime later the second lion returned from an unsuccessful chase after the horse, having followed the spoor of its mate and Wolhuter to the foot of the tree. The lion now made clear his intention to pull Wolhuter from his perch, but each time the lion turned to Wolhuter, his dog began a furious assault on the lion from behind. Wolhuter had secured himself as best as he could in the tree with a large handkerchief from around his neck, and it was in this position that he was found by his native bearers at first light.

After only being able to dress superficially his extensive wounds in camp, it took a week to get Wolhuter to hospital for treatment by which time, inevitably, blood poisoning had set in. Quite remarkably, Wolhuter survived this also, and was eventually able to return to work in the bush.

Because of the putrefied and decaying matter lodged under a man-eater's claws, any wound thus inflicted turns septic and before the discovery of anti-biotics this was usually the fatal aftermath of any physical encounter with a man-eater, even if miraculously the actual mauling was survived.

A station appropriately named Simba along the Uganda railway, so often associated with man-eater incidents, was the setting for another remarkable escape from a lion attack. Simba station was being plagued by lions and a hunter, C H Stigand, came to help eliminate the problem. The lions normally visited the station at night and on a particular moonlit night Stigand eventually succeeded in shooting two of the suspected man-eaters and badly wounding a third.

Using a light, Stigand walked forward to investigate something he could just make out at the bottom of the railway embankment which he thought might be the wounded lion. He approached carefully, but relied on being able to stop any charge with ease, as the lion would have to rush up the embankment. But what Stigand could not see in the dark was that the embankment at that point was no more than a few feet high. Stigand later wrote that the lion, when it did charge, subsequently got to him much faster than expected and before a shot could be fired from a safe distance.

As the lion sprang I fired into his chest, and he landed on me, his right paw over my shoulder, and he seized my left arm in his teeth. As my left arm was advanced in the firing position, it was the first thing he met. The weight of his spring knocked me down and I next found myself lying on my back, my left arm being bitten, and my rifle still in my left hand underneath his body. I scrambled round with my left arm still in his mouth until I was kneeling alongside of him, and started pummelling him with my right fist on the back of the neck. He gave me a final shake and then quickly turned round and disappeared in the grass a little nearer to the station than I was.

Drenched with blood and his coat and breeches torn to shreds, Stigand staggered to the station where his wounds were washed out with potassium permanganate. He then sat waiting for six hours until the Nairobi to Mombasa train came at five in the morning. Helped by the station master, but exhausted by loss of blood, he fell into a railway compartment where the rudely awakened passengers, assuming they had to deal with a drunkard, tried to push him out again until they realised what had happened. In Nairobi, Stigand's arm duly turned septic but it was saved after a long period in hospital.

Physical strength was obviously an important factor helping to save the lives of Wolhuter and Stigand. Similarly, a tiger attack in India, related to Jim Corbett by an unarmed villager who successfully fought off a man-eater and resulting remarkably in the tiger's death, was only possible because of the man's exceptional strength and physique.

In this case, the villager was stooping to cut grass for fodder on an almost perpendicular hillside when he was attacked by a tiger which, seizing him by the head, sank one canine into his face below the right eye, another into his chin, and the other two into the back of his neck. Struck with great force by the tiger's jaws, the man fell over onto his back, with the tiger lying on top of him, chest to chest, and its belly between his legs. As he fell backwards, however, he flung out his arms, clutching hold of a sapling with his right hand. Despite his agony, as the tiger crushed all the bones on the right side of his face, the man remained sufficiently in control of his senses to draw up his legs very cautiously until his bare feet were against the tiger's belly. Then, pressing his left hand against the tiger's chest and pushing and kicking upwards with all his strength, he hoisted the tiger right off the ground and, tearing his head free, with the loss of half his face, hurled the tiger down the hill.

In spite of this extraordinary escape, once at close quarters a man-eater's bite through the neck or chest of his victim will normally be instantaneously fatal. As an Indian game warden has noted, it is the culmination of a final spring by an animal of vast muscular proportions, weighing four to five hundred pounds, which then applies all its momentum at the instant that it seizes its victim.

The tiger does not usually strike (like the lion) but it merely seizes with its claws, and uses them to clutch firm hold, and to lacerate its victim. I have seen several examples of the tiger's attack upon man, and in no instance has the individual suffered from the shock of any blow; the tiger has seized, and driven deeply its claws into the flesh, and with this tremendous purchase it has held the victim, precisely as the hands of a man would clutch a prisoner; at the same time it has taken a firm hold with its teeth, and killed its victim by a crunch of the jaws.

In attacking man, the tiger generally claws the head. An Indian is generally slight, and shallow in the chest, therefore the widespread jaws can include both chest and back when seized in the tiger's mouth. I have seen men who were thus attacked, and each claw has cut down to the skull, leaving clean incisions from the brow across the forehead and over the scalp, terminating at the back of the neck. These cuts were as neatly drawn across the skull as though done by a sharp pruning-knife; the fatal wound was the bite, through the neck or through the back and chest penetrating the lungs.

To pursue the trail of a man-eater into the bush, rather than sitting in a machan over a recent victim's remains and waiting for the man-eater to return to his kill, is particularly fraught with risk, even more so if the animal has been wounded. If a firearm malfunctions in any way or if a shot is fired too late during the man-eater's final charge, the hunter is in a potentially fatal predicament. Arthur Strachan, a tea planter, found himself in such a situation when in Assam, northern India, during the 1930's.

In the third year of my residence in Sylhet a worker was killed on a neighbouring estate, and the evidence pointed to the fact that a tigress with small cubs was the culprit.

Shortly after the tragedy had occurred on August 12th I received word from the assistant of the estate in question saying that one of his cattle had been killed by a tiger that morning, and asking me to sit with him over the carcass in the afternoon. I was the more willing to do so as I believed that by sharing this vigil I might have an opportunity of avenging the man's death.

Little did I dream that my decision was to affect the whole of my future life, or that it was to result in bringing my opportunities for seeing tigers in all the beauty of their natural surroundings to a sudden and violent end.

It was about 4.30 p.m. when I arrived at the estate assistant's bungalow, and at once proceeded with him to the scene of our prospective vigil. The victim, a fully grown bullock, was lying with its head twisted under it in a small open space between the tea and the jungle, and a machan had been cunningly constructed in a tree growing conveniently amongst the tea bushes about twenty paces distant from the spot where the kill lay. We lost no time in climbing to this vantage point with as little noise as possible, as it was quite likely that the tiger might be in the immediate vicinity at this late hour in the afternoon. Our platform was some fifteen feet from the ground, and commanded an excellent view of all approaches to the kill, besides the carcass of the bullock itself. We had brought cushions and settled down in comparative comfort.

The jungle immediately behind the spot where the tiger's victim was lying appeared to be almost impenetrable, while to our left was an extensive patch of long grass from three to four feet high. It looked likely country for the tiger to return before dark and we were hopeful of at least obtaining a shot.

Every detail of the scene is deeply engraved upon my memory.

On the neighbouring trees a large number of vultures had already collected and were sitting patiently awaiting the lead of the most venturesome to commence their meal.

The faint, distant voices of the estate workers returning to the lines after finishing their various tasks could be distinctly heard; while from the lines themselves the barking of a pariah dog, mingling with the spasmodic beat of a tom-tom could be heard on the evening air.

A couple of crows paid a brief visit of inspection, but finding the skin of the carcass still unbroken, and too tough for their beaks to penetrate, they soon went off in quest of a more manageable meal.

The sun was rapidly nearing the horizon and the dead bullock was already in shadow before the first vulture ventured to descend; but its example was immediately followed by others, and in a few minutes the kill was completely blotted out by a seething, squabbling mass of the birds. Fighting, chattering, and tearing whenever they could obtain a hold on some part of the bullock's anatomy, they would soon have stripped it to the bones had the noisy feast been allowed to go on unchecked. But this was not to be.

Suddenly, from the black shadow at the jungle edge, a dark form sprang clear into the midst of the struggling birds. In absolute silence, like an avenging monster from the lower regions, it came, scattering the noisy rabble in the utmost confusion. There was a roar of flapping wings as the vultures frantically endeavoured to rise out of reach of the death-dealing paws, and in less time than it takes to tell, a few quivering bodies were all that remained of the throng, the survivors having completely disappeared.

The whole incident happened so quickly that for the moment my companion and I scarcely realised that the tiger had actually appeared on the scene, but it did not take us long to appreciate the fact. There, within twenty yards of where we sat, stood the unmistakable form, broadside-on, with head raised and its tail twitching from side to side. It appeared almost black in the last remnant of the rapidly fading daylight.

Whispering to my companion that this was our opportunity, we raised our weapons simultaneously. Aiming as nearly as I could judge in the dim light at the angle of the shoulder, I pressed the trigger. I was not conscious of any report from my companion's gun and I afterwards discovered that he had not fired at all as he had forgotten to release his safety-catch.

At the shot it seemed as if pandemonium had suddenly been let loose about us. With a succession of the most terrifying roars, the tigress (as it proved to be) came rapidly straight towards our tree in a series of somersaults, roaring all the time. It was evident that she was wounded, but by the time I had picked up the 12-bore which was beside me, loaded with ball and slugs, the animal had passed under our platform where it was impossible to get another shot at her. The last we saw of her that night was as she fell head-over-heels into the long grass on our left, and as the uproar suddenly ceased we surmised that she must be dead or nearly so.

After waiting for some considerable time, during which she had made no sign to indicate that she was still alive, we descended from our perch - not without misgivings that she might still have sufficient vitality left to charge. It was now almost dark and such a predicament would have been decidedly unpleasant, so in our descent we took very good care to advertise our movements as little as possible. On reaching the ground we listened intently for any sign of life, and not without a certain amount of trepidation, but as none was forthcoming we were of the opinion that she must be dead. However, as it is folly to take risks by remaining in the vicinity of a wounded tiger that you do not positively know to be incapable of doing damage, we quickly slipped away to a healthier neighbourhood.

Of course nothing more could be done that night, but on the way back to the bungalow we arranged our plan of action for the morrow. It was decided that we should ask one of the best shots in the district to accompany us, as he had had experience of this dangerous sport. Though all the evidence seemed to indicate that the beast was past doing damage, there was always the possibility that the wound was not as severe as it appeared to be and it was essential that we should be prepared for such a contingency. We also arranged for a gang of ten estate workers to be ready at 9 a.m. to act as trackers or beaters in case of need.

By that hour on the 13th (note the date) the three of us met at the bungalow and at once set off for the scene of action, each accompanied by his pet shikari to act as gun-bearer. Ticka was again my henchman, and my battery consisted of a 405 magazine rifle and a 12-bore that I invariably used for this sort of work, and in whose stopping power I had every confidence. My companions also had a gun and rifle each, but their rifles were the old army pattern 303 Lee-Enfield. On the way we picked up our bank of trackers, each of whom carried a large machete with which to cut our way through the jungle, though we hoped that these would not be necessary.

When we arrived at the spot where the tigress had been wounded the previous evening, there was little difficulty in following her tracks to the edge of the patch of grass into which she had disappeared. Apart from the well-defined track she had made during her struggles, there was a good deal of blood spattered on the leaves and branches of the tea bushes through which she had gone.

Before entering the high grass we took the precaution of making the Indians bombard the spot where we thought the beast had fallen with lumps of earth and stones, while the three of us stood with guns at the ready in case of a charge. There was no response to this fusillade, so we proceeded cautiously behind my man, Ticka, who was slowly following the spoor under cover of our weapons. My companions and I felt sure that we would find the tigress lying dead at the spot where she appeared to fall the night before, but we discovered that, though she had apparently lain here for a considerable time and lost a great quantity of blood, she had eventually gone on. This was rather a blow to our hopes, and the knowledge that she was still alive and probably capable of being aggressive caused us grave misgivings about the wisdom of following her through such country. There was no alternative, however, as we could not leave her in her wounded condition.

Stopping every few minutes to listen for some indication of her whereabouts, we cautiously traversed the grassland without any sign from our quarry beyond the blood-tracks we had so patiently followed. On entering bamboos the going was very much easier for a time. The spoor was more difficult to follow, but the work was much less trying to the nerves, as the jungle here was comparatively open and we could see some distance ahead of us. The fact that she had gone so far without lying down again was conclusive proof that she had a considerable amount of vitality left, so it was imperative that we should be doubly careful.

In the sandy margin of a small stream we found, for the first time, the deep impressions of her pugs. It was evident that she had crossed this some time previously, as her tracks where she had emerged on the other side were quite dry. This might mean that we still had a long way to go before coming up with her, and our hopes of the early morning had almost vanished. The trail took up along the bank of the stream for a distance of a hundred yards or so, then entered a dense patch of undergrowth through which the Indians had to cut a path. Here it was necessary to go in single file, so I took the lead as I had wounded the animal.

I had seen and shot many tigers, one or two of which I had followed up after being wounded. Though I had been growled at and roared at threateningly more than once, I had never been charged by one of these animals, so it was perhaps a case of familiarity breeding contempt. Anyhow, I did not think the risk was very great when the beast had three guns to face should it prove nasty.

I had the 12-bore in my hands with Ticka immediately behind with my rifle; then came my two companions, each with his gun-bearer. Two of the Indians were clearing a path with their machetes immediately ahead of us. I had just emerged into a small open space when I was greeted with a sound I am never likely to forget.

From the jungle to my right came a succession of short, coughing roars – the unmistakable challenge of a tiger that means mischief. I could see nothing, owing to the density of the undergrowth. In the belief that we could put her out of action before she could charge home I stood my ground.

I was quite unconscious of the fact that I stood alone. My companions had, on the first intimation that the tigress meant to charge, removed themselves to a safer distance, not unnaturally believing that I was following in their footsteps.

The intimidating roars increased in volume as the man-eater drew rapidly nearer, but still I could see nothing but the shaking of the undergrowth as she rushed towards me. There could be no doubt about her intentions, but I had no opportunity to stop her.

The first view I got of her was when she bounded over the scrub straight at me. All I had time to do was to snap both barrels of my gun at her as she was in the air. Before I had time to lower my weapon a snarling tigress' face loomed through the smoke from my cartridges and I went down. My gun was sent spinning from my grasp, and though none of the blows aimed at me struck me fairly, their force hurled me backwards. This probably saved my life, as the upper part of my body fell away from her where she collapsed, her back broken by my hasty shots. Unfortunately for me, she still had the use of her forepaws with which she caught me by the legs and dragged me towards her, then biting through my left foot.

It has been said that in moments such as this all the sins and omissions of one's past life flash through the mind. Though I was perfectly conscious all the time, I have no recollection of this being the case, and my one thought was 'how long is this chewing-up process going to last?'

I had no feeling of fear, and felt comparatively little pain from the wounds inflicted by the tigress. On the report of a rifle-shot, however, a red-hot iron seemed to pass through the foot which was in the brute's mouth, and I am afraid that I added considerably to the anxiety of my rescuers by shouting to them that I had been shot. At the report the animal sank inert and lifeless, but I was still held a prisoner, as her jaws were tightly closed upon my foot, and the claws of her left paw were sunk deep in the muscle of my right leg.

When at last her mouth was prised open, and her claws removed, I was able to get up and survey the damage that had been done. It was quite extensive, and I realised that my future prospects did not look rosy.

There was a deep gash in my right arm extending from the elbow to the wrist, and every bone in the hand appeared to be broken, apparently by her teeth, though I was not aware that it had ever been in her mouth. One of her forepaws had ripped my coat across the chest, inflicting minor flesh wounds. With the other she had struck at my head, but luckily only succeeded in leaving the impression of her paw and claws in my pith helmet, which was picked up some yards away.

Her huge canine teeth had pierced the heavy shooting boot I was wearing at the time, and met in my left foot; and the bullet which had ended her life had at the same time made rather a mess of my big toe on its way through her head. There were also deep claw wounds in the flesh of my right leg.

My friends, to whose courage and steadiness under the most trying possible circumstances I owe my life, wanted to carry me, but I managed to walk, as I was not suffering a great deal of pain, and stopped to bathe my injuries in the stream. It was nearly one and a half miles back to the bungalow, so I lost a considerable amount of blood before I reached the foot of the hill on which it was situated. Here I had to be carried the last lap of the journey.

The Indians, carrying the dead tigress, formed the rear of the slow procession, and I have recollections that their epithets regarding her and her antecedents were anything but polite. As these had frequently been accompanied by vigorous slashes from their machetes the skin was not improved, but at the time my interest in the trophy was not particulary great.

She was a short, thick-set tigress, and as there were no further attacks on human beings up to the time I left the district, it seemed that it was she who had been responsible for the death of the unfortunate native.

My two injured limbs had, of course, to be amputated, but the claw wounds gave me little trouble, and, thanks to the skill and devoted attention of the doctor who pulled me through, I was able to leave for home on the 5th of November.

CHAPTER SEVEN

The Bellundur Ogre

IN RIDDING A VILLAGE in Mysore state, south-central India, of a man-eating tigress, circumstances compelled Kenneth Anderson to lie alongside a human victim's remains all night, awaiting the animal's possible return to the kill. The tigress did return that night – but together with its tiger mate.

Bellundur is a hamlet situated on the shoulder of a hill and about three miles from the village of Tagarthy, in the district of Shimoga, in Mysore State. For centuries this part of Mysore has been the home of tigers.

In Bellundur there lived a necromancer who was reputed for his ability to provide charms and talismans of all sorts for all purposes. These were said to be particularly efficacious in procuring a loved one, or contrarily, in ridding yourself of one whom you did not love quite so well.

Among his other abilities, this magician was famous for possessing the power, by charms and incantations, to 'tie up' the jungle, so that any hunter operating in that area would meet with total failure. The game animals would not appear before his rifle; or if they did, the rifle would not go off; or if it did go off, the bullet would not strike the quarry even at a few yards range. Like most members of his calling, he enjoyed a little flattery. I had always found him quite friendly and found nothing wrong in his weakness. After all, we all like to be flattered.

The 'Ogre of Bellundur' began its career as a very ordinary and inoffensive tiger. Nothing was heard of it in its younger days. Evidently it had confined its attentions to killing and eating spotted deer, sambar and pig. Then the government began encouraging programmes of cattle-rearing, and as rich pasturage abounded,

herds of cattle were introduced to the detriment of the wild deer
and pig that previously had grazed undisturbed.

The ogre, as it came to be known later, now made its presence
felt by varying its taste for wild game with a liking for good prime
beef, and this inclination grew rapidly to the exclusion of any other
kind of meat. It killed and it ate, and it ate and it killed, till it had
accounted for many head of cattle and the villagers at last began to
feel that something should be done.

The Indian villager is a man of unbounded patience, an attribute
easier to understand if one observes his complete apathy, his
capacity for resignation and for accepting whatever misfortune it
may be the will of God to bestow upon him. So, when at last the
villagers had had enough of this tiger and were determined to put
a stop to its depredations, you will realise that the ogre had really
gone too far. They decided to set a trap, catch it and then kill it.

A deep rectangular hole was dug in the centre of a game trail; the
mouth was carefully concealed by thin interlaced bamboos covered
with leaves and twigs, and the bait, in the form of the least valuable
calf in the village, was tied to a stake at the farther end of the
rectangular pit. A direct appraoch to the bait from any other
direction except across the rectangular pit was made impracticable
for the tiger by a vast mass of thorns packed tightly around it on
both sides and beyond, leaving only the one approach open.

Eveything went according to plan and on the third night the tiger
fell into the pit.

The following morning all the inhabitants of Bellundur village
turned out, including the necromancer, to gloat over their enemy
and throw firebrands at it, before putting it to death by the simple
but rather slow process of spearing it from above. Evidently
nobody had a gun, and the question of cruelty, of course, did not
occur to anybody. For was not this animal the tiger who had killed
and devoured so many of their cattle?

Not only did the inhabitants of Bellundur have no guns, but they
did not appear to be very rich in spears either. I discovered
afterwards that just two people had spears, or articles that might
pass as such. One was a short affair, less than four feet long and

entirely blunt at the end. The description fitted more a crowbar than a spear. The second was a true spear and belonged to the local temple. It was reputed to have been used in a war two and a half centuries before but was now as blunt as the crowbar, having been employed many times for digging up yams. In any case, the shafts of both weapons were too short to reach the tiger from the surface of the pit, but this mattered little, as each of their owners was confident that, with a single throw of his particular weapon, he could transfix and kill the imprisoned beast.

Much argument is said to have arisen as to who should cast his weapon first. Finally, the owner of the crowbar won the dispute. Taking careful aim, he hurled his weapon; no sooner had it left his hand than its blunt point was deflected and the side of the weapon, rather than its blunt point, struck the tiger's flank.

The tiger did not take lightly to this form of treatment. It roared its defiance and glared up at its tormentors. There was widespread tittering amongst the assembled crowd as the second spearman, after glancing contemptuously at the crestfallen owner of the crowbar, prepared to make his cast. The 250-years-old spear flew downwards to its target, the blunt point embedding itself fairly in the tiger's hindquarters.

Now Bellundur was totally unarmed. And the ogre lost its temper. With a burst of unexpected energy, it sprang upwards to the rim of the pit, groping with the talons of its forefeet. They reached it, held and embedded themselves in the soft soil. The hindfeet, kicking the air madly, found purchase against the sides of the pit and levered the beast upwards. And the next moment the tiger was free, leaping out of the mouth of the pit like a demon from hell, and far more dangerous.

Just one of the crowd stood stood in its path to freedom; all the rest had fled. The tiger leaped over the man before it, kicking backwards with all four feet extended, and the claws of one of those dreadful feet met the back of the man's skull before he, in turn, could gather his wits to run. It was only a glancing blow, comparatively light considering the force that the tiger had put into it, for if the paw had struck the head fully the skull would have been smashed like an eggshell. As it was, the tips of the claws caught in the skin at the back of the man's neck, and the weight of the tiger, as it leaped over the man's head, did the rest.

Then the tiger had gone. The man fell where he had been standing, but he was quite alive. The whole of his scalp, removed neatly from the bone, now hung over his face, the long hair streaming down before him instead of behind. It took three days for this man to die, for to the very last moment he lived in the hope that his scalp could be put back. He was the ogre's first victim, although unintentionally so.

Naturally, with the healing of his wound, the tiger grew cunning. Other baits were tied out for it with various forms of traps, but they were studiously ignored. All its killings of cattle thereafter were done in broad daylight, generally in the afternoons while the herds were placidly resting after having grazed all morning and their attendants were huddled asleep in the shade of the bushes. Those who were awake, or had been awakened by the short cry of the stricken victim, at first attempted to drive the ogre off by shouting and throwing stones. But the ogre soon put a stop to such tactics by leaping upon one of the graziers and mauling him severely. Strangely enough, this man made a complete recovery, though the lesson that had been given was salutary enough. Thereafter, at sight or sound of the tiger all herdsmen fled, leaving their charges to its mercy.

The situation at Bellundur went from bad to worse. Cattle owners could no longer trust their animals to the forest grazing, but endeavoured to feed them at home and this cost a lot of money. Correspondingly, the tiger's hunger grew as the supply of Bellundur beef was cut down, so it extended the range of its operations to include Tagarthy and some of the smaller neighbouring hamlets. Its fame and daring as a cattle-lifter began to spread far and wide.

That was how a gentleman, whom we shall call Mr Johnson, came to hear about the tiger. Johnson was an officer in railway service who had lately been transferred to the area from some other part of India where tigers did not exist. This made him very keen to attempt to bag the beast that was the talk of the neighbourhood, and as he had a rifle he made his way to Bellundur, which was only about seven miles from the railway track, on the few days' leave during which he hoped to succeed. And this is where old Buddiah, the necromancer, comes into my story.

Hearing that a white man had arrived and was making inquiries about the tiger, Buddiah donned his ceremonial saffron robe, plaited the long roll of filthy false hair that he kept for such occasions in a coil around the crown of his head, smeared ashes liberally across his forehead, which he further decorated with vermilion marks of a religious significance. He hung his chain of large amber and wooden beads around his neck, and holding his gnarled walking-stick, blackened by being soaked in oil, presented himself before Johnson. Offering his services, he claimed that they were absolutely indispensable if the white man wishes to succeed in shooting the tiger.

Now the situation was really very simple. To anyone of moderate experience, it was obvious that old Buddiah was endeavouring to earn a few rupees, but more than that he was taking the opportunity to impress his fellow villagers with his greatness as a magician. He wanted them to feel that even the white man had to come to him for help. If Johnson had used a little psychology and common sense, he would have recognised these things and given the old man a boost with a few rupees to humour him. Instead, Johnson lost his temper and told the magician to get out of his presence, and when Buddiah began to remonstrate indignantly Johnson made matters worse by threatening to break Buddiah's neck.

So the necromancer stalked away in fury: his prestige with the villagers, which he had been endeavouring to enhance, had been severely lessened by the white man's words. He felt his companions would laugh at him secretly, although he was still confident that they feared him too much to do so openly.

The villagers, on the other hand, felt abashed. Although none of them had any liking for Buddiah, who had exploited them systematically since childhood he was, nevertheless, their own magician and one of themselves. To be spoken to in such a fashion by the white man, and to be threatened with a beating, reflected scant respect for their magician and incidentally for themselves and the village as a whole. Thus by his hasty words Johnson made enemies all around instead of friends. The villagers left him where he stood and refused to have anything more to do with him. Nor would anyone sell or hire him a bait to tie out for the tiger.

Being of a determined nature, Johnson made up his mind to succeed in spite of local non-co-operation. He made his way back to Tagarthy where, by exercising the tact he should have displayed at Bellundur, he was able to buy two ancient bulls. Engaging herdsmen, he had these two animals driven back to the outskirts of Bellundur, where he tied each up in a nullah said to be frequented by the tiger, or so he was told by the herdsmen he had engaged. But as these men were from Tagarthy and not from Bellundur, they did not know very much about the tiger's movements.

The following morning Johnson and his herdsmen visited the baits. One had disappeared. It certainly had not been taken by the tiger, for there were no pug marks to be seen in the sandy bed of the nullah, which bore a number of human footprints instead. Had these been made by his own men the previous day, or by others? The other bait had not been touched.

Johnson rightly came to the conclusion that the villagers of Bellundur had stolen his first bait. He stalked into the village with loaded rifle, demanded the return of the bull, and then threatened to inform the police. To all of which the villagers assumed an air of injured innocence. They maintained that the human footprints he had seen in the sandy ravine were those of his own men when they had tied the bait and asked him to prove otherwise. To Johnson's furious threats to shoot the thieves the yokels turned a deaf ear and smiled.

Fearing the second bait would also disappear, Johnson ordered his two men to construct a machan over it, in which he sat that same afternoon, perhaps more to protect his bait from being robbed than in serious hope of bagging the tiger. But the unexpected happened. I am told the tiger turned up while it was still daylight. Johnson fired, succeeding only in wounding the animal, which got away.

Throughout the next week Johnson, with commendable determination, scoured the jungles in search of the tiger. No one came forward to assist him; even his two henchmen refused to accompany him on the plea that it was too dangerous. Unaided, the white man lost his way on one occasion and was compelled to spend the night in the forest. In the end, bitterly disappointed, Johnson had to return to duty without bagging his tiger.

Everything was quiet for some time after that. The ogre did not show up and the villagers of Bellundur had to admit that, in spite of their best efforts at non-co-operation, the sahib had rid them of the pest that had been exacting such a heavy toll of their cattle. Buddiah, the magician, was more aggrieved than ever. He felt his pride and reputation at a still lower ebb, for he had announced boastfully that the sahib would not or could not shoot the tiger; he had done so nevertheless and had rid Bellundur of the hated cattle-lifter.

So the cattle were driven out to the jungles once again each day for grazing. That is, until the inevitable happened. Early one afternoon a herd rushed pell-mell back to the village minus one of its members – and minus the nineteen-year-old youth who had gone out with the animals that morning to graze them. Nobody worried about the matter till nightfall. Then the relatives of the boy grew a little anxious about him, while the owner of the missing cow grew far more anxious about his valuable animal. A search the next morning revealed the cow lying dead: her neck had been neatly broken by a large tiger whose pug marks were clearly to be seen in the field where she had been struck down. A hundred yards away, hidden under a bush, was the body of the missing youth.

There was, however, an important difference between the two carcasses: the cow had not been eaten, while rather more than half of the boy had been devoured by the tiger. The familiar pattern had appeared once more; an innocent tiger had been turned into a man-eater through being wounded and left to fend for itself. Tragedy succeeded tragedy after that and the pattern of events was repeated. The people of Bellundur locked themselves in their huts at sundown while the cattle were kept starving in their pens. Old Buddiah's prestige was at its lowest ebb.

Lack of human prey drove the tiger into extending his operations towards Tagarthy and more distant villages, and that was when the beast began to be referred to as 'the ogre', a name that was whispered with bated breath behind locked doors and only during daylight hours. Otherwise it would surely hear and bring dreadful vengeance upon the man who dared refer to the creature as a tiger.

After darkness the ogre was about. It roamed everywhere and a man was not safe even in a locked room. The ogre, or one of its spies, perhaps an evil spirit of the air in the form of a bat or an owl, or one of the many devils that lived in the jungle, might hear what was being said and carry words to the dreaded man-eater. Then the man who had spoken against it was indeed undone. It would be only a matter of time before the ogre exacted a terrible revenge. His fate was sealed and there was no means of escape. That was the universal opinion.

At this stage my old friend, Doctor Stanley, the medical officer of Tagarthy village, wrote a long letter to me and related this story, inviting me to join him in an attempt to end the ogre's career. This doctor, who owned only a 12-bore shotgun and no rifle, had shot many tigers himself in his younger days. Now that he had grown older, he felt that his rather antiquated gun might not be quite up to the mark for a man-eater.

I met him three days later in the front room of his dispensary-cum-hospital, after motoring to Tagarthy in my Studebaker. The first step was to visit Bellundur and pick up the trail from there. We had a hard time to reach this village. The track, which was always bad, had become really terrible after the last rains. The doctor, who sat next to me, said we should have walked. Reaching Bellundur at last, I immediately set about undoing some of the mischief that had been done by the tactless Johnson and I called upon Buddiah, who was sulking in his hut. I presented him with ten rupees to cover incidental expenses and asked him to don his ceremonial robes and make pooja for me, repeating all the mantras he knew to enable me to succeed in shooting the man-eater.

He brightened up at once. In no time at all he stalked out into the market place, all dressed up for the occasion, where the first thing he did was to demand another five rupees from me to cover the cost of a black fowl and a bottle of arrack, the local spirit. The fowl was to be killed, cooked and eaten by him, presumably to placate the spirits of the jungle, and the arrack was to be drunk, also by Buddiah, presumably for the same purpose. The old man declared that only thereafter would he be in a proper condition to utter the mantras that would lead to the downfall of the man-eater. Dr Stanley and I, knowing what state that would be, pretended hearty agreement.

I handed over the money and resigned myself to a further delay of another hour at least, which would be the shortest possible time for the cock to be half-cooked while Buddiah had conditioned himself with arrack for saying his mantras. But the old man, and the villagers of Bellundur especially, had to be humoured if the damage done by Johnson was to be repaired.

The doctor and I chatted while the unfortunate black cock was procured, slaughtered before our eyes, par-boiled into a curry and then devoured by the greedy old necromancer. With scarcely an interval he then proceeded to empty the bottle of arrack.

This done, the magician staggered to his feet. He was dead drunk and could hardly stand erect. With blood-shot eyes and an inane smile, he produced what looked like a bracelet of twisted and dried jungle vines from a filthy cloth bag that he brought out from somewhere on his person. Asking for my rifle, he proceeded to pass this bracelet over the end of the muzzle and down the length of the barrel three or four times. He was so drunk that he missed his aim once or twice, but I was able to rectify the error unostentatiously by quickly guiding the end of the barrel so as to allow it to be encircled by the bracelet.

That was the end of the mantra. The tiger's doom was sealed! It would fall to my rifle! The spirits of the jungle, in the person of old Buddiah, had eaten and drunk well. The crowd of villagers, who had been watching every detail while they stood around us in a circle, breathed their assurance loudly. In any case the mantra, together with their assurances, ended just in time, for the next moment old Buddiah fell to earth as if pole-axed.

The important thing was that good feeling had been restored. Buddiah's prestige was up again, as was that of the villagers and of Bellundur village itself. Dr Stanley and I were smiled upon as 'good fellers', while the activities of the ogre were momentarily eclipsed. Just then it was no more than an ordinary tiger, waiting to be shot.

It was now dark, and the trip back to Tagarthy in the Studebaker was a nightmare. Stanley procured two baits at Tagarthy, which we duly tied out the next day at suitable points near the track to Bellundur. The tiger was, by this time, operating throughout the area. After lunch we walked the seven miles to Bellundur and there were able, without any difficulty, to procure another three animals as additional baits. Obviously the little show we had organised with Buddiah the previous evening had had its good effects. These baits were tied out at points which the villagers informed us were often visited by the ogre.

Time was against us, however, and we were in too much of a hurry to be able to set up a machan above any one of the five baits we had laid that day. This is against my usual practice, which is to construct a machan and tie the bait in full view of it. This has two advantages. Firstly a kill, if it occurs, is in proper view f the machan and does not have to be shifted. Secondly, no noise is made in building the machan which otherwise could arouse the suspicion of a tiger if it is lying up after a kill or lurking within hearing.

It was again pitch-dark when we walked back to Tagarthy, keeping a sharp lookout with our torches against surprise attack by the man-eater, but the only animal we encountered was a pangolin foraging amongst the dead leaves, out much earlier than usual for these creatures.

None of the five baits we had tied out was touched that night, but late in the morning of the third day a man came running to the doctor's dispensary to announce that his cousin had been taken by the tiger. The victim and his wife, together with our informant and his wife, lived in two huts constructed side by side and only a short mile away along the track to Bellundur. It was midday when this cousin, who was returning from a visit to Tagarthy for provisions, came into full view of the other three members of the little community, gathered before their huts and chatting together. They had been about to call out to him when he screamed loudly and then vanished into thin air.

Our informant stated he had then grabbed his axe and set out to see what was the matter, accompanied by his cousin's wife, wringing her hands and lamenting aloud. The thought of the man-eater had never occurred to them. Rather they suspected that an evil spirit from the forest had done away with their companion.

Reaching the spot where the man had disappeared, they were terrified to find the pug marks of a tiger in the soft sand of the trail. Prevented by fear from going farther, they were about to turn back when the wails of the woman, which had now increased in volume, annoyed the man-eater who had just begun to taste his victim not far away. The tiger growled fiercely, whereupon both the man and the victim's wife fled. Stopping long enough to enable the two women to lock themselves into one of the huts, the man had come running to Tagarthy by a round-about route to inform the doctor and me of what had happened. The ogre would be there still, he affirmed, feasting upon his cousin, if only we would come at once and shoot it.

Grabbing rifle, torch and warm coat, I set out at a jog-trot with our informant, Stanley bringing with him the 12-bore gun and another torch. Minutes later, with the man in the middle, Stanley to the left of him and me to the right, we approached the place where the tragedy had taken place, determined to flush the man-eater on its kill.

The tiger sensed we were coming long before we knew where it was, for we heard no sounds of eating or the breaking of bones. As likely as not it had seen our arrival at the two huts, which were, as I have said, in full view of the spot where the ogre had seized its victim. When we were quite close, the man-eater began to growl, and its protests grew to hideous volume. Clearly, it was bent upon driving us away. If we beat a retreat now, while the going was good, all would be well. But if we continued to advance, it would either rush us, or its courage might fail at the last moment and it would then run away.

We hesitated only a second before Stanley and I nodded to each other. With my left arm I thrust back the man who had called us, motioning to him with my hand to go away. Then we advanced, shoulder to shoulder. We could not see the tiger yet. Roar followed upon roar, and the bushes in front of us shook violently. We stopped, gun and rifle to respective shoulders, awaiting the onslaught that was inevitable.

It never came. At the last moment the man-eater shirked the encounter. It was accustomed to chasing and killing men. Never before had human beings deliberately followed and approached it. With a final shattering roar the tiger sprang away from the spot and I was just able to catch a fleeting glimpse of a reddish-brown form hurtling into a bush; then it disappeared. I could have fired. Why I did not do so I just cannot say, but I was to regret my mistake.

The tiger must have been really hungry, for we discovered it had made the most of its opportunity by devouring over half its victim, leaving only the head, arms, legs and a few ribs uneaten. Stanley and I did not speak to each other. We were both experienced enough to know that the human voice carries a long way. Instead, I looked about to see if there were any possible places to conceal myself and await the man-eater's return, should it decide to come back to finish what scraps were left.

But the ogre put an end to my reflections by its next action, as unexpected as it was sudden. It might have been hunger or natural ill-nature, or maybe the fact that as it fled it saw that only two humans and not a crowd had dared to follow. Anyway, this extraordinary animal stopped in its tracks, turned about and started to come for us, roaring louder and louder as it approached. The ground shook with the intensity of the sound, while its ever-increasing volume indicated that the tiger was getting dangerously close. All this time we could not see the beast, for it was hidden by the bushes which shook violently as it came closer and closer.

Standing shoulder to shoulder once more, the doctor and I turned to face the man-eater, which was making things easy for us and solving the problem by attacking. In another second or two the tiger would have to show itself and then all would be over. But the moment never came. For the ogre was wily beyond expectation. At the last moment it changed its mind once more and began to circle us and the remains of its meal without showing itself, still snarling and roaring for all it was worth. The animal's tactics were now clear. Again its courage had failed when it had been about to press home its attack. Now its intention was to drive us away with the noise it was making.

Then I had an idea. Its success depended on just how observant the tiger had been, how persistent was its memory, and how alert its instinct. It had seen the two of us approaching. That much was evident. Now if one of us went away and the other hid in the grass somewhere near the remains of the victim, would the tiger be aware of the fact? Would it think the coast was clear and return to its meal? Would it be tempted to follow and attack the one who was retreating? Would it see through the trick we were trying to play by stalking whichever one of us had remained behind and leaping upon that person from the rear?

There were many imponderables in the situation. Stanley solved the problem for me by whispering to me to hide while he would go away, motioning impatiently towards the bushes for me to hide. The tiger was creeping about now, circling our position and continuing to snarl and roar alternately. A single bush, not more than four feet high, grew about thirty feet or so away, its base hidden by the usual carpet of grass and greenery. There was no other large tree or rock that offered shelter. I tiptoed to the bush and took up my position behind it, crouching on the ground with my weapon ready. We waited till the tiger had reached a point that was opposite the direction in which the doctor would have to go to regain the track leading towards the two huts. Then I motioned for him to get away quickly.

With the purpose of letting the man-eater know that he was departing and that the coast would be clear to return to the meal, Stanley coughed slightly and began to talk to himself as he began to back slowly towards the track. I watched him looking intently in the direction where the man-eater was still demonstrating, his 12-bore gun ready for instant action should the animal charge.

But Stanley had made the mistake by talking. Instead of returning to its kill now that the coast was clear, as the doctor had hoped, this most unusual animal did the unexpected thing once again. Circling the scant clearing in which the remains of its victim reposed, and incidentally myself, the tiger began to follow the departing doctor. Worse still, it stopped roaring and snarling. Clearly, the man-eater now meant business. Whatever the ogre was doing at that moment, or intended to do at the next, was going to be done in silence. Stanley, already handicapped with only a shotgun, was going to be still further handicapped by not knowing from which direction the man-eater would attack him.

This thought worried me. It was hard to sit idly behind a bush while my friend's life might at that moment be in great danger. Without weighing the consequences I decided to creep after the tiger. No greater folly could have been committed than by my action at that moment.

Try to imagine the doctor stepping backward, a foot at a time, with his shotgun loaded in both barrels ready for instant use and pointed towards where he thinks the tiger is, the latter creeping upon him unseen and in silence. Stanley does not know that I have left my shelter in the bush and am following him and the tiger. Then put yourself in the tiger's place, your composure now regained after an exhibition of bad temper. You move softly and silently, bent upon putting an end to this interfering human being who has dared to follow you. At the same time, you are aware that you are close enough for a final spring, but instinct warns you that to do so will court disaster. And you do not know that a second human being is following you. Behind both Stanley and the tiger am I, creeping forward with equally great caution, my Winchester cocked and ready for use at the first glimpse of the tiger. But I cannot see it, nor Stanley. All I can hear is the faint rustle of a bush here and there before me, as either Stanley or the tiger brushes against it despite their caution. Finally, do not forget that the distance between the doctor and myself cannot be more than forty or fifty yards now, with the tiger somewhere in between.

If only that tiger had had a little reasoning power, what amusement it could have had that day at our expense. All it had to do was to conceal itself and then mimic the roaring sound of a charging tiger. Stanley and I would have opened fire. One or other would have shot his companion. Perhaps with a spot of luck – or bad luck – we might have shot each other. What headlines for the newspapers: 'Shikaris after man-eater shoot each other! Man-eater eats both!'

So intent was I on following the tiger that these possibilities did not dawn upon me at the time. The man-eater, unaware of being followed, kept steadfastly after Stanley. He meanwhile, naturally worried by the silence that had succeeded the tiger's threatening roars, was wondering if he would reach the track to the huts before the attack came.

Then things happened. The doctor reached the track. The tiger broke the silence with a shattering roar. Seeing nothing but hearing everything, I did not know right away whether the man-eater was launching its attack upon the doctor or myself. The doctor fired, and slugs from his gun spattered through the undergrowth uncomfortably close to me. The tiger, frightened by the sound, lost its nerve, turned, and dashed past me at full gallop. I saw the tiger coming, threw the rifle to my shoulder, and pressed the trigger at almost point-blank range. Stanley told me a few minutes later that my bullet whizzed past his head within inches. Inadvertently the ogre had almost succeeded in accomplishing what it had been unable to do intentionally. The doctor and I had narrowly escaped shooting each other.

We still had hopes that one of us must have wounded the tiger at least. We both had considerable hunting experience. Both had been ready to fire when we had actually pressed our triggers. Both had fired at point-blank range. The tiger must be lying mortally wounded close by, perhaps it was even dead. So we searched far and wide, but not a speck of blood did we come across. Of dead or wounded tiger there was neither sight nor sound. Then it dawned upon us. In the excitement we had overlooked the fact that I had heard the slugs from Stanley's gun, while he had heard my bullet. We had both missed, although the ogre had met us almost face to face.

We made our way in silence back to the huts, where to the man and the two women still hiding there we confided all that had happened. We were half a furlong from Tagarthy before my mind, numbed with disappointment, started to function again.

Normally a tiger, after being fired upon, would avoid the place where that had happened for a long time. This tiger, it should be remembered, had been fired upon not once, but twice. Therefore, by all the rules, it should leave the neighbourhood and not appear there again. But was there just a small chance to the contrary? The ogre had already shown itself to be of a most unusual disposition on two occasions. It had fled and then turned and crept back again. And it had deliberately followed Stanley when the way was clear to return to its kill. Would it once again display its singular nature by returning to a place where, at least instinct must tell it, it had suffered two narrow escapes? The chances were ninety-nine per cent against. That left a one per cent chance that the tiger might return.

I halted in my tracks as the thought came home to me. The doctor stopped also, wondering what was the matter. I told him. He was too much of a hunter himself not to realise the chance was one that could not, must not, be missed. So we retraced our steps to the two huts. The man and the two women, now all locked together in one of the huts for mutual safety, were surprised at our early return. When we told them why we had come, they were pleased but they were honest enough to say they did not think we had any chance of success. It was the man's opinion that the tiger would be many miles away by now.

Stanley and I retraced our steps to the place where the remains of the man-eater's victim lay strewn about, exercising extreme caution while negotiating the patch of jungle through which the doctor, the tiger and I had played our strange game of hide-and-seek. There was neither sight nor sound of our quarry. A strange mixture of relief and disappointment filled us, relief that the ogre had not launched another attack and disappointment at the feeling that it might never return.

My earlier survey of the possibilities of concealment, although made in such a hurry, had about summed up the chances accurately. Apart from the four-foot high bush where I had stood while the doctor retreated there was no other place in which to conceal myself. Hiding behind that bush in daylight from a man-eater, as I had done already, was one thing; but remaining there after darkness was quite another. The tiger, with its ability to see at night, would spot me immediately it approached what was left of its victim from any angle other than directly opposite the bush behind which I would be hiding, while for me to see it would be impossible. Further, should it return in spite of being shot at twice only a few hours earlier, the man-eater would undoubtedly make an extremely cautious approach and I would not be able to hear it. Lastly, there was no possibility of erecting any sort of shelter behind that scanty bush that would not immediately betray my presence.

What could I do? I was reluctant to forgo that tiny possibility of the man-eater's return. To commit suicide, and that in a most painful manner in the jaws of the tiger, I was still more reluctant to do. There seemed no solution as we thought about the matter without speaking, till suddenly the doctor had an idea: would it not be possible, with the help of the man and the two women in the nearby huts, to dig a narrow hole just where the human remains were scattered? He would hide in the hole which would be wide and deep enough to conceal him, wait until the tiger returned, and shoot it at point-blank range.

Several obstacles to the execution of this plan presented themselves. Firstly, the tiger might discover the hole and shy away; worse still, the tiger might decide to investigate it. Secondly, admitting that the man-in-the-hole was hidden from the tiger, the tiger was equally hidden from the man-in-the-hole, who would necessarily have to stand erect to be able to shoot the beast, during which process the latter would surely spot him when he appeared, as it were, out of the very ground. When that happened, much would depend upon the reflexes of the feasting tiger. It would be frightened, yes; but it would also be decidedly annoyed. What transpired after that would depend upon which of these reflexes gained the upper hand.

Well, there was no use spending time thinking about it. The chance, and the risk, would have to be taken or the whole plan dropped. Time was passing and it was now after 3 p.m. We would have to work fast. We hurried back to the huts, where the inmates gladly volunteered to help us, but stated they had no implements of any sort to dig with. The doctor, who in his capacity of village medic wielded much influence, solved this by returning to Tagarthy at the double; he came back in an incredibly short time with six helpers, two with pickaxes, two with crowbars, and two with large baskets in which to remove all traces of the earth we dug out. With the three earlier helpers and ourselves, all eleven of us set to work, with the result that the hole had soon been dug and all traces of loose earth removed and thrown far away.

I knew that as father of the plan, Stanley had prepared the hole to sit in it himself. I also knew that no amount of argument would dissuade him. If I tried to tell him that his shotgun was not an effective weapon against so dangerous a quarry, he would reply that it was just the right thing at such close range. Nor would I be able to gainsay the truth of his assertions as, in reality, at point-blank range a 12-bore gun has its merits. So I resigned myself to inactivity for once by spending the night at Tagarthy.

Our helpers were just gathering their tools together, prior to departing with me, when chance once again took a hand in this strange adventure. Two men burst upon us, having ran all the way from Tagarthy in search of the doctor. One was the village patel, the other was his servant. The patel announced that his wife, who was heavily pregnant, had slipped and fallen while carrying her pot of water from the well. She had aborted and was bleeding profusely. The doctor must come at once.

While he was still speaking, the young man summed up the position and realised that Stanley was preparing to sit up for the tiger. So as to make his summons more forceful, he started lamenting aloud that the doctor, as his best friend, must come to his aid at once to save his wife's life, while in the same breath he denounced the woman as a stubborn wench. How often had he told her not to carry weights, particularly the water-pot from the well? Was he not the village patel? Did he not have servants enough for this task? Yet in her wilfulness she would never listen to him. Now this was the result. And never mind the tiger; was his wife's life not far more important?

Stanley looked at me, chagrin written large upon his face. In another minute Stanley and the other members of the group, which had grown to twelve, were lost to sight. I was alone with the remains of the dead man. Dusk was fast approaching and there was not a moment to be lost as I slipped into the hole we had prepared, to squat at the bottom and look upwards at a circle of sky above my head. By canting my Winchester, loaded and cocked, at an angle with the butt against my right thigh and the foresight-guard leaning against the wall of the hole opposite me, we had made sure, by means of measuring Stanley's 12-bore gun in the same position, that the end of the muzzle would not be visible above ground level.

In the excitement and hurry of forming and executing what I now began to realise was a rather insane plan, we had overlooked the fact that it would be terribly hot inside that hole. The earth around had been exposed to the sun's rays all day, no air could enter, and with my body in close proximity to the sides of the cavity, air could not circulate anywhere. I soon began to perspire profusely.

Fortunately in those days there were no wild elephants around Tagarthy or, for that matter, in any of the districts to the north-west of Mysore State. Those were the times when tigers roamed in hundreds, but things have since changed and carnivora are scarce, but 'jumbo' in his wild state has extended his wanderings into those jungles and herds of elephants have now made their home there, where once there were none.

I remember that it was almost deathly silent inside the hole and I could scarcely hear the roosting calls of peafowl, jungle-cocks and other birds as they settled down for the night. To hope to hear the man-eater's arrival by any faint sound that it might make was out of the question. I would only be able to hear it if it roared or snarled nearby, and the ogre was hardly likely to do that – or so at least I thought till I recollected that the tiger had in fact done just that only a few hours earlier. How I hoped it would repeat its performance rather than decide upon a silent approach.

It was almost dark when the circle of sky above my head was crossed by an elongated black form that passed silently by. A nightjar, with wings outstretched, had flown low over the spot, evidently to investigate the possibility of devouring the insects that were already assembling to feed upon the exposed flesh that hung in shreds from the human bones and undevoured portions of the carcass of the tiger's unfortunate victim. I could hear the bluebottles as they buzzed across the opening above my head to settle on the mess, while the stench of decaying flesh, increased by the sun's rays in which it had been baking all day, clung to the ground and drifted into my hole.

Would the tiger come? Would it start eating right away? Or would it know that something unusual was afoot? It might have been watching us from cover of some distant bush. It might even know, at that very moment, that one of its hated foes, a man, had gone into hiding somewhere in the ground. Now would be an excellent opportunity for the tiger to unearth and devour that enemy. The thought was a very sobering one.

Where there had been an oval of sky above, two stars now twinkled down upon me; night had fallen. They seemed so serene and peaceful up there, oblivious to my predicament down in the hole. My thoughts focused upon them and I wondered what other tragedies, taking place at that moment in other remote corners of the earth, they also twinkled upon so impartially.

That was when I first heard the sound: faint but distinctly heavy breathing. It had to be the tiger. It had located me and was creeping upon its stomach to get close enough to pull me out of my hiding place. Involuntarily, my hand reached towards the rifle. The touch of metal and wood, warm like everything else in that wretched pit, was very comforting to my nerves.

The sound ceased for a while. Then I heard a sudden, loud hiss, followed by silence again. Could this be a passing panther? Panthers were scarce in this area as the tigers had driven them out. Nevertheless, there were one or two to be found here and there, and it was possible that an odd member had happened to be passing and had stumbled upon the exposed kill, creeping forward to snatch a mouthful from the tiger's kill.

I did not hear anything more for quite a long time. Then came a dull, scraping sound, as of something gliding over the ground above my head. Could a large snake be the cause? A hamadryad? There were quite a number of them to be found in these forests, where the vegetation and jungles were of the wet variety, unlike the drier forests farther south.

Silence followed, while I strained my ears to pick up the faintest of sounds, and my eyes stared upwards at the faint light of the hole above me till they ached. The two stars still twinkled down upon me, but whether in disdain or mockery I did not know. I saw that they had shifted farther towards the edge of the circle above me and would soon disappear from view. Would their place be taken by other stars, I wondered?

This thought was still in my mind when at last the heavy silence was broken. There was a loud crack, and the man-eater began to gnaw the bone it had just broken.

The noise made by a feeding tiger indicates its mood. Generally it is one of great contentment, and the sounds of mastication, gnawing, chewing and the tearing and rendering of flesh follow one another as the feast progresses. Should there be a second tiger present, or the killer be a tigress with cubs, there is a lot of growling and wrangling, accompanied by threatening snarls when the other tiger, or a cub, approaches too closely. Despite the ties of mother love, which are considerable - and instances have been known where a tigress has sacrificed her life for her cubs - when it comes to eating, instinct seems to tell a feasting tigress that food is something not to be shared too soon, and to urge her to eat her fill before allowing her companion, mate, or even her cubs to approach and eat what may be left.

The tiger above me began to growl. I knew then that it could not be alone. Perhaps there were cubs, perhaps another tiger accompanying the man-eater. The situation was decidedly complicated and more than I had bargained for. None of us had considered the possibility earlier in the evening, when this sitting-in-the-hole idea had occurred to Stanley.

I thought hard what to do next. Obviously, in order to take a shot at the tiger, I would have to locate it first by peeping over the edge of the hole, and then by drawing the rifle right out of the hole and placing it on the ground outside so as to take aim. All this would entail considerable movement; I might even make a sound of some sort; the rifle might knock against the ground. The feeding animal would hear me and attack before I could free my weapon. There might be a slight hope of escaping the tiger's attention should he, or she, happen luckily to be facing the other way.

But there was a second tiger present. Even cubs could give the game away if they saw my head and shoulders, followed by my rifle, emerging from the ground. It was certainly straining imagination and luck too far to hope that all the animals above me would have their backs to me and be looking in the wrong direction. And if there should be two tigers above me, which of them was the man-eater? A silly question, that: obviously the one that was eating. But had both developed the man-eating habit, or only one? I must not kill the wrong tiger and leave the man-eater. Therefore, I must shoot both to take no chances.

The alternative course of action was to sit in silence in the hole, allow the animals to finish their meal and afterwards go about their business, then call it a day. But I had come here to shoot the man-eater; not to hide from it. I thought of the man it had killed and was now eating. What would Stanley and the villagers say of me when they came in the morning to find the ground covered with tiger pug marks, the scraps of the man otherwise completely devoured, and me hiding in the hole?

Well, here goes, I said to myself, and a millimetre at a time I began to position my feet so as to support me. Then slowly, very very slowly, I started to raise myself, bringing my head to ground level. This in itself took a long time, for I had to avoid making the slightest sound, and my thighs and legs were cramped from squatting so long on my haunches. The tiger continued feeding, growling and snarling now and again to keep the other tiger, or perhaps the cubs, away.

At last I was on my knees and toes and I stretched my two hands downwards to help support my weight on my outstretched fingers. Then, very slowly, I began to raise myself. Time had passed, and the strain on my hands and legs began to tell. But I must not hurry. Even now, as my ears came closer to the surface above, the tiger's growls grew stronger. I began to be frightened.

My hands were beginning to tremble with the sustained strain of supporting my weight, when I sensed that the top of my head must have reached about ground level. I could not delay longer, for the tiger or tigers would be able to see me should they be looking in my direction, whilst I would not be able to see them. I therefore quickly raised my head, until my eyes were level with the earth.

A terrifying sight confronted me. Luckily, through sitting in the darkness of the hole for so long my eyes had grown accustomed to the gloom, so that I could see only a few feet away and lying broadside on the enormous form of a tiger extended on its belly, chewing some part of the victim which it was holding between its front paws. Worse still, there was another form, also at full stretch, slightly farther away from me and a few feet from the feasting tiger, but facing it, and watching anxiously as the latter swallowed mouthful after mouthful. This second tiger, facing the first, was also facing me, and could not fail to see the top of my head popping out of the earth.

It let out a snarl of surprise and scrambled to its feet. I ducked into my hole like a jack-in-the-box, grabbed my rifle, and looked upwards, expecting to find one or both tigers attacking the opening. I was wondering whether to sit tight, or to raise myself and the rifle quickly to ground level and risk a shot, but I remembered there were two tigers, not one, outside. So I funked it and decided to sit tight.

All this occupied only a few seconds, but in that time the feasting tiger had not been idle. Hearing its companion snarl, and seeing it spring to its feet, this animal, not knowing that the sight of me was the cause of the excitement, concluded that its companion had decided to fight for a share of the kill. There was a second loud roar, followed by a fearful din as the feaster, who was obviously the man-eater, attacked the tiger that had spotted me.

Now is my chance, I said to myself, for their attention was so distracted that they would not notice me.

I quickly raised myself. First the rifle, then head and shoulders, reached ground level. For a moment I could see nothing and do nothing because of the dust that was raised by the fighting animals. But neither tiger was anywhere in sight, nor was there any growling or snarling to be heard.

I could not understand it. Perhaps the second tiger had fled with the first in pursuit. But if that was so, I should hear some sounds at least, snarls and growls as one animal chased the other away. Perhaps they saw the rifle, or even the top of my head emerging from the hole, and fled at such an unexpected apparition. Then, too, there should have been growling and snarling; at least some sounds of departure.

As it was, the jungle was silent. I could not fathom it; it was eerie. The thought then occurred to me that, if the man-eater had chased its companion away, it would undoubtedly return to finish what was left of the kill. So I ducked back into the hole to await its return and the renewed sounds of eating. I waited in vain. Maybe half an hour passed when suddenly I heard a loud, sustained human scream. It shattered the silence, rose to a crescendo, and then faded into choking sobs and was still. Then I heard other yells and shouts, and could make out a deeper voice and a more shrill one. These were the voices of the man and one of the two women from the two huts not far away. They were screaming for help.

That was when I grasped what had happened. The second woman had been taken by the man-eater! In chasing its companion away from the feast, or perhaps in its headlong flight after seeing my rifle and myself appear out of the ground, the man-eater must have passed the two huts where the man and his wife, and the widow of the late victim, were sheltering. But how did the ogre get its second victim? Perhaps it was in such a towering rage that it just dragged her out of the hut in which she was sleeping. This tiger certainly was not hungry enough to justify such an action, as it had been feasting all this while.

I wondered what to do. Should I remain where I was, or hasten to the huts? In either event, there was not much that I could do. There was little chance that the man-eater would return to the bones of its first victim when it had a fresh one at its disposal. And I would not be able to follow it up with the second kill, because of the darkness. That could be done only after daybreak. I decided to remain where I was. It was just possible that the second tiger – the one that had been chased away – might return to the scant remains lying above me. If it did so, I would shoot; even if it were not the ogre itself, this second tiger would undoubtedly become a man-eater in time. I remembered how, a short while ago, it lay anxiously waiting for a chance to eat the human remains, though held at bay by the feasting man-eater.

I spent a sleepless night after that, uncomfortably hot and stung by tiny ants and other insects that had decided to share my shelter. Nothing came, and no sound disturbed the silence until about four o'clock. Then a hyena discovered the bones above me and a great commotion began. The hyena smelt the tigers and knew it was about to commit the unpardonable crime of robbery. It also knew that to be caught by the owner or owners would mean death. It was undecided, therefore, between satisfying its hunger and its fear of being killed. The tiger did not show itself, but might come at any moment, and that moment would be the hyena's last if it lingered.

The opening above me grew a little brighter with the coming of the false dawn before the hyena finally summoned up enough courage to start eating. I heard the crunch of a few bones for a short while, then fear must have returned to its craven heart, for I heard the pattering sound of its departure. I could picture the poor beast slinking quickly away, a human bone between its jaws, for gnawing later in the safety of its shelter among the rocks or in a hole in the ground, far from this place of danger and lurking death.

I awaited the advent of the true dawn before raising the Winchester and myself very cautiously above ground level. The coast was clear and I dragged my cramped legs out of that awful hole, stamped about for a few minutes to restore the circulation, and set off for the huts to see what had happened. There I came upon a dreadful sight.

The terrified man and his wife, still hiding in a corner of one of the huts, told me a very harrowing tale. Along with the widow of the man-eater's earlier victim, they had decided to sleep in one of the huts, the one they felt was the more secure of the two. The man had taken good care to sleep in the centre of the floor, equidistant from all the walls while his wife had slept to the left of him. Modesty forbade the second woman to lie down to the right of the man, so she had been compelled to sleep as far away as possible from the couple which meant lying down near to the wall of the hut and opposite their feet.

The hut was comparatively small. It was roughly a square, about twelve feet by twelve. Allowing six feet for the man and his wife who were sleeping in the centre of the hut, and another three feet in order to be clear of their legs, the second woman was, therefore, lying not more than a yard from the wall. The foot of the walls of such huts, in the damper parts of India, are kept a few inches from the ground so that termites cannot climb them overnight and destroy a large part of the structure by daylight. This practice leaves a slight opening around all four sides at ground level.

The man-eater, who had passed very close to the hut either in pursuit of its companion or in flight from me, was probably in a great rage. It must have caught a glimpse of the sleeping woman, or sensed her presence through this small opening, and had decided to drag her out. It had inserted one of its paws under the opening, grabbed the woman and had begun to pull her out.

Her screams and wails, which I had heard, had awakened her two companions, who in turn had started to yell and call for help. Meanwhile the man-eater had succeeded in dragging the woman's head and neck outside the hut, and had killed her by tearing out her gullet. But the rest of her body was stuck inside, for in dying the woman had clung to two of the bamboos supporting the wall of the hut. These had broken, and the end of one of them, piercing her sari and jacket, had gone right into the flesh of her side, thus wedging her body against the bamboo wall.

The pandemonium caused by her wails, and the shouts of her companions, seemed to have acted as a deterrent; the tiger changed its mind and abandoned the victim. The carcass of the woman as it lay before me was a dreadful sight. The tiger's claws had pierced the chest and torn one breast to ribbons. Then the ogre had bitten right through her gullet and had wrenched out her windpipe, leaving just the bones of her neck and the skin behind to keep her head from being totally severed. She lay in a pool of her own blood, most of which had soaked into the dry earth.

The two survivors, man and wife, crouched wide-eyed and paralysed with fear in a far corner of the hut, expecting the man-eater to return at any moment. In fact, they were so terrified as to be oblivious of the fact that it was already daylight outside. Hearing my approaching footsteps and thinking they heard the tiger returning, they started to gibber in fear. I called aloud to reassure them. The man and the woman then hurled themselves at the door of the hut, opened it, and rushed outside, to fall on the ground trembling and crying in terror and relief. They were quite hysterical and took a long while to calm down enough to tell their story.

I had entered the hut and was reviewing the dreadful sight inside when Stanley and some of the men who had helped us the previous evening arrived upon the scene. Stanley had been awake all night but had not heard any report from my rifle, the sound of which would have carried to Tagarthy village. He therefore concluded that the tiger had not returned - or that I had been killed - and was hurrying to find out what had happened. I fear my first question took the good doctor aback: 'How is the patel's wife?' He looked rather pained at my irrelevance, then muttered, 'She's safe. But what has happened?' I told the story. Our subsequent plans were then soon laid.

We bundled the two survivors and their belongings out of the hut, an action that did not require much persuasion, and advised them to return with the rest of our party to the village. Stanley would hide in the other hut while I would conceal myself in the one with the corpse of the slain woman. Ordinarily, the man-eater might be expected to return to its kill, but as there was a second tiger which was potentially a man-eater, if not already one, the doctor would be available to deal with it.

We laid our plans carefully. To begin with, neither of us would fire in the direction where the other was hiding. Secondly, should Stanley see one of the tigers, or both of them first, he was to hold his fire till the actual man-eater approached the carcass of its victim in order to give me the chance of a shot at the real culprit. As soon as I had fired, the doctor was to shoot the second tiger if it was still within sight. These precautions were necessary to avoid a mistake at the last moment, for should the doctor fire first he might shoot the wrong tiger and the man-eater would escape. We had to account for the ogre primarily, although for reasons I have already given the second tiger had to be shot too. But the confirmed man-eater must die first and we could not risk his escape.

As I was tired after a sleepless night, while Stanley was less so, even though he had spent a good part of the night attending to the patel's wife, it was agreed that I should go back to Tagarthy for a meal and some sleep. I would return by three o'clock, bringing the doctor's lunch and some food for both of us to eat later on, besides drinking-water, tea and the torch that Stanley was to fit to the barrels of his shotgun. It was wise that one of us should remain on guard, just in case either of the tigers took the unusual step of returning to the kill by day.

Another idea then occurred to me. We took a sack from one of the huts and walked down to the remains of the earlier kill. My plan was to remove all that was left of it, so that should either of the tigers, or both of them, think of revisiting the old spot, they would find nothing. That would urge them to come to the huts, where we would be in hiding.

A slight hitch arose when we asked our men to do this job. Being of high caste, they recoiled with horror and flatly refused. There was nothing but for Stanley and myself to do the job ourselves. Stanley did not mind, for he was a doctor, but it was an unpleasant undertaking for me. What little remained of the flesh was two days old and stank abominably. Further, bluebottles had laid their eggs in the remains, and in the hot sun maggots had already hatched in myriads; the flesh was covered with a seething mass.

We gathered all the bits and pieces and put them into the sack. Since none of our followers would touch it, I had the unhappy task of conveying this nasty burden on my shoulder all the way to the village. It was surprising how heavy those pieces turned out to be, although they represented so very little of their owner.

I smelled dreadfully and was in a bath of perspiration; some sticky fluid had oozed through the sacking from the putrefying flesh and bones within. It was on my hands, shoulders and neck when I dumped my grisly burden at the entrance to the local police chowki. The constable on sentry gazed at me goggle-eyed. For once in his life he was too taken aback to ask for a statement. I remembered about the statement well enough, but did not care to remind him. Why should I? There was going to be a hell of a row in any case, when the Sub-Inspector and other busybodies from headquarters arrived at Tagarthy. Why had we removed the remains from the scene of the tragedy? How were the police to know the man had been killed by a tiger? Had he been murdered? Perhaps he had committed suicide? Time enough to answer these questions later. What I wanted was a bath, tea, a hot meal and some sleep.

I hastened to the little quarters occupied by the doctor, which he had invited me to share with him, and yelled to his servant-boy to prepare a gallon of tea. Then I divested myself of my stinking clothes, washed my shirt and had a bath.

I told the boy to put the doctor's lunch aside and to make dinner for both of us, saying that I would take the three meals with me to the two huts at three o'clock. I told him to awaken me at 2.30 sharp.

When I got up the meals were ready and packed, together with two flasks of tea and two canteens of water. I had only to pick up the doctor's torch and place it in a large bag with the food and flasks, sling the canteens and my rifle over my shoulders, and set out for the huts. Walking fast, I soon arrived to find a very hungry doctor who had no news of the tigers. He swallowed his lunch while we reviewed our plans in whispers and drank some water. The flasks of tea we decided to keep for the night.

At four o'clock we separated. I went to the neighbouring hut where the woman's body lay, taking my rifle, torch, dinner and a flask of tea with half a canteen of water, leaving Stanley in the other hut with his tea, water and food. Taking up my position at the farther end, as far away as possible from the spot where the corpse was lying half-in and half-out of the little structure, I made myself comfortable in preparation for the long vigil of fourteen hours till dawn.

As tigers have only a very poor sense of smell, what I had to be careful about was that the man-eater should not discover my presence by sight or sound. After the adventure of the previous night, we could expect both tigers to be very cautious. It is remarkable how instinct enables a man-eater to differentiate between a possible victim, helpless and defenceless, and a would-be hunter capable of taking its life.

Having been sheltered from the sun the corpse was not smelling yet, and it was otherwise pleasant inside the hut, offering a great relief from the conditions of the previous night in that hot and tight-fitting hole. Everything about me was quiet for, in fear of the man-eater, the herdsmen of Tagarthy and the neighbouring villages for miles around had abandoned their usual habit of driving their herds out to the jungles to graze.

The afternoon passed in silence except for the buzzing of flies that had discovered the dead body and were busy laying their eggs in the raw flesh. Dusk was accentuated within the hut and it soon became difficult to see, although I could perceive the lingering daylight outside, visible right round me through the few inches of space between the base of the walls of the hut and the floor. Jungle-fowl swarmed in this area and their calls, together with those of spurfowl and peafowl, told me the sun was about to set. Silently,

I munched the food I had brought with me for dinner and drank some tea.

In due course the cries of the birds died away, to be replaced by the calls of a near-by herd of spotted deer and the belling of a more distant sambar stag. This told me the sun had set, although by now it was already quite dark inside the hut.

Soon the nightjars began their teasing cries and a night-heron wailed in the little stream at the bottom of the valley. Night had fallen and I could now see nothing. If the man-eater came and started to remove the cadaver of the woman, I would be compelled to use my torch.

This raised a problem. When I used the torch, its beam would necessarily strike against the inside of the wall of the hut and be reflected back into my eyes. I would not be able to see beyond, or to look through the gap between the wall and the floor. In other words, the man-eater would not be visible to me. The thought began to trouble me and I decided to change my position. I would lie prone on the floor, as close as possible to that part of the woman's body which remained inside. This would give me a great advantage. By keeping my rifle extended on the ground before me, all I would need to do, when the tiger came, would be to point the barrel in the animal's direction and press the trigger. The man-eater could not avoid making some noise when it began to pull the woman's carcass out of the hut, for the end of one of the bamboos of the hut wall was still embedded in her flesh after the struggle of the previous night. The tiger would have to tear the body free from this obstruction.

Gathering the flask of tea and my weapon, I crept quietly across the floor till I reached the woman's body and then lay down beside it, the rifle on the ground before me with the butt under my armpit and the end of the barrel only a few inches from the opening. Accidentally my shoulder touched something that was cold and hard and very stiff. It was the corpse's leg and I drew a few inches away.

Three hours passed with no sign of any tiger. It was well after ten o'clock. Tigers generally return to their kills around eight, and I was beginning to think our quarries had decided to keep clear of the huts when the leg which had touched my shoulder three hours ago touched it again.

That cold, stiff leg was now moving very distinctly. It was not only rubbing against my shoulder but moving gently away from me.

Not a sound could I hear. But the leg moved again. The hair at the back of my neck stood on end. Panic seized me. I was on the verge of scrambling to my hands and knees and getting as far away as possible from that awful, mangled human thing that had come to life. Then reason returned. I could feel myself trembling and the perspiration was pouring down my face as I realised what was happening. The leg and its owner had not come back to life, nor was it moving of its own volition. The man-eater was taking it.

I could see nothing. There was no sense in sticking the barrel of my rifle forward and firing blindly; that would only scare the tiger away, to continue its depredations elsewhere. At most I might wound it. I had first to make certain what I was firing at.

Then it was that I heard a faint scratching sound, coming from somewhere very close to me and a little to my right. I could still see nothing. I was tempted to switch on my torch, but remembered in time that to do so might result in dazzling myself. Yet it was imperative that I should find out where the scratching sound came from and what was causing it.

I then did an extremely stupid thing. Not being able to see, I thought I might be able to feel what was going on, and with this in mind, I stretched my right arm very slowly forwards in the direction of the scratching.

I did not have far to reach. My questing fingertips contacted something hairy, something sinewy, and the next instant all hell was let loose. The man-eater, perhaps remembering its difficulty of the night before to free the body of its victim, or maybe in an endeavour to secure a better grip on the corpse, had extended its paw into the gap below the wall and was groping for a hold on something solid. That movement of its paw was the cause of the scratching sound I had heard a moment before. When my fingertips touched its skin, not having heard of ghosts, the tiger knew there was something alive inside the hut.

An ordinary tiger would have bolted. But the ogre, who was no ordinary tiger and had always done the unexpected, lost its temper. It let out a terrific roar, then grasped the wall of the hut in its jaws and began to tear it apart.

My task after that was easy. A great hole appeared before me and the beam of my torch revealed a horrifying tiger-face with the matting of the wall still stuffed in its mouth. With only a few inches to find its target, the bullet of my 405 entered high into the throat; then I rolled over and over with my rifle to get out of range of what I knew would follow. I was near the far end of the hut when the ogre hurled itself through the gap. But I had time to put two more shots straight into its head. With the dying animal threshing about the floor, I rushed to the door of the hut, flung it open and leaped out, only to be confronted by yet another terrifying spectacle.

Another tiger was there, about twenty feet away and to one end of the farther hut. But it was lying on the ground, stretched on its side and still twitching. Stanley had killed the second tiger, almost at point-blank range, with lethal ball fired simultaneously from both barrels of his shot-gun. Because of the noise made by my own rifle, and because of my own excitement, I had entirely failed to hear Stanley's shots.

The doctor related afterwards that he heard the man-eater's roar, followed by the report of my first shot. Then the sounds of the hut wall being demolished. Disregarding our agreement, he had dashed out to my aid, to be confronted by the sight of the second tiger, standing broadside on to him a few yards away, watching its mate and obviously undecided what to do. He had fired both barrels of his shotgun into the animal's heart, killing it instantly.

As we suspected, the man-eater turned out to be a tigress, the other animal her mate.

There was much tom-tomming and rejoicing at Tagarthy until dawn and when the news reached Bellundur next day old Buddiah strutted about, filled with pride. Was he not the greatest of all man-eater and also of her mate? Buddiah was happy indeed. With his fame as a necromancer soaring once again, he could look forward to many feasts of cock curry and many more bottles of that fiery arrack for which the villagers of Bellundur were famed. He was dead drunk at midday when I called to thank him.

CHAPTER EIGHT

Lions at Tsavo

In 1898 THE UGANDA RAILWAY was under construction which was to run from Mombasa on the coast inland to Nairobi. In April of that year a pair of man-eating lions began to lay siege to the camps of the workers engaged in the construction of the line and over a nine month period succeeded in killing 28 Indian workers, plus an uncounted number of Africans, finally succeeding in bringing all work on the railway to a halt.

Though the lions ranged substantial distances between workers' camps to find their victims, their efforts were concentrated around the vicinity of Tsavo, a stop on the line towards Nairobi.

This is the account of the engineer in charge of the line, J H Patterson, to whom fell the task of dealing with the two man-eating lions.

I had only been a few days at Tsavo when I first heard that the two lions had been seen in the neighbourhood. Shortly afterwards one or two Indian workers mysteriously disappeared, and I was told that they had been carried off by night from their tents and devoured by lions. At the time I did not credit this story, and was more inclined to believe that the unfortunate men had been the victims of foul play at the hands of some of their comrades. They were, as it happened, very good workmen and had each saved a fair number of rupees, so I thought it quite likely that some scoundrels from the gangs had murdered them for the sake of their money.

This suspicion, however, was soon dispelled. About three weeks after my arrival in April 1898, I was roused one morning about daybreak and told that one of my jemadars, a fine powerful Sikh named Ungan Singh, had been seized in his tent during the night, dragged off and eaten.

Naturally I lost no time in making an examination of the place and was soon convinced that the man had indeed been carried off by a lion – its pug marks were plainly visible in the sand, while the furrows made by the heels of the victim showed the direction in which he had been dragged away. Moreover, the jemadar shared his tent with half a dozen other workmen and one of his bedfellows had actually witnessed the occurrence. He graphically described how, at about midnight, the lion suddenly put its head in at the open tent door and seized Ungan Singh – who happened to be nearest the opening – by the throat. The unfortunate fellow cried out 'Choro' (Let go) and threw his arms up round the lion's neck. The next moment he was gone, and his panic-stricken companions lay helpless, forced to listen to the terrible struggle which took place outside. Poor Ungan Singh must have died hard; but what chance had he? As a workman gravely remarked, 'Was he not fighting with a lion?'

On hearing the dreadful story I at once set out to try to track the animal accompanied by Captain Haslem who happened to be staying at Tsavo at the time, and who, poor fellow, himself met with a tragic fate very shortly afterwards. We found it an easy matter to follow the route taken by the lion, as he appeared to have stopped several times before beginning his meal. Pools of blood marked these halting places, where he doubtless indulged in the man-eater's habit of licking the skin off so as to get at the fresh blood. (I have been led to believe that this is their custom from the appearance of two half-eaten bodies which I subsequently rescued: the skin was gone in places, and the flesh looked dry, as if it had been sucked.)

On reaching the spot where the body had been devoured, a dreadful spectacle presented itself. The ground all round was covered with blood and morsels of flesh and bones, but the unfortunate jemadar's head had been left intact save for the holes made by the lion's tusks on seizing him, and lay a short distance away from the other remains, the eyes open with a startled, horrified look in them. The place was considerably cut up and on closer examination we found that two lions had been there and had probably struggled for possession of the body. It was the most gruesome slight I had even seen. We collected the remains as well as we could and heaped stones on them, the head with its fixed, terrified stare seeming to watch us all the time, for it we did not bury, but took back to camp for identification before the medical officer.

Thus occurred my first experience of man-eating lions, and I vowed there and then that I would spare no pains to rid the neighbourhood of them. I little knew the trouble that was in store for me or how narrow were my own escapes from sharing poor Ungan Singh's fate.

That same night I sat up in a tree close to the late jemadar's tent, hoping that the lions would return to it for another victim. I was followed to my perch by a few of the more terrified workers who begged to be allowed to sit up in the tree with me; all the other workmen remained in their tents, but no more doors were left open. I had with me my 303 and a 12-bore shotgun, one barrel loaded with ball and the other with slug.

Shortly after settling down to my vigil, my hopes of bagging one of the man-eaters were raised by the sound of their ominous roaring coming closer and closer. Presently this ceased, and quiet reigned for an hour or two, as lions always stalk their prey in complete silence. All at once, however, we heard a great uproar and frenzied cries coming from another camp about half a mile away; we knew then that the lions had seized a victim there, and that we should see or hear nothing further of them that night.

Next morning I found that one of the lions had broken into a tent at railhead camp - from where we had heard the commotion during the night - and had made off with a poor wretch who was lying there asleep. After a night's rest, therefore, I took up my position in a suitable tree near this tent. I did not at all like the idea of walking the half-mile to the place after dark, but all the same I felt fairly safe as one of my men carried a bright lamp close behind me. He in his turn was followed by another leading a goat, which I tied under my tree in the hope that the lion might be tempted to seize it instead of a worker.

A steady drizzle commenced shortly after I had settled down to my night of watching and I was soon thoroughly chilled and wet. I stuck to my uncomfortable post, however, hoping to get a shot, but I well remember the feeling of impotent disappointment I experienced when I heard screams and cries and a heartrending shriek, which told me that the man-eaters had again eluded me and had claimed another victim elsewhere.

At this time the various camps for the workmen were very scattered, so that the lions had a range of some eight miles on either side of Tsavo to work upon; and as their tactics seemed to be to break into a different camp each night, it was most difficult to forestall them. They almost appeared, too, to have an extraordinary and uncanny faculty of finding out our plans beforehand, so that no matter in how likely or how tempting a spot we lay in wait for them, they invariably avoided that particular place and seized their victim for the night from some other camp. Hunting them by day, moreover, in such a dense wilderness as surrounded us, was an exceedingly tiring and really foolhardy undertaking. In a thick jungle of the kind round Tsavo the hunted animal has every chance against the hunter, as however careful the latter may be, a dead twig or something of the sort is sure to crackle just at the critical moment and so give the alarm.

I never gave up hope of some day finding their lair, however, and accordingly continued to devote all my spare time to crawling about through the undergrowth. Many a time when attempting to force my way through this bewildering tangle I had to be released by my gun-bearer from the fast clutches of the 'wait-a-bit'. Often with immense pains I succeeded in tracing the lions to the river after they had seized a victim, only to lose the trail from there onwards owing to the rocky nature of the ground which they seemed to be careful to choose in retreating to their den.

At this early stage of the struggle, I am glad to say, the lions were not always successful in their efforts to capture a human being for their nightly meal, and one or two amusing incidents occurred to relieve the tension from which our nerves were beginning to suffer. On one occasion an enterprising Indian trader was riding along on his donkey late one night, when suddenly a lion sprang out on him knocking over both man and beast. The donkey was badly wounded, and the lion was just about to seize the trader when in some way or other his claws became entangled in a rope by which two empty oil tins were strung across the donkey's neck. The rattle and clatter made by these as he dragged them after him gave him such a fright that he turned tail and bolted off into the jungle, to the intense relief of the terrified trader, who quickly made his way up the nearest tree and remained there, shivering with fear, for the rest of the night.

Shortly after this episode, a Greek contractor named Themistocles Pappadimitrini had an equally marvellous escape. He was sleeping peacefully in his tent one night when a lion broke in, seizing and making off with the mattress on which he was lying. Though rudely awakened, the Greek was quite unhurt and suffered from nothing worse than a bad fright. This same man, however, met with a melancholy fate not long afterwards. He had been to the Kilimanjaro district to buy cattle, and on the return journey attempted to take a short cut across country to the railway but perished miserably of thirst on the way.

On another occasion fourteen workers who slept together in a large tent were one night awakened by a lion suddenly jumping onto the tent and breaking through it. The animal landed with one claw on a worker's shoulder, which was badly torn. But instead of seizing the man himself, in his hurry he grabbed a large bag of rice which happened to be lying in the tent, and made off with it, dropping it in disgust some little distance away when he realised his mistake.

These, however, were only the earlier efforts of the man-eaters. Later on, as will be seen, nothing flurried or frightened them in the least, and except as food they showed a complete contempt for human beings. Having once marked down a victim, they would allow nothing to deter them from securing him, whether he were protected by a thick fence, or inside a closed tent, or sitting round a brightly burning fire. Shots, shouting and firebrands they alike held in derision.

All this time my own tent was pitched in an open clearing, unprotected by a fence of any kind round it. One night when the medical officer Dr Rose was staying with me, we were awakened about midnight by hearing something tumbling about among the tent ropes, but on going out with a lantern we could discover nothing. Daylight, however, plainly revealed the pug marks of a lion, so that on that occasion I fancy one or other of us had a narrow escape.

Warned by this experience, I at once arranged to move my quarters, and went to join forces with Dr Brock who had just arrived at Tsavo to take medical charge of the district. We shared a hut of palm leaves and boughs, which we had constructed on the eastern side of the river, close to the old caravan route leading to Uganda; and we had it surrounded by a circular boma, or thorn fence, about seventy yards in diameter, well made, thick and high. Our personal servants also lived within the enclosure and a bright fire was always kept up throughout the night.

For the sake of coolness, Brock and I used to sit out under the verandah of this hut in the evenings; but it was rather trying to our nerves to attempt to read or write there as we never knew when a lion might spring over the boma, and be on us before we were aware. We therefore kept our rifles within easy reach and cast many an anxious glance out into the inky darkness beyond the circle of the firelight. On one or two occasions we found in the morning that the lions had come quite close to the fence, but fortunately they never succeeded in getting through.

By this time, too, the camps of the workmen had also been surrounded by thorn fences. Nevertheless the lions managed to jump over or break through some of these and regularly every few nights a man was carried off, the reports of the disappearance of this or that workman coming in to me with painful frequency. So long as railhead camp - with its two or three thousand men scattered over a wide area – remained at Tsavo, the workers appeared not to take much notice of the dreadful deaths of their comrades. Each man felt, I suppose, that as the man-eaters had such a large number of victims to choose from, the chances of their selecting him in particular were very small. But when the large camp moved ahead with the railway, matters altered considerably. I was then left with only some few hundred men to complete the permanent works; and as all the remaining workmen were naturally camped together, the attentions of the lions became more apparent and made a deeper impression.

A regular panic consequently ensued and it required all my powers of persuasion to induce the men to stay on. In fact, I succeeded in doing so only by allowing them to knock off all regular work until they had built exceptionally thick and high bomas round each camp. Within these enclosures fires were kept burning all night, and it was also the duty of the night-watchman to keep clattering half a dozen empty oil tins suspended from a convenient tree. These he manipulated by means of a long rope, while sitting in safety within his tent; and the frightful noise thus produced was kept up at frequent intervals during the night in the hopes of terrifying away the man-eaters. In spite of all these precautions, however, the lions would not be denied and men continued to disappear.

When the railhead workmen moved on, their hospital camp was left behind. It stood rather apart from the other camps, but in a clearing about three-quarters of a mile from my hut protected by a good thick fence and to all appearances was quite secure. It seemed, however, as if barriers were of no avail against the 'demons', for before very long one of them found a weak spot in the boma and broke through. On this occasion the hospital assistant had a marvellous escape. Hearing a noise outside, he opened the door of his tent and was horrified to see a great lion standing a few yards away looking at him. The animal made a spring towards him, which gave the assistant such a fright that he jumped backwards, and in doing so luckily upset a box containing medical stores. This crashed down with such a loud clatter of breaking glass that the lion was startled for the moment and made off to another part of the enclosure.

Here, unfortunately, he was more successful as he jumped on to and broke through a tent in which eight patients were lying. Two of them were badly wounded by his spring, while a third poor wretch was seized and dragged off bodily through the thorn fence. The two wounded Indians were left where they lay, a piece of torn tent having fallen over them, and in this position the doctor and I found them on our arrival soon after dawn next morning. We at once decided to move the hospital closer to the main camp; a fresh site was prepared, a stout hedge built round the enclosure, and all the patients were moved in before nightfall.

As I had heard that lions generally visit recently deserted camps, I decided to sit up all night in the vacated boma in the hope of getting an opportunity of bagging one of them; but in the middle of my lonely vigil I had the mortification of hearing shrieks and cries coming from the direction of the new hospital, telling me only too plainly that our dreaded foes had once more eluded me. Hurrying to the place at daylight I found that one of the lions had jumped over the newly erected fence and had carried off the hospital water-carrier, and that several other workers had been unwilling witnesses of the terrible scene which took place within the circle of light given by the big camp fire.

The water-carrier, it appears, had been lying on the floor with his head towards the centre of the tent and his feet nearly touching the side. The lion managed to get its head in below the canvas, seizing him by the foot and pulling him out. In desperation the unfortunate water-carrier clutched hold of a heavy box in a vain attempt to prevent himself being carried off, and dragged it with him until he was forced to let go by its being stopped by the side of the tent. He then caught hold of a tent rope and clung tightly to it until it broke.

As soon as the lion managed to get him clear of the tent, he sprang at his throat and after a few vicious shakes the poor man's agonising cries were silenced for ever. The brute then seized him in his mouth, like a huge cat with a mouse, and ran up and down the boma looking for a weak spot to break through. This he presently found and plunged into, dragging his victim with him and leaving shreds of torn cloth and flesh as ghastly evidence of his passage through the thorns. Dr Brock and I were easily able to follow his track and soon found the remains about four hundred yards away in the bush. There was the usual horrible sight. Very little was left of the unfortunate victim - only the skull, the jaws, a few of the larger bones and a portion of the palm with one or two fingers attached. On one of these was a silver ring and this, with the teeth (a relic much prized by certain castes), was sent to the man's widow in India.

Again it was decided to move the hospital; and again, before nightfall, the work was completed, including a still stronger and thicker boma. When the patients had been moved I had a covered goods-waggon placed in a favourable position on a siding which ran close to the site which had just been abandoned, and in this Brock and I arranged to sit up that night. We left a couple of tents still standing within the enclosure, and also tied up a few cattle to it as bait for the lions, who had been seen in no less than three different places in the neighbourhood during the afternoon.

This was on April 23. Four miles from Tsavo the lions had attempted to seize a workman who was walking along the line. Fortunately, however, he had just time to escape up a tree, where he remained, more dead than alive, until he was rescued by the traffic manager who caught sight of him from a passing train. They next appeared close to Tsavo Station, and a couple of hours later some workmen saw one of the lions stalking Dr Brock as he was returning about dusk from the hospital.

In accordance with our plan, the doctor and I set out after dinner for the goods-waggon, which was about a mile away from our hut. In the light of subsequent events, we did a very foolish thing in taking up our position so late; nevertheless, we reached our destination in safety and settled down to our watch about ten o'clock. We had the lower half of the door of the waggon closed, while the upper half was left wide open for observation: we faced, of course, in the direction of the abandoned boma, but which we were unable to see in the inky darkness.

For an hour or two everything was quiet and the deadly silence was becoming very monotonous and oppressive when suddenly, to our right, a dry twig snapped and we knew that an animal of some sort was about. Soon afterwards we heard a dull thud, as if some heavy body had jumped over the boma. The cattle, too, became very uneasy, and we could hear them moving about restlessly. Then again came dead silence.

At this juncture I proposed to my companion that I should get out of the waggon and lie on the ground close to it, as I could see better in that position should the lion come in our direction with his prey. Brock, however, persuaded me to remain where I was; and a few seconds afterwards I was heartily glad that I had taken his advice, for at that very moment one of the man-eaters – although we did not know it – was quietly stalking us and was even then almost within springing distance. Orders had been given for the entrance to the boma to be blocked up, and accordingly we were listening in the expectation of hearing the lion force his way out through the bushes with his prey. However, the doorway had not been properly closed, and while we were wondering what the lion could be doing inside the boma for so long, he was outside all the time, silently reconnoitring our position.

Presently I fancied I saw something coming very stealthily towards us. I feared to trust to my eyes, which by that time were strained by prolonged staring through the darkness, so under my breath I asked Brock whether he saw anything, at the same time covering the dark object as well as I could with my rifle. Brock did not answer; he told me afterwards that he, too, thought he had seen something move, but was afraid t say so lest I should fire and it turn out to be nothing after all. After this there was intense silence again for a second or two then, with a sudden bound, a huge body sprang at us. 'The lion!' I shouted and we both fired almost simultaneously – not a moment too soon, for in another second the animal would assuredly have landed inside the waggon. As it was, he must have swerved off in his spring, probably blinded by the flash and frightened by the noise of the double report which was increased a hundredfold by the reverberation of the hollow iron roof of the truck. Had we not been very much on the alert, he would undoubtedly have got one of us, and we realised that we had a very lucky and very narrow escape. The next morning we found Brock's bullet embedded in the sand close to a footprint; it could not have missed the lion by more than an inch or two. Mine was nowhere to be found.

Thus ended my first direct encounter with one of the man-eaters.

The lions seemed to have got a bad fright the night Brock and I stayed up in wait for them in the goods-waggon, for they kept away from Tsavo and did not molest us in any way for some considerable time - not, in fact, until long after Brock had left me and gone on safari to Uganda. In this breathing space it occurred to me that should the lions renew their attacks, a trap would perhaps offer the best chance of getting at them, and that if I could construct one in which a couple of Indians might be used as bait without being subjected to any danger, the lions would be quite daring enough to enter it in search of them and thus be caught.

I accordingly set to work at once and in a short time managed to make a sufficiently strong trap out of wooden sleepers, tram-rails, pieces of telegraph wire, and a length of heavy chain. It was divided into two compartments - one for the men and one for the lion. A sliding door at one end admitted the former, and once inside this compartment they were perfectly safe: between them and the lion, if he entered the other, ran a cross wall of iron rails only three inches apart and embedded both top and bottom in heavy wooden sleepers. The door which was to admit the lion was, of course, at the opposite end of the structure, but otherwise the whole thing was very much on the principle of the ordinary rat-trap, except that it was not necessary for the lion to seize the bait in order to send the door clattering down.

This part of the contrivance was arranged in the following manner. A heavy chain was secured along the top part of the lion's doorway, the ends hanging down to the ground on either side of the opening; and to these were fastened, strongly secured by stout wire, short lengths of rails placed about six inches apart. This made a sort of flexible door which could be packed into a small space when not in use and which abutted against the top of the doorway when lifted up. The door was held in this position by a lever made of a piece of rail, which in turn was kept in its place by a wire fastened to one end and passing down to a spring concealed in the ground inside the cage. As soon as the lion entered sufficiently far into the trap, he would be bound to tread on the spring. His weight on this would then release the wire and in an instant down would come the door behind him; and he could not push it out in any way as it fell into a groove between two rails firmly embedded in the ground.

In making this trap, which cost us a lot of work, we were rather at a loss for want of tools to bore holes in the rails for the doorway, so as to enable them to be fastened by the wire to the chain. It occurred to me, however, that a hard-nosed bullet from my 303 would penetrate the iron, and on making the experiment I was glad to find that a hole was made as cleanly as if it had been punched out.

When the trap was ready I pitched a tent over it in order to deceive the lions, and built an exceedingly strong boma round it. One small entrance was made at the back of the enclosure for the men, which they were to close on going in by pulling a bush after them; and another entrance just in front of the door of the cage was left open for the lions. The wiseacres to whom I showed my invention were generally of the opinion that the man-eaters would be too cunning to walk into my parlour; but, as will be seen later, these predictions proved false. For the first few nights I baited the trap myself, but nothing happened except that I had a very sleepless and uncomfortable time and was badly bitten by mosquitoes.

As a matter of fact, it was some months before the lions attacked us again, though from time to time we heard of their depredations in other quarters. Not long after our night in the goods-waggon, two men were carried off from railhead, while another was taken from a place called Engomani about ten miles away. Within a very short time, this latter place was again visited by the animals, two more men being seized, one of whom was killed and eaten, and the other so badly mauled that he died within a few days. As I have said, we at Tsavo enjoyed complete immunity from attack. The workers, believing that their dreaded foes had permanently deserted the district, resumed all their usual habits and occupations and life in the camps returned to its normal routine.

But we were suddenly startled out of this feeling of security. One dark night the familiar terror-stricken cries and screams awoke the camps, and we knew that the 'demons' had returned and had commenced a new list of victims. On this occasion a number of men had been sleeping outside their tents for the sake of coolness, thinking, of course, that the lions had gone for good, when suddenly in the middle of the night one of the animals was discovered forcing its way through the boma. The alarm was at once given, and sticks, stones and firebrands were hurled in the direction of the intruder. All was of no avail, however, for the lion burst into the midst of the terrified group, seizing an unfortunate wretch amid the cries and shrieks of his companions and dragging him off through the thick thorn fence.

He was joined outside by the second lion and so daring had the two become that they did not trouble to carry their victim any further away, but devoured him within thirty yards of the tent where he had been seized. Although several shots were fired in their direction by the jemadar of the gang to which the Indian belonged, the lions took no notice of these and did not attempt to move until their horrible meal was finished. The few scattered fragments that remained of the body I would not allow to be buried at once, hoping that the lions would return to the spot the following night; and on the chance of this I took up my station at nightfall in a convenient tree.

Nothing occurred to break the monotony of my watch except that I had a visit from a hyena, and the next morning I learned that the lions had attacked another camp about two miles from Tsavo – for by this time the camps were again scattered as I had works in progress all up and down the line. There the man-eaters had been successful in obtaining a victim, whom, as in the previous instance, they devoured quite close to the camp. How they forced their way through the bomas without making a noise was, and still is, a mystery to me; I should have thought that it was next to impossible for an animal to get through it all. Yet they continually did so and without a sound being heard.

After this occurrence, I sat up every night for over a week near likely camps, but all in vain. Either the lions saw me and then went elsewhere, or else I was unlucky, for they took man after man from different places without ever once giving me a chance of a shot at them. This constant night watching was most dreary and fatiguing work, but I felt that it was a duty that had to be undertaken, as the men naturally looked to me for protection.

In the whole of my life I have never experienced anything more nerve-racking than to hear the deep roars of these dreadful monsters growing gradullay nearer and nearer, and to know that some one or other of use was doomed to be their victim before morning dawned. Once they reached the vicinity of the camps, the roars completely ceased, and we knew that they were stalking for their prey. Shouts would then pass from camp to camp. ' *Khabar dar, bhaieon, shaitan ata'* (Beware brothers, the devil is coming). But the warning cries would prove of no avail, and sooner or later agonising shrieks would break the silence and another man would be missing from roll-call next morning.

I was naturally very disheartened at being foiled in this way night after night, and was soon at my wits' end to know what to do; it seemed as if the lions really were 'devils' after all and bore a charmed life. As I have said before, tracking them through the jungle was a hopeless task; but as something had to be done to keep up the men's spirits, I spent many a weary day crawling on my hands and knees through the dense undergrowth of the exasperating wilderness around us. In fact, if I had come up with the lions on any of these expeditions it was much more likely that they would have added me to their list of victims than that I should have succeeded in killing either of them, as everything would have been in their favour. About this time, too, I had many helpers, and several came to Tsavo from the coast and sat up night after night in order to get a shot at our daring foes. All of us, however, met with the same lack of success; the lions always seemed capable of avoiding the watchers while succeeding at the same time in obtaining a victim.

I have a very vivid recollection of one particular night when the man-eaters seized a man from the railway station and brought him close to my camp to devour. I could plainly hear the animals crunching the bones, and the sound of their dreadful purring filled the air and rang in my ears for days afterwards. The terrible thing was to feel so helpless; it was useless to attempt to go out, as of course the poor fellow was dead, and in addition it was so pitch-dark as to make it impossible to see anything. Some half a dozen workmen, who lived in a small enclosure close to mine, became so terrified on hearing the lions at their meal that they shouted and implored me to allow them to come inside my boma. This I willingly did, but soon afterwards I remembered that one man had been lying ill in their camp and on making enquiry I found that they had callously left him behind alone. I immediately took some men with me to bring him to my boma, but on entering his tent I saw by the light of the lantern that the poor fellow was beyond need of safety. He had died of shock at being deserted by his companions.

From this time matters gradually became worse and worse. Hitherto, as a rule, only one of the man-eaters had made the attack and had done the foraging, while the other waited outside in the bush. But now they began to change their tactics, entering the bomas together and each seizing a victim. In this way two Swahili porters were killed during the last week of November, one being immediately carried off and devoured. The other was heard moaning for a long time, and when his terrified companions at last summoned up sufficient courage to go to his assistance, they found him stuck fast in the bushes of the boma, through which for once the lion had apparently been unable to drag him. He was still alive when I saw him next morning, but so terribly mauled that he died before he could be got to the hospital.

Within a few days of this the two lions made a most ferocious attack on the largest camp in the section, which for safety's sake was situated within a stone's throw of Tsavo station and close to a permanent way inspector's iron hut. Suddenly in the dead of night the two man-eaters burst in among the terrified workmen, and even from my boma some distance away, I could plainly hear the panic-stricken shrieking of the workers. Then followed cries of 'They've taken him, they've taken him' as the brutes carried off their unfortunate victim and began their horrible feast close beside the camp. The Inspector, Mr Dalgairns, fired over fifty shots in the direction in which he heard the lions, but they were not to be frightened and calmly lay there until their meal was finished.

After examining the spot in the morning, we at once set out to follow the lions, Mr Dalgairns feeling confident that he had wounded one of them, as there was a trail on the sand like that of the toes of a broken limb. After some careful stalking, we suddenly found ourselves in the vicinity of the lions and were greeted with ominous growlings. Cautiously advancing and pushing the bushes aside, we saw in the gloom what we at first took to be a lion cub. Closer inspection, however, showed it to be the remains of the unfortunate Indian, which the man-eaters had evidently abandoned at our approach. The legs, one arm and half the body had been eaten, and it was the stiff fingers of the other arm trailing along the sand which had left the marks we had taken to be the trail of a wounded lion. By this time the lions had retired far into the thick jungle where it was impossible to follow them, so we had the remains of the Indian buried and once more returned home disappointed.

Not even the bravest men in the world will stand constant terrors of this sort indefinitely. The whole district was by this time thoroughly panic-stricken, and I was not at all surprised, therefore, to find on my return to camp that same afternoon (December 1) that the men had all struck work and were waiting to speak to me. When I sent for them, they flocked to my boma in a body and stated that they would not remain at Tsavo any longer for anything or anybody; they had come from India on an agreement to work for the Government, not to supply food for either lions or 'devils'.

No sooner had they delivered this ultimatum than a regular stampede took place. Some hundreds of them stopped the first passing
train by throwing themselves on the rails in front of the engine and
then, swarming on to the trucks and throwing in their possessions
anyhow, they fled from the accursed spot.

After this the railway works were completely stopped, and for the
next three weeks practically nothing was done but build 'lion-
proof' huts for those workmen who had sufficient courage to
remain. It was a strange and amusing sight to see these shelters
perched on the top of water-tanks, roofs and girders - anywhere
for safety - while some even went so far as to dig pits inside their
tents, into which they descended at night, covering the top over
with heavy logs of wood. Every good-sized tree in the camp had
as many beds lashed on to it as its branches would bear - and
sometimes more. I remember that one night when the camp was
attacked, so many men swarmed on to one particular tree that
down it came with a crash, hurling its terror-stricken load of
shrieking workers close to the very lions they were trying to avoid.
Fortunately for them, a victim had already been secured, and the
man-eaters were too busy devouring him to pay attention to
anything else.

Some little time before the flight of the workmen, I had written
to Mr Whitehead, the District Officer, asking him to come up and
assist me in my campaign against the lions and to bring with him
any of his askaris that he could spare. He replied accepting the
invitation, and told me to expect him about dinner-time on
December 2, which turned out to be the day after the exodus. His
train was due at Tsavo about six o'clock in the evening, so I sent
my 'boy' up to the station to meet him and to help in carrying his
baggage to the camp. In a very short time, however, the 'boy'
rushed back trembling with terror, and informed me that there was
no sign of the train or of the railway staff, but that an enormous
lion was standing on the station platform.

This extraordinary story I did not believe in the least, as by this
time the workers - never remarkable for bravery - were in such a
state of fright that if they caught sight of a hyena, or a baboon, or

even a dog, in the bush, they were sure to imagine it was a lion. But I found out next day that it was an actual fact, and that both station master and signalman had been obliged to take refuge from one of the man-eaters by locking themselves in the station building.

I waited some little time for Mr Whitehead, but eventually, as he did not put in an appearance, I concluded that he must have postponed his journey until the next day, and so had my dinner in my customary solitary state. During the meal I heard a couple of shots, but paid no attention to them, as rifles were constantly being fired off in the neighbourhood of the camp. Later in the evening I went out as usual to watch for our elusive foes, and took up my position in a crib made of sleepers which I had built on a big girder close to a camp which I thought was likely to be attacked.

Soon after settling down at my post, I was surprised to hear the man-eaters growling and purring and crunching up bones about seventy yards from the crib. I could not understand what they had found to eat, as I had heard no commotion in the camps, and I knew by bitter experience that every meal the man-eaters obtained from us was announced by shrieks and uproar. The only conclusion I could come to was that they had pounced upon some poor unsuspecting native traveller. After a time I was able to make out their eyes glowing in the darkness, and I took as careful aim as was possible in the circumstances and fired; but the only notice they paid to the shot was to carry off whatever they were devouring and to retire quietly over a slight rise, which prevented me from seeing them. There they finished their meal at their ease.

As soon as it was daylight, I got out of my crib and went towards the place where I had last heard them. On the way, whom should I meet but my missing guest, Mr Whitehead, looking very pale and ill, and generally dishevelled.

'Where on earth have you come from?' I exclaimed. 'Why didn't you turn up to dinner last night?'

'A nice reception you give a fellow when you invite him to dinner,' was his only reply.

'Why, what's up?' I asked.

'That infernal lion of yours nearly did for me last night,' said Whitehead.

'Nonsense, you must have dreamed it!' I cried in astonishment.

For answer he turned round and showed me his back. 'That's not much of a dream, is it?' he asked.

His clothing was rent by one huge tear from the nape of the neck downwards and on the flesh there were four great claw marks, showing red and angry through the torn cloth. Without further parley, I hurried him off to my tent, and bathed and dressed his wounds; and when I had made him considerably more comfortable, I got from him the whole story of the events of the night.

It appeared that his train was very late, so that it was quite dark when he arrived at Tsavo Station, from which the track to my camp lay through a small cutting. He was accompanied by Abdullah, the sergeant of askaris, who walked close behind him carrying a lighted lamp. All went well until they were about half-way through the gloomy cutting, when one of the lions suddenly jumped down upon them from the high bank, knocking Whitehead over like a ninepin and tearing his back in the manner I had seen. Fortunately, however, he had his carbine with him, and instantly fired.

The flash and the loud report must have dazed the lion for a second or two, enabling Whitehead to disengage himself; but the next instant the brute pounced like lightning on the unfortunate Abdullah, with whom he at once made off. All that the poor fellow could say was: '*Eh, Bwana, simba*' (Oh, Master, a lion). As the lion was dragging him over the bank Whitehead fired again, but without effect, and the lion quickly disappeared into the darkness with his prey. It was, of course, this unfortunate man whom I had heard the lions devouring during the night. Whitehead himself had a marvellous escape; his wounds were happily not very deep, and caused him little or no inconvenience afterwards.

On the same day, December 3, the forces arrayed against the lions were further strengthened. Mr Farquhar, the superintendent of police, arrived from the coast with a score of sepoys to assist in hunting down the man-eaters, whose fame had by this time spread far and wide; the most elaborate precautions were taken, his men

being posted on the most convenient trees near every camp.
Several other officials had also come up on leave to join in the
chase, and each of these guarded a likely spot in the same way, Mr
Whitehead sharing my post inside the crib on the girder. Further,
in spite of some chaff, my lion trap was put in thorough working
order, and two of the sepoys were installed as bait.

Our preparations were quite complete by nightfall and we all
took up our appointed positions. Nothing happened until about
nine o'clock, when to my great satisfaction the intense stillness was
suddenly broken by the noise of the door of the trap clattering
down. 'At last,' I thought, 'one at least of the man-eaters is done
for.' But the sequel was an ignominious one.

The bait-askaris had a lamp burning inside their part of the cage
and were each armed with a Martini rifle, with plenty of ammunition. They had also been given strict orders to shoot at once if
a lion should enter the trap. Instead of doing so, however, they
were so terrified when he rushed in and began to lash himself
madly against the bars of the cage, that they completely lost their
heads and were actually too unnerved to fire. Not for some
minutes – in fact not until Mr Farquhar, whose post was close by,
shouted at them and cheered them on – did they at all recover
themselves.

When at last the bait-askaris did begin to fire, they fired with a
vengeance – anywhere, anyhow. Whitehead and I were at right
angles to the direction in which they should have shot, and yet
their bullets came whizzing all round us. Altogether they fired over
a score of shots and in the end succeeded only in blowing away one
of the bars of the door, thus allowing our prize to make good his
escape. How they failed to kill him several times over is, and always
will be, a complete mystery to me, as they could have put the
muzzles of their rifles absolutely touching his body. There was,
indeed, some blood scattered about the trap, but it was small
consolation to know that the man-eater, whose capture and death
seemed so certain, had only been slightly wounded.

Still we were not unduly dejected and when morning came a
hunt was at once arranged. Accordingly we spent the greater part

of the day on our hands and knees following the lions through the dense thickets of thorny jungle, but though we heard their growls from time to time, we never succeeded in actually coming up with them.

Of the whole party, only Farquhar managed to catch a momentary glimpse of one as it bounded over a bush. Two days more were spent in the same manner, with equal lack of success, and then Farquhar and his sepoys were obliged to return to the coast. Mr Whitehead also departed for his district and once again I was left alone with the man-eaters.

A day or two after the departure of my allies, as I was leaving my boma soon after dawn on December 9, I saw a Swahili running excitedly towards me, shouting out 'Simba! Simba!' and every now and again looking behind him as he ran. On questioning him I found that the lions had tried to snatch a man from the camp by the river, but being foiled in this had seized and killed one of the donkeys and were at that moment busy devouring it not far off. Now was my chance.

I rushed for the heavy rifle which Farquhar had kindly left with me for use in case an opportunity such as this should arise and, led by the Swahili, I started most carefully to stalk the lions who I earnestly hoped were confining their attention strictly to their meal. I was getting on splendidly, and could just make out the outline of one of them through the dense bush, when unfortunately my guide snapped a rotten branch. The wily beast heard the noise, growled his defiance, and disappeared in a moment into a patch of even thicker jungle close by. In desperation at the thought of his escaping me once again, I crept hurriedly back to the camp, summoned the available workmen and told them to bring all the tom-toms, tin cans and other noisy instruments of any kind that could be found.

As quickly as possible I posted them in a half-circle round the thicket, and gave the head jemadar instructions to start a simultaneous beating of the tom-toms and cans as soon as he judged that I had had time to get round to the other side. I then crept round by myself and soon found a good position and one which the lion was most likely to retreat past, as it was in the middle of a broad animal path leading straight from the place where he was concealed. I lay down behind a small anthill and waited expectantly. Very soon I heard a tremendous din being raised by the advancing line of workers and almost immediately, to my intense joy, out into the open path stepped a huge maneless lion. It was the first occasion during all these trying months upon which I had a fair chance at one of the man-eaters.

Slowly he advanced along the path, stopping every few seconds to look round. I was only partially concealed from view and if his attention had not been fully occupied by the noise behind him, he would have observed me. As he was oblivious to my presence, however, I let him approach to within about fifteen yards of me, and then covered him with my rifle. The moment I moved to do this, he caught sight of me and seemed much astonished at my sudden appearance. He stuck his forefeet into the ground, threw himself back on his haunches and growled savagely. As I covered his brain with my rifle, I felt that at last I had him absolutely at my mercy - but never trust an untried weapon! I pulled the trigger. To my horror I heard the dull snap that tells of a misfire.

Worse was to follow. I was so taken aback and disconcerted by this untoward accident that I entirely forgot to fire the left barrel, lowering the rifle from my shoulder with the intention of reloading - if I should be given time. Fortunately for me, the lion was so distracted by the terrific din and uproar of the coolies behind him that instead of springing on me, as might have been expected, he bounded aside into the jungle again. By this time I had collected my wits and just as he jumped I let him have the left barrel. An answering angry growl told me that he had been hit; but nevertheless he succeeded once more in getting clear away, for although I tracked him for some little distance, I eventually lost his trail in a rocky patch of ground.

Bitterly did I regret the decision to rely on a borrowed weapon, and in my disappointment and vexation I abused owner, maker, and rifle with fine impartiality. On extracting the unexploded cartridge, I found that the pin had not struck home, the cap being only slightly dented; so the whole fault did indeed lie with the rifle, which I later returned to Farquhar with polite compliments. However, my continued ill-luck was most exasperating and the Indians were more than ever confirmed in their belief that the lions were really evil spirits, proof against mortal weapons. Certainly, they did seem to bear charmed lives.

After this dismal failure there was, of course, nothing to do but to return to camp. Before doing so I looked at the dead donkey, which I found to have been only slightly devoured at the quarters. It is a curious fact that lions always begin at the tail of their prey and eat upwards towards the head. As their meal had thus been interrupted evidently at the very beginning, I felt pretty sure that one or other of the brutes would return to the carcass at nightfall. Accordingly, as there was no tree of any kind close at hand, I had a staging erected some ten feet away from the body. This machan was about twelve feet high and was composed of four poles stuck into the ground and inclined towards each other at the top, where a plank was lashed to serve as a seat. Further, as the nights were still pitch-dark, I had the donkey's carcass secured by strong wires to a neighbouring stump, so that the lions might not be able to drag it away before I could get a shot at them.

At sundown I took up my position on my airy perch and much to the disgust of my gun-bearer, Mahina, I decided to go alone. I would gladly have taken him with me but he had a bad cough, and I was afraid that he might make an involuntary noise or movement which might spoil everything. Darkness fell almost immediately and everything became extraordinarily still. The silence of an African jungle on a dark night needs to be experienced to be realised; it is most impressive, especially when one is absolutely alone and isolated from one's fellow creatures, as I was then. The solitude and stillness, and the purpose of my vigil, all had their effect on me, and from a condition of strained expectancy I gradually fell into a dreamy mood which harmonised well with my surroundings.

Suddenly I was startled out of my reverie by the snapping of a twig and, straining my ears for a further sound, I fancied I could hear the rustling of a large body forcing its way through the bush. 'The man-eater' I thought to myself, 'surely tonight my luck will change and I shall bag one of the brutes.' Profound silence again succeeded; I sat on my eyrie like a statue, every nerve tense with excitement. Very soon, however, all doubt as to the presence of the lion was dispelled. A deep long-drawn sigh – sure sign of hunger – came up from the bushes, and the rustling commenced again as he cautiously advanced. In a moment or two a sudden stop, followed by an angry growl, told me that my presence had been noticed; and I began to fear that disappointment awaited me once more.

But no; matters quickly took an unexpected turn. The hunter became the hunted; and instead of either making off or coming for the bait prepared for him, the lion began stealthily to stalk me. For about two hours he horrified me by slowly creeping round and round my crazy structure, gradually edging his way nearer and nearer. Every moment I expected him to rush it; and the staging had not been constructed with an eye to such a possibility. If one of the rather flimsy poles should break, or if the lion could spring the twelve feet which separated me from the ground – the thought was scarcely a pleasant one. I began to heartily repent my folly in having placed myself in such a dangerous position.

I kept perfectly still hardly daring even to blink my eyes, but the long-continued strain was telling on my nerves. My feelings may be imagined when about midnight suddenly something came flop and struck me on the back of the head. For a moment I was so terrified that I nearly fell off the plank, as I thought that the lion had sprung on me from behind. Regaining my senses in a second or two, I realised that I had been hit by nothing more formidable than an owl, which had doubtless mistaken me for the branch of a tree – not a very alarming thing to happen in ordinary circumstances, I admit, but coming at the time it did, it almost paralysed me. The involuntary start which I could not help giving was immediately answered by a sinister growl from below.

After this I again kept as still as I could, though absolutely trembling with excitement, and in a short while I heard the lion begin to creep stealthily towards me. I could barely make out his form as he crouched among the whitish undergrowth; but I saw enough for my purpose. Before he could come any nearer, I took careful aim and pulled the trigger. The sound of the shot was at once followed by a most terrific roar and then I could hear him leaping about in all directions. I was no longer able to see him, however, as his first bound had taken him into thick bush, but to make assurance doubly sure, I kept blazing away in the direction in which I heard him plunging about. At length came a series of mighty groans, gradually subsiding into deep sighs, and finally ceasing altogether. I began to feel convinced that one of the 'devils' who had so long harried us would trouble us no more.

As soon as I ceased firing, a tumult of inquiring voices was borne across the dark jungle from the men in camp about a quarter of a mile away. I shouted back that I was safe and sound and that one of the lions was dead, whereupon such a mighty cheer went up from all the camps as must have astonished the jungle for miles around. Shortly I saw scores of lights twinkling through the bushes; every man in camp turned out, and with tom-toms beating and horns blowing came running to the scene. They surrounded my eyrie and to my amazement prostrated themselves on the ground before me, saluting me with cries of '*Mabarak! Mabarak!*' meaning blessed one or saviour.

I refused to allow any search to be made that night for the body of the lion, in case his companion might be close by. Besides, it was possible that he might be still alive and capable of making a last spring. Accordingly we all returned in triumph to the camp, where great rejoicings were kept up for the remainder of the night, the Swahili and other African natives celebrating the occasion by an especially wild and savage dance.

For my part, I anxiously awaited the dawn and even before it was thoroughly light I was on my way to the eventful spot, as I could not completely persuade myself that even yet the 'devil' might not have eluded me in some uncanny and mysterious way. Happily my fears proved groundless and I was relieved to find that my luck - after playing me so many exasperating tricks - had really turned at last. I had scarcely traced the blood for more than a few paces when, on rounding a bush, I was startled to see a huge lion right in front of me, seemingly alive and crouching for a spring. On looking closer, however, I satisfied myself that he was really and truly stone-dead, whereupon my followers crowded round, laughing and dancing and shouting with joy like children and then bore me in triumph shoulder-high round the dead body.

These thanksgiving ceremonies being over, I examined the body and found that two bullets had taken effect – one close behind the left shoulder, evidently penetrating the heart, and the other in the off-hind leg. The prize was indeed one to be proud of: his length from tip of nose to tip of tail was nine feet eight inches, he stood three feet nine inches high and it took eight men to carry him back to camp. The only blemish was that the skin was much scored by the boma thorns through which he had so often forced his way in carrying off his victims.

The news of the death of one of the man-eaters soon spread far and wide over the country. Telegrams of congratulation came pouring in and scores of people flocked from up and down the railway to see the skin for themselves.

It must not be imagined that with the death of this lion our troubles at Tsavo were at an end; his companion was still at large and very soon began to make us unpleasantly aware of the fact. Only a few nights elapsed before he made an attempt to get at the permanent way inspector, climbing up the steps of his bungalow and prowling round the verandah. The inspector, hearing the noise and thinking it was a drunken worker, shouted angrily 'Go away!' but, fortunately for him, did not attempt to come out or to open the door. Thus disappointed in his attempt to obtain a meal of human flesh, the lion seized a couple of the inspector's goats and devoured them there and then.

On hearing of this occurrence I determined to sit up the next night near the inspector's bungalow. Fortunately there was a vacant iron shanty close at hand, with a convenient loophole in it for firing from; and outside this I placed three full-grown goats as bait, tying them to a half-length of rail, weighing about 250lbs. The night passed uneventfully until just before daybreak, when at last the lion turned up, pounced on one of the goats and made off

with it, at the same time dragging away the others, rail and all. I
fired several shots in his direction, but it was pitch-dark and quite
impossible to see anything, so I only succeeded in hitting one of
the goats. I often longed for a flashlight on such occasions.

Next morning I started off in pursuit and was joined by some
others from the camp. I found that the trail of the goats and rail was
easily followed, and about a quarter of a mile away we soon came
up to where the lion was still busy at his meal. He was concealed
in some thick bush and growled angrily on hearing our approach.
Finally, as we got closer, he suddenly made a charge, rushing
through the bushes at a great pace. In an instant, every man of the
party scrambled hastily up the nearest tree, with the exception of
one of my assistants, Mr Winkler, who stood steadily by me
throughout. The animal, however, did not press his charge home
and on throwing stones into the bushes where we had last seen
him, we guessed by the silence that he had slunk off. We therefore
advanced cautiously, and on getting up to the place discovered that
he had indeed escaped us, leaving two of the goats scarcely touched.

Thinking that in all probability the lion would return as usual to
finish his meal, I had a very strong scaffolding put up a few feet
away from the dead goats and took up my position on it before
dark. On this occasion I brought my gun-bearer, Mahina, to take
a turn at watching, as I was by this time worn out for want of sleep,
having spent so many nights on the look-out. I was just dozing off
comfortably when suddenly I felt my arm seized and on looking up
saw Mahina pointing in the direction of the goats. 'Sher!' was all
he whispered. I grasped my double smooth-bore, which I had
charged with slug, and waited patiently.

In a few moments I was rewarded for, as I watched the spot where
I expected the lion to appear, there was a rustling among the
bushes and I saw him stealthily emerge into the open and pass
almost directly beneath us. I fired both barrels practically together
into his shoulder and to my joy could see him go down under the
force of the blow. Quickly I reached for the magazine rifle, but
before I could use it he was out of sight among the bushes and I
had to fire after him quite at random. Nevertheless I was confident

of getting him in the morning and accordingly set out as soon as it was light. For over a mile there was no difficulty in following the blood-trail and, as he had rested several times, I felt sure that he had been badly wounded. In the end my hunt proved fruitless, however, for after a time the traces of blood ceased and the surface of the ground became so rocky that I was no longer able to follow the spoor.

As it happened, there was no sign of our enemy for about ten days after this, and we began to hope that he had died of his wounds in the bush. All the same we still took every precaution at night, and it was fortunate that we did so, as otherwise at least one more victim would have been added to the list. On the night of December 27 I was suddenly aroused by terrified shouts from my trolley men, who slept in a tree close outside my boma, to the effect that a lion was trying to get at them. It would have been madness to have gone out, as the moon was hidden by dense clouds and it was absolutely impossible to see anything more than a yard in front of one; so all I could do was to fire off a few rounds just to frighten the brute away. This apparently had the desired effect, for the men were not further molested that night, but the man-eater had evidently prowled about for some time. In the morning we found that he had gone right into every one of their tents, and round the tree was a regular ring of his footmarks.

The following evening I took up my position in this same tree, in the hope that he would make another attempt. The night began badly, as while climbing up to my perch I very nearly put my hand on a venomous snake which was lying coiled round one of the branches. As may be imagined, I came down again very quickly, but one of my men managed to despatch it with a long pole. The night fortunately was clear and cloudless and the moon made every thing almost as bright as day. I kept watch until about 2 a.m., when I roused Mahina to take his turn.

For about an hour I slept peacefully with my back to the tree, and then woke suddenly with an uncanny feeling that something was wrong. Mahina, however, was on the alert and had seen nothing, and although I looked carefully round us on all sides, I too could discover nothing unusual. Only half satisfied, I was about to lie back again, when I fancied I saw something move a little way off among the low bushes. On gazing intently at the spot for a few seconds, I found I was not mistaken. It was the man-eater, cautiously stalking us.

The ground was fairly open round our tree, with only a small bush here and there. From our position it was a most fascinating sight to watch this great brute stealing round us, taking advantage of every bit of cover as he came. His skill showed that he was an old hand at the terrible game of man-hunting, so I determined to run no undue risk of losing him this time. I accordingly waited until he got quite close - about twenty yards away - and then fired my 303 at his chest. I heard the bullet strike him but unfortunately it had no knockdown effect, for with a fierce growl he turned and made off with great long bounds. Before he disappeared from sight, however, I managed to have three more shots at him from the magazine rifle, and another growl told me that the last of these had also taken effect.

We awaited daylight with impatience and at the first glimmer of dawn we set out to hunt him down. I took a native tracker with me, so that I was free to keep a good look-out, while Mahina followed immediately behind with a Martini carbine. Splashes of blood being plentiful, we were able to get along quickly and we had not proceeded more than a quarter of a mile through the jungle when suddenly a fierce warning growl was heard right in front of us. Looking cautiously through the bushes, I could see the man-eater glaring out in our direction, and showing his tusks in an angry snarl. I at once took careful aim and fired. Instantly he sprang out and made a most determined charge on us. I fired again and knocked him over, but in a second he was up once more and coming for me as fast as he could in his crippled condition. A third shot had no apparent effect, so I put out my hand for the Martini, hoping to stop him with it. To my dismay, however, it was not there.

The terror of the sudden charge had proved too much for Mahina and both he and the carbine were by this time well on their way

up a tree. In the circumstances there was nothing to do but follow
suit, which I did without loss of time and but for the fact that one
of my shots had broken a hind leg, the man-eater would most
certainly have had me. Even as it was, I had barely time to swing
myself up out of his reach before he arrived at the foot of the tree.

When the lion found he was too late, he started to limp back to
the thicket but by this time I had seized the carbine from Mahina,
and the first shot I fired from it seemed to give him his quietus, for
he fell over and lay motionless. Rather foolishly, I at once scrambled down from the tree and walked towards him. To my surprise
and no little alarm he jumped up and attempted another charge.
This time, however, a Martini bullet in the chest and another in
the head finished him for good and all. He dropped in his tracks
not five yards away from me, and died gamely, biting savagely at
a branch which had fallen to the ground.

By this time all the workmen in the camp, attracted by the sound
of the firing, had arrived on the scene, and so great was their
resentment against the brute who had killed such numbers of their
comrades that it was only with the greatest difficulty that I could
restrain them from tearing the dead body to pieces. Eventually,
amid the wild rejoicings of the natives and coolies, I had the lion
carried to my boma, which was close at hand. On examination we
found no less than six bullet holes in the body, and embedded only
a little way in the flesh of the back was the slug which I had fired
into him from the scaffolding about ten days previously. He
measured nine feet six inches from tip of nose to tip of tail and
stood three feet eleven and a half inches high. As in the case of his
companion, the skin was disfigured by being deeply scored all over
by the boma thorns.

The news of the death of the second 'devil' soon spread far and
wide over the country, and natives actually travelled from up and
down the line to have a look at my trophies and at the 'devil-
killer', as they called me. Best of all, the workers who had ab-
sconded came flocking back to Tsavo. Much to my relief work was
resumed and we were never again troubled by man-eaters. It was
amusing to notice the change which took place in the attitude of

the workmen towards me after I had killed the two lions. Instead of wishing to murder me, as they once did, they could not now do enough for me, and as a token of their gratitude they presented me with a beautiful silver bowl, as well as with a long poem written in Hindustani describing all our trials and my ultimate victory. The bowl I shall always consider my most highly prized and hardest won trophy. The inscription on it reads as follows:

SIR, - We, your Overseer, Timekeepers, Mistaris and Workmen, present you with this bowl as a token of our gratitude to you for your bravery in killing two man-eating lions at great risk to your own life, thereby saving us from the fate of being devoured by these terrible monsters who nightly broke into our tents and took our fellow-workers from our side. In presenting you with this bowl, we all add our prayers for your long life, happiness and prosperity. We shall ever remain, Sir, Your grateful servants,

Baboo PURSHOTAM HURJEE PURMAR,
Overseer and Clerk of Works,
on behalf of your Workmen.

Dated at Tsavo, January 30, 1899

Before I leave the subject of the man-eaters, it may be of interest to mention that these two lions possess the distinction, probably unique among wild animals, of having been specifically referred to in the House of Lords by the prime minister of the day. Speaking of the difficulties which had been encountered in the construction of the Uganda Railway, the late Lord Salisbury said:

The whole of the works were put a stop to for three weeks because a party of man-eating lions appeared in the locality and conceived a most unfortunate taste for our porters. At last the labourers entirely declined to go on unless they were guarded by an iron entrenchment. Of course it is difficult to work a railway under these conditions, and until we found an enthusiastic sportsman to get rid of these lions, our enterprise was seriously hindered.

Well had the two man-eaters earned all this fame: they had devoured between them no less than twenty-eight Indian workers, in addition to scores of unfortunate African natives of whom no official record was kept.

CHAPTER NINE

Man-eater of Mamandur

THE DESCENT OF ONE PARTICULAR TIGER from cattle lifting to man-eating was not attributable to any of the conventional causes. The animal also failed to return to its uneaten human kills. For Kenneth Anderson, pursuit required an unorthodox and desperate response: stalking the man-eater at night, against all the rules.

This animal was a female, and young at that; so there was no apparent reason for her becoming a man-killer.

She made her first attempt at killing a human being when she attacked a herdsman, who attempted to succour a fine milk-cow, which she had chosen to attack from amongst his herd of cattle, and whose neck she had just skilfully broken. The herdsman, very bravely but foolishly, attempted to frighten the tigress away from the fallen cow by shouting and brandishing his staff in the air. Mostly such tactics have the desired effect of frightening the tigress away, but in this case the effect was just the reverse. Instead of bounding away, the tigress bounded towards the herdsman, covering the short twenty yards that separated them at incredible speed. The herdsman turned tail and bolted, but the tigress dealt him a raking blow with her front paw that opened the flesh from shoulder to buttocks. The weight of the blow bore him to the ground; but in this, her first attack on a human being, the tigress apparently considered she had inflicted enough damage, because she then turned back to the cow she had just killed.

With returning consciousness, the herdsman could hear the crunch of bones a mere forty yards away, as the tigress fed on the cow.

Fortunately, the man kept his head and did not attempt to get to his feet. In all probability any such movement would have provoked a second, and this time fatal, attack. So he lay as he had fallen, on his face, but by stealthily moving his head very slowly and slightly, he was able to see the tigress as she fed.

He told me afterwards that he would never forget the next hour for the rest of his life. Apparently the tigress stopped eating every now and then, raised her head and glanced in his direction. Once she got to her feet and even took a few steps towards him. The poor fellow almost screamed with terror and nearly made the mistake of moving. Perhaps his very terror saved his life by making him incapable of movement. Fortunately, the tigress then changed her mind and returned to the cow.

It was more than an hour, the herdsman told me, before the tigress eventually decided she had eaten enough. She then leisurely sat on her haunches, licked her forepaws thoroughly and began to clean her face. With a final backward glance at his recumbent figure, she at last got to her feet, stretched herself contentedly and walked off into the jungle. The herdsman lay still for another ten minutes, to make perfectly sure she had really gone. Then he got to his feet and dashed homewards as fast as he could run.

There is at least one other, equally remarkable, end to this story: the deep scratches the tigress had inflicted healed completely in spite of the absence of any proper medical treatment, apart from some crushed herbs, mixed with cow-dung, which a native doctor rubbed into the wounds. Perhaps the shawl he had been wearing, draped across his shoulders, had prevented the poisonous matter under the claws from entering the bloodstream.

This incident had occurred scarcely four miles from Mamandur railway station, where a rocky escarpment fell sharply for about 300 feet into a forest glen, through which ran a little stream.

The next incident was also one of mauling, but this time the victim was not so lucky. Again it was a cowherd who was involved, an elderly man who died of his wounds. The events were much the same as in the earlier case. The tigress had dashed into a herd of cattle that was grazing a mile to the west of the railway line that cut through the forest, and had once more selected a milk-cow for her victim. As the frightened cattle stampeded past the elderly herdsman, he ran in the direction from which they had come to learn the cause of their alarm.

Soon he came upon the tigress, astride the dead cow. This time no attempt was made to frighten her off; the herdsman just stopped in his tracks in surprise. But evidently the tigress resented his appearance on the scene, for she attacked and mauled him severely. Then she walked back to the dead cow and dragged it away into the undergrowth.

It was three hours before help came to the old man, the cattle having meanwhile stampeded across the railway line. The old man's brother, coming in search of him, saw that the cattle had moved and that their owner was nowhere to be seen. Standing on the railway embankment, he called loudly to his brother, but got no response. Then, sensing that something was wrong, he hurried back to Mamandur village for help.

The search-party, by following the tracks of the stampeding cattle, came upon the mauled man. He was unconscious and almost dead from loss of blood. They carried him to the village and then to the station, eventually putting him in the guard's van of a goods train that was due in half-an-hour, bound for the town of Renigunta nine miles away where there was a hospital. But the old herdsman died before the goods train reached Mamandur.

Only at her third killing of cattle did this tigress develop obvious man-eating tendencies. She again attacked a herdsman, on this occasion at about nine in the morning. How it happened was related by a second herdsman, who was standing beside the first at the time of the attack. The tigress dashed out amongst the herd as usual and leapt upon a young bull. Somehow, she failed in her initial attempt to bring the bull down. The bull, with the tigress on his back, dashed madly to where the two herdsmen were standing. One of them – the man who lived to tell the tale – bolted. The other just did nothing, but appeared to be rooted to the spot with surprise. The fleeing man looked back only once, in time to see the tigress leap from the bolting bull on to the terror-stricken herdsman. He saw no more, turning away and running as fast and as far from the spot as he could.

When the rescue-party turned up some hours later, armed with sticks and matchlocks, the body of the victim was not to be seen. So the party went back for reinforcements. Another three hours elapsed before the rescuers, now numbering nearly a hundred men, arrived at the scene of the attack. They followed a clear trail and found the corpse, lying on its face in the sandy bed of a narrow nullah. A part of the chest and buttocks had been eaten.

Three further human kills followed during the next couple of months. Of these, one was a herdsman, one a traveller on the Renigunta road, and the third a Lumbani, who had gone out to gather wild honey. Thereafter, all cattle grazing stopped, as did also the collection of wild honey. No more travellers dared to move by road or on foot, coming by train instead.

Mr Littlewood, the district forest officer at that time, then wrote to me, suggesting I might spend a few days at the beautiful forest bungalow at Mamandur and try to bag this tigress. With fifteen days privilege leave to my credit I caught the night mail-train from Bangalore, but it was 3.30 p.m. next day before I alighted from a slow passenger train at the little wayside station of Mamandur.

The forest bungalow lies a bare seven furlongs away on the top of a small hillock. The path to the bungalow traverses the small village of Mamandur, where I stopped for some time to make it widely known that I had come especially to shoot the tigress. My object was to get the news to spread from mouth to mouth, so that I would not only pick up all available known details about the animal but, more particularly, would be acquainted with the news of any fresh kills that took place, either animal or human. I also negotiated the purchase of three buffalo heifers, which I paid for in cash, placing them in the charge of the local shikari, a man by the name of Arokiaswamy, whom I had engaged on earlier visits to Mamandur.

The bungalow had a wide and well-sheltered verandah. From its hillock fire-lines radiated in five directions. Those south and south-westwards ran close to the village and railway embankment respectively. The other three stuck far into the forest, and the eye could travel along them for many miles. The fire-line to the north stretched away towards the escarpment where the very first herds-man had been mauled by the tigress. Those to the east and south-east travelled in almost straight lines into the labyrinth of jungle, like the spokes of some giant wheel. The country in both these directions was flat. In years gone by, when game was far more plentiful, I had spent many a pleasant early morning or late evening, standing on the verandah or on the plinth of the bungalow with a pair of powerful binoculars, looking along those forest-lines. It was very common to see sambar, spotted deer and peafowl cross from one side to another. I had seen bear on three occasions, early in the morning, and a tiger crossing the northern fire-line at five in the evening.

It was too late that evening to tie out more than one of the three buffaloes, which only arrived at 5.30 p.m. This buffalo I took for two miles along the northern fire-line, where I tied it at the foot of a large and leafy tamarind tree. It was past seven when I got back, so I kept the other two buffaloes in the garage and asked Arokiaswamy to sleep in the kitchen.

Early next morning we were astir. First we took the bait which we had tied two miles away the previous night, and which was still alive, right up to the foot of the escarpment where the very first attack had taken place. There we had secured it to the roots of a tree, in a beautiful glade of rank, green grass; we then came back to the bungalow and took the second heifer along the fire-line stretching to the east. Returning for the second time to the bungalow, we took the third and last heifer across the railway line to the west, and tied it near the spot where the elderly herdsman had been killed.

It was past midday when I got back to the bungalow for the third time, and blazing hot too. Taking off my sweat-soaked shirt, I ate a belated cold lunch and awaited the advent of the sea breeze, which I knew would start at about two; when it began, it turned that boiling-hot verandah to the likeness of the shores of some distant South Sea island.

The next two days were uneventful. I visited all three baits each day, but none of them were touched. The evening of the fifth day, however, brought a tragedy.

The semaphores along the railway lines of southern India are lit at night by kerosene oil lamps, except in the shunting yards of the larger railway junctions. Every ordinary railway station has two sets of signals on each side of it: the near or home signal and a more distant outer signal. Normally, the kerosene oil lamps at these signals are cleaned, trimmed, re-filled and lit by a pointsman or other railway employee appointed for the purpose, who does his job at about six each evening. But owing to the presence of the tigress at Mamandur, and the fact that both the outer signals in the direction of Renigunta to the south and Settigunta to the north-west were surrounded by forest, it had become the custom to light these lamps well before five while the sun was still up.

That evening two pointsmen had set out on this task at 4 p.m., one walking towards Renigunta and the other in the opposite direction. The second man never came back.

Shortly before six a body of seven men came running to the forest bungalow, sent by the station master, to tell me what had happened. Hastily grabbing my rifle, torch and a few other necessities for a night-long vigil, I sent the seven men back to the station, and Arokiaswamy along with them as he absolutely refused to stay in the bungalow alone that night. Then I hurried up the forest-line that led to the west, which I knew met the railway track almost midway between the inner and outer signals. When I reached the railway line, which here ran along an embankment ten feet high, I looked to my left and saw the inner signal, with its red light twinkling.

'Stupid man,' I thought. 'Instead of attending to the outer light first while it was still early, and coming back to the inner on his way to the station, he wasted time on the inner light, and then went to the outer when it was considerably later.'

Turning to the right, I walked along the embankment towards the outer semaphore, which came into view when I turned a corner. As I walked, I looked along and about the track for signs of the attack that must have taken place while the pointsman was approaching the outer signal. I found nothing. Then I came to the foot of the signal, and looked up. The light was burning. So the man had been attacked on his way back after he had attended to the outer signal, and not before. Added to this was the fact that the light of the inner signal was also burning. Perhaps he had not attended to that light first, as I had originally thought. Perhaps he had lit the outer, then the inner, and had been attacked somewhere between the inner signal and the station yard.

But was that likely in view of the fact that all the area from the station up to the inner signal, and even a little beyond it, was open cultivated land? Would any tiger, even if it was a man-eater, walk about thus boldly on absolutely open land in broad daylight? It was possible, but rather unlikely. My watch showed 6.55 p.m. and it was rapidly growing dark as I began to retrace my steps towards the inner signal, keeping now a sharper look-out than ever. An early moon had risen, which was indeed fortunate, or it would have become quite dark by this time. Almost at the spot where I had first come on to the embankment from the forest-line was a small culvert, crossing a narrow but deep nullah. Something white there caught my eye, fluttering between the sleepers of the railway track as it spanned this nullah. I stopped, stooped, and peered between the sleepers.

It was the white dhoty worn by the railwayman. Wedged under a boulder, twenty feet away and clear of the embankment, lay an elongated, dark shape, which I knew to be the body of the victim. Even in that uncertain light I could tell that the body had been partly devoured in the short time that had elapsed since the kill had taken place. The neck had been bitten through, and the head lay about a yard away. Because the tigress might perhaps be in the vicinity at that moment, or even watching me from the cover of the bushes, it would be unnecessarily dangerous to descend the embankment and make a closer examination of the body.

A hasty survey of the position made me decide to lie at right angles across the railway lines and exactly in the middle of the culvert. I would thus be safe from attack from the front or rear, as to do this the tigress would have to leap a clear fifteen feet from the bottom of the nullah onto the track. This left her the choice of attacking me along the track, either to my right or left. The span of the culvert was about twenty feet; not much, but it would at least give me time to see the tigress. There was also the possibility that she would creep up at an angle to the embankment and attack me obliquely, either from in front, or worse still, from behind; and either to the left or right of me. It was a chance that had to be taken.

I had already clamped my torch to the rifle while walking from the bungalow. I placed my haversack beneath my chest, to soften contact with the rail. This section of track was broad gauge, which means that the lines were five feet six inches apart. By spreading my legs widely, I found my soles just touched the other rail and did not overlap it. The teak-wood sleeper, on which I lay, was perhaps eight inches wide: not over-comfortable to lie on and awfully hard.

The moon was shining brightly by this time and lit the scene clearly. The corpse and its severed head were clearly visible against the lighter colour of the rock and the finely-grained white sand of the nullah in which it lay. Everything was deathly silent. The red light glimmered from the friendly inner signal; it seemed to remind me that help was close – but yet so distant.

The hours ticked by. A sambar stag called from the jungle to the west. Perhaps it heralded that the tigress was on the move? No, for it was answered by another stag, further away to the north-east, and then by another to the east. Periodically, the spotted deer also gave vent to their sharp cries of alarm, '*Aiow! Aiow! Aiow!*'

But the cries did not come from any one direction; if they had done so, that would have indicated definitely that a carnivore was afoot in that area. They came from all sides, far and near, indicating that several carnivores were on the move. Also, being a brilliant moonlight night, it was possible that packs of wild dogs were on the hunt. These animals chase their prey by day and never on a dark night except on brilliant moonlight nights, in certain jungles, when occasionally they reverse their habit and hunt by moonlight.

At midnight silence reigned again. I looked down between the sleepers. I then felt the hair at the back of my neck begin to rise: the severed head had rolled onto its side.

All this time it had been staring heavenwards; now its lifeless eyes and face were turned to me. Yet no animal had touched it, for it lay in the open, clearly visible in the bright moonlight. I felt myself tremble and grow cold. I licked my dry lips and stared at that awful head. Again it moved. It rolled halfway to its former position and then, as if it lacked the strength to complete the move, it had rolled back again and was staring me in the face.

Now I am a very practical person, not superstitious, nor afraid of the dark. I had spent many a night in a similar or even more dangerous position; I had sat over half-eaten human bodies before, and on earlier occasions I had imagined that I had seen them move. But never before in my life had I seen a severed human head actually turn around of its own accord.

I almost cried out and for quite a while was seized with a powerful urge to get up and run towards the twinkling, friendly red light of the inner signal. Then common sense reasserted itself. A dead head, human or otherwise, cannot move of its own accord. Something must have moved it.

I stared at the head intently, and the bright moonlight showed me the answer to the riddle. Two black objects could be seen moving in the white sand. They were rhinoceros beetles: large insects, more than an inch-and-a-half long, each with a great spike on its nose resembling the horn of a rhinoceros. Generally these beetles are nocturnal, although one frequently sees them on forest roads, early in the morning, and again late at evening, busily rolling a ball of cow-dung, perhaps three times their own size, to some unknown destination.

These two little creatures by their combined strength had succeeded in rolling this head over once, but the second time they had not quite succeeded. I had been so absorbed by what I had seen that I had forgotten all about the tigress; she could easily have surprised me during that time.

It was now 1.40 a.m. and the rail beneath my chest began to tremble. Then I heard a distant rumbling sound which gradually grew louder and nearer. A sharp whistle rent the air and soon the brilliant headlight of an engine fell full upon me. It was the night mail from Madras to Bombay.

Stiffly I got to my feet, lifted my haversack, walked to the end of the culvert, and then a couple of feet down the embankment. But I had entirely forgotten to take into account the vigilance of the driver of the train. He had clearly seen me in the bright headlight of the engine, although he had not noticed my rifle. As he was to tell me in a few minutes, he took me for a would-be suicide, deliberately lying on the track in order to be run over, whose courage had failed him at the last moment. I may mention, incidentally, that this method of committing suicide is rather popular in India.

With a grinding of brakes and violent hissing of steam, the train drew up just after the engine had passed me. The next thing I heard was the loud thudding of boots on the hard ground as figures ran towards me. It was the driver and his two firemen from the engine.

They charged up and grabbed me. Only then did they realise that I was obviously not what they had taken me to be. In the meantime, heads popped out of carriage windows, and a hundred voices began to question and conjecture. The guard came up from the rear with his bulls-eye lantern, so I had no alternative but to tell them what I was doing.

'Where is the man who has been eaten by the tiger?' asked the driver, a middle-aged Anglo-Indian. I pointed the corpse out to him. `And you have been lying here in the open by yourself since evening?' he asked, incredulously. When I replied in the affirmative, he added very simply: `You're quite mad,' and tapped his forehead significantly. His two firemen, and the Indian guard of the train, nodded heartily in agreement. A few minutes later, the mail puffed onwards, on its long journey to Bombay, and I was left alone once more. But I had little hope of the tigress putting in her appearance after so great a disturbance.

At 2.30 a.m. the rails began to rumble again. This time I lay flat on the embankment, hiding my rifle, before the engine's headlight betrayed my presence. As a result, the goods train passed me by without stopping. At 4 a.m. again the rails rumbled and trembled, and I hid once more. It was the return mail, from Bombay to Madras, thundering by at full speed as mail trains do not halt at Mamandur.

The false-dawn came and went. The distant call of awakening peafowl fell on the air, as they cried, *'Mia-a-oo - Aaow'* across the forest valleys to be answered by the cheery *'Whe-e-e-e-Kuck - Kaya-Khuck'm'* of that most lovely bird, the grey jungle cock.

A pale shell-pink tinted the sky above the eastern hills now standing sharply outlined in black. Meanwhile, the moon, which had held sway all night and was now about to set, began losing some of her brilliance. In the east the shell-pink turned to mauve, then to a deep rose, tinged at its edges by the palest of greens and the purest of blues. The rose became orange-purple, then orange alone, then deep red, and finally flame, as the glowing tip of the sun peeped above the hill tops to the east. Beams of sunlight touched the clouds with all the colours of the spectrum. Then, suddenly, the sun surmounted the hills, driving before it the wisps of mist from the damp jungle below. A chorus of song burst from the birds of the forest all around me. Every bush and tree throbbed with life, fresh, clean and new. It was the marvel of an Indian jungle sunrise.

The head still stared up at me, but it was still now; the two rhinoceros beetles that had worked so diligently through the night had long since abandoned the unequal task and gone to rest.

I made my way to the station, disappointed and slowly, to tell the station master he could allow the relations of the dead man to remove the remains for cremation, and by eight I was asleep on the verandah of the bungalow. In the afternoon the sea breeze lulled me to a deeper slumber and at 4 p.m. I awoke, feeling refreshed and fit. I ate a quick lunch-cum-tea while listening to Arokiaswamy's report that he, with four others, had visited all the baits and had found them alive. It certainly looked as if this tigress was not going to kill any of the heifers I had tied out.

Then came sunset and bright moonlight. I felt like taking a walk. If I kept to the centre of any one of those five radiating forest fire-lines, I felt I would be safe enough, provided I maintained a sharp watch while I walked. There was also the definite chance of attracting the tigress, should our trails cross during the night.

I dressed for the occasion. In my own kit I had only khaki clothes and a black shirt which was useful for night machan work. So I went with Arokiaswamy to his hut, where I slipped on a long white shirt, allowing the shirt-tails to flutter loosely outside my khaki trousers. Arokiaswamy further completed the disguise by tying a white turban round my head. I did not know what the tigress would take me for if we met but I know I was a source of considerable amusement to the villagers, who were somewhat shocked to hear of my plan.

I debated for a moment which fire-line to walk up first and decided to follow the one leading in the easterly direction. It was 7.30 p.m. when I set out. I kept in the centre of the line, and as I moved I allowed my eyes to rove freely around and about the bushes and undergrowth on both sides. Occasionally I glanced backwards.

Although the moonlight was brilliant, the bushes cast long black shadows and clumps of thorns and grass looked ghostly grey around me. I realised that, for all the moonlight, my eyes could never pick out a lurking carnivore in that unreal light, even if it showed itself, which it would not. I should have to rely on my sense of hearing - and that other, my sixth sense. At ten-minute intervals I whistled a bar of some tune or other to advertise my presence to the tigress; but only for half-a-minute at a time, so as not to impede my own ears, that were attuned to catch the slightest sound.

Many a subtle rustle did I hear in the grassy hillocks as I passed them. Invariably, the nocturnal bamboo-rat was the culprit, as he scampered for cover at my approach. Then an indefinable, pro-longed, slithering rustle: a snake, probably a Russell's Viper, coiling comfortably around and around himself in the grass, to be cosy and warm. Something heavy descended from the sky neatly onto the back of a hare as it scampered across the fire-line. The hare squealed, and the great horned owl, which had attacked it, pecked it sharply on the forehead. I approached the owl, which extended both its wings to the ground to hide the hare from me, much in the same way as does a hen with chickens. I approached closer and the owl glowered; drew closer still and the owl flew away. I picked up the limp hare and rubbed its back briskly. With returning consciousness, it began to kick vigorously and I let it go in the long grass.

There were no bison in these jungles, nor elephants, but in their stead bear were plentiful. Nor was it long before I came upon bruin, engaged in his favourite pastime of sucking white ants out of their hills. A distant sound, midway between a buzzing and a humming, a queer noise rather like someone inflating a bag-pipe, or the sound of angry swarming bees, first told me that a bear was afoot. It grew louder and louder and was punctuated by grunts, coughs, whimpers of impatience and growls of annoyance.

There, to one side of the line and to my right was a white anthill. Standing up against it, with its head inside a hole, was a shaggy, black shape. It was the bear, blowing, sucking, grumbling, swearing and complaining, as he met with little or no success. Occasionally there would be a chuckle of sheer joy as something succulent went down. He was deeply engrossed in his task as I padded silently on my way, and the sounds of his feast receded behind me, growing fainter and fainter. I walked for two hours along that line, then turned and retraced my steps. Bruin had gone home by the time I came to the anthill again and it was then only half its original height, due to his efforts. I saw nothing else till I reached the forest lodge.

Next, I turned up the northern fire-line and walked towards the escarpment. This line did not run straight like the one I had just abandoned. Rather, it twisted and turned considerably as I approached the escarpment. A stream intersected it at the third mile, in which a trickle of clear, cold water sparkled like silver in the moonlight. Stooping down, I drank, bringing the water to my mouth in my left palm; my right hand held the rifle with its butt to the ground, while my eyes watched the jungle and my ears strained to catch the slightest sound. There was nothing visible, and the only sound was the gurgle of the water. I went on.

The bait I had tied was around the next corner. It was alive, and as I passed it looked at me with dumb reproach for the cruel fate to which I had exposed it. I had no answer, no excuse. That I was guilty there was no doubt. I turned my eyes away, but could not rid myself of the sense of guilt.

At last the base of the escarpment was reached. Here the fire-line stopped and became a narrow game trail that plunged abruptly into the labyrinth of greenery. It was too dangerous to go any further under such conditions and I turned back.

All I passed on the return journey was a large cobra in the process of swallowing a bamboo-rat in the middle of the fire-line. Three-quarters of the rat were already down the cobra's throat, with only the hindquarters and tail protruding when I came upon the scene. The snake saw me and raised its head two feet above the ground, simultaneously erecting the fine bones of its neck to form that most beautiful and at the same time most enthralling of sights, the cobra's hood. The hind legs and tail of the rat still dangled incongruously from its mouth. The beady, black eyes glittered in the phosphorescent light. I rapidly stamped my feet and clapped my hands. The cobra became nervous and finally panicked. It vomited the rat, lowered itself to the ground with deflated hood, and slithered away into the bushes to one side of the fire-line.

Once more I was back at the bungalow. I had covered twenty miles and it was 2.45 a.m. Two fire-lines remained to be tried, but there would only be time to negotiate one: either the fire-line running to the south-east, up which I had not yet been since my arrival, or the line to the south-west crossing the railway embankment, where I had sat the previous night over the dead body. I chose the latter.

I reached the railway track, crossed it, and had walked over a mile further towards the west, when suddenly the silence was shattered by the moaning call of a tigress. It appeared to come from a point no more than a couple of furlongs in front of me. Perhaps the beast was walking along the same fire-line; she may have been going away, or perhaps coming towards me. Doubling forward for the next fifty yards, I hid behind the trunk of a large wood-apple tree, cocked the rifle and raised it into position. Then I gave the deep-lunged moan of a male tiger.

Almost immediately it was answered, from much closer than I thought - perhaps a hundred yards away. I did not dare to call again, for fear that I should be recognised as an imposter.

Tiger-calling should not be indulged in at close quarters, for fear that the tiger should discover a difference in the timbre of the call and become suspicious, when he may just fade away. One hundred yards is about the closest range at which such mimicry can be tried. Of course, man-eating propensities, and also the curiosity, from which all animals suffer to some degree, might still cause the tiger to come forward, but there is always the risk that suspicion may drive him off. So I remained silent - and still.

Thirty seconds later, a tigress strode down the forest-line towards me, the moonlight playing upon the black stripes of her coat. She came abreast of me, then began to pass. I shot her behind the ear.

At Mamandur no human being has been killed now for some years. The tigress, which was young, was in the best of condition and there was no reason why she should have become a man-eater.

CHAPTER TEN

The Thak Man-eater

JIM CORBETT SPENT a large part of his life from boyhood in the Indian jungle. In so doing he became closely in tune with the jungle's inhabitants, particularly the tiger which he studied all his adult life, much of the time when he was in pursuit of man-eaters. Corbett became aware of extra sensory phenomenon and receptive to such communication. It was a phenomenon which he experienced nowhere more completely than in the pursuit of the man-eater of Thak, the last man-eater he hunted before his retirement in 1938.

Peace had reigned in the Ladhya valley for many months when in September 1938 a report was received in Naini Tal that a girl, twelve years of age, had been killed by a tiger at Kot Kindri village.

The report which reached me through Donald Stewart of the forest department gave no details, and it was not until I visited the village some weeks later that I was able to get particulars of the tragedy. It appeared that, about noon one day, this girl was picking up wind-falls from a mango tree close to and in full view of the village, when a tiger suddenly appeared. Before the men working nearby were able to render any assistance, it carried her off. No attempt was made to follow up the tiger, and as all signs of drag and blood trail had been obliterated and washed away long before I arrived on the scene, I was unable to find the place to which the tiger had taken the body.

Kot Kindri is about four miles south-west of Chuka, and three miles due west of Thak. During the summer of 1938 the forest department had marked all the trees in this area for felling, and it was feared that if the man-eater was not accounted for before

November – when the felling of the forest was due to start – the contractors would not be able to secure labour, and would repudiate their contracts. It was in this connection that Donald Stewart had written to me shortly after the girl had been killed. I must confess that it was more in the interests of the local inhabitants than in the interest of the contractors that I gave my promise to go to Kot Kindri.

My most direct route to Kot Kindri was to go by rail to Tanakpur, and from there by foot via Kaldhunga and Chuka. This route, however, though it would save me a hundred miles of walking, would necessitate my passing through the most deadly malaria belt in northern India; to avoid it I decided to go through the hills to Mornaula, and from there along the abandoned Sherring road to its termination on the ridge above Kot Kindri.

While my preparations for this long trek were still under way a second report reached Naini Tal of a kill at Sem, a small village on the left bank of the Ladhya and distant about half a mile from Chuka.

The victim on this occasion was an elderly woman, the mother of the headman of Sem. This unfortunate woman had been killed while cutting brushwood on a steep bank between two terraced fields. She had started work at the further end of the fifty-yard-long bank, and had cut the brushwood to within a yard of her hut when the tiger sprang on her from the field above. So sudden and unexpected was the attack that the woman only had time to scream once before the tiger killed her and, taking her up the twelve-foot-high bank, crossed the upper field and disappeared with her into the dense jungle beyond.

The woman's son, a lad some twenty years of age, was at the time working in a paddy field a few yards away and witnessed the whole occurrence, but was too frightened to try to render any assistance. I response to the lad's urgent summons the headman arrived at Sem two days later, accompanied by eighty men he had collected. Following up in the direction the tiger had gone, he found the woman's clothes and a few small bits of bone. This kill had taken place at 2 p.m. on a bright sunny day, and the tiger had eaten its victim only sixty yards from the hut where it had killed her.

On receipt of this second report Ibbotson (Deputy Commissioner of the three Districts of Almora, Naini Tal, and Garhwal) and I held a council of war, the upshot of which was that Ibbotson, who was on the point of setting out to settle a land dispute at Askot on the border of Tibet, changed his tour programme and, instead of going via Bagaswar, decided to accompany me to Sem, and from there go on to Askot.

The route I had selected entailed a considerable amount of hill-climbing, so we eventually decided to go up the Nandhour valley, cross the watershed between the Nandhour and Ladhya and follow the latter river down to Sem. The Ibbotsons accordingly left Naini Tal on 12 October, and the following day I joined them at Chaurgallia.

Going up the Nandhour we arrived on the fifth day at Durga Pepal. Here we left the river and after a very stiff climb camped for the night on the watershed. Making an early start next morning we pitched our tents that night on the left bank of the Ladhya, twelve miles from Chalti. The monsoon had given over early, which was very fortunate for us, for owing to the rock cliffs that run sheer down into the valley the river has to be crossed every quarter of a mile or so. At one of these fords my cook, who stands five feet in his boots, was washed away and only saved from a watery grave by the prompt assistance of the man who was carrying our lunch basket.

On the tenth day after leaving Chaurgallia we made camp on a deserted field at Sem, two hundred yards from the hut where the woman had been killed and a hundred yards from the junction of the Ladhya and Sarda rivers. Gill Waddell, of the police, whom we met on our way down the Ladhya, had camped for several days at Sem and had tied out a buffalo that MacDonald of the forest department had very kindly placed at our disposal, and though the tiger had visited Sem several times during Waddell's stay, it had not killed the buffalo.

The day following our arrival at Sem, while Ibbotson was inter-viewing forest guards, and headmen of the surrounding villages, I went out to look for pug marks. Between our camp and the junction, and also on both banks of the Ladhya, there were long stretches of sand. Here I found the tracks of a tigress, and of a young male tiger. The tigress had crossed and recrossed the Ladhya a number of times duing the last few days, and the previous night had walked along the strip of sand in front of our tents. It was this tigress the villagers suspected of being the man-eater, and as she had visited Sem repeatedly since the day the headman's mother had been killed they were probably correct.

An examination of the pug marks of the tigress showed her as being an average-sized animal in the prime of life. Why she had become a man-eater would have to be determined later, but one of the reasons might have been that she had assisted to eat the victims of an earlier man-eater when they were together the previous mating season, and having acquired a taste for human flesh and no longer having a mate to provide her with it, had now turned a man-eater herself. This was only a surmise, and proved later to be incorrect.

Before leaving Naini Tal I had written to the tahsildar of Tanakpur and asked him to purchase four young male buffaloes for me, and to send them to Sem. One of these buffaloes died on the road, the other three arrived on the 24th and we tied them out the same evening together with the one MacDonald had given us. On going out to visit these animals next morning I found the people of Chuka in a great state of excitement. The fields round the village had been recently ploughed, and the tigress the previous night had passed close to three families who were sleeping out on the fields with their cattle; fortunately in each case the cattle had seen the tigress and warned the sleepers of her approach. After leaving the cultivated land the tigress had gone up the track in the direction of Kot Kindri, and had passed close to two of our buffaloes without touching either of them.

The headman, forest guards, and villagers had told us on our arrival at Sem that it would be a waste of time tying out our young buffaloes, as they were convinced the man-eater would not kill them. The reason they gave was that trying to shoot the man-eater by this method had been used by others without success, and that in any case if the tigress wanted to eat buffaloes there were many grazing in the jungles for her to choose from. In spite of this advice, however, we continued to tie out our buffaloes, and for the next two nights the tigress passed close to one or more without touching them.

On the morning of the 27th just as we were finishing breakfast, a party of men led by Tewari, the brother of the headman of Thak, arrived in camp and reported that a man of their village was missing. They stated that this man had left the village at about noon the previous day, telling his wife before leaving that he was going to see that his cattle did not stray beyond the village boundary, and as he had not returned they feared he had been killed by the man-eater.

Our preparations were soon made and at ten o'clock the Ibbotsons and I set off for Thak, accompanied by Tewari and the men he had brought with him. The distance was only about two miles, but the climb was considerable, and as we did not want to lose more time than we could possibly help we arrived at the outskirts of the village out of breath and in a lather of sweat.

As we approached the village over the scrub-covered flat bit of ground which I have reason to refer to later, we heard a woman crying. The wailing of an Indian woman mourning her dead is unmistakable, and on emerging from the jungle we came on the mourner – the wife of the missing man – and some ten or fifteen men, who were waiting for us on the edge of the cultivated land. These people informed us that from their houses above they had seen some white object, which looked like part of the missing man's clothing, in a field overgrown with scrub thirty yards from where we were now standing. Ibbotson, Tewari, and I set off to investigate the white object, while Mrs Ibbotson took the woman and the rest of the men up to the village.

The field, which had been out of cultivation for some years, was covered with a dense growth of scrub not unlike chrysanthemum, and it was not until we were standing right over the white object that Tewari recognized it as the loin-cloth of the missing man.

Near it was the man's cap. A struggle had taken place at this spot, but there was no blood. The absence of blood where the attack had taken place and for some considerable distance along the drag could be accounted for by the tigress having retained her first hold, for no blood would flow in such a case until the hold had been changed.

Thirty yards up the hill above us there was a clump of bushes roofed over with creepers. This spot would have to be looked at before following up the drag, for it was not advisable to have the tigress behind us. In the soft earth under the bushes we found the pug marks of the tigress and where she had lain before going forward to attack the man.

Returning to our starting point we agreed on the following plan of action. Our primary object was to try to stalk the tigress and shoot her on her kill: to achieve this end I was to follow the trail and at the same time keep a lookout in front, with Tewari – who was unarmed – a yard behind me keeping a sharp lookout to right and left, and Ibbotson a yard behind Tewari to safeguard us against an attack from the rear. In the event of either Ibbotson or I seeing so much as a hair of the tigress we were to risk a shot.

Cattle had grazed over this area the previous day, disturbing the ground, and as there was no blood and the only indication of a tigress's passage was an occasional turned-up leaf or crushed blade of grass, progress was slow. After carrying the man for two hundred yards the tigress had killed and left him, returning and carrying him off several hours later, when the people of Thak had heard several sambar calling in this direction. The reason for the tigress not having carried the man away after she had killed him was possibly that his cattle had witnessed the attack on him and driven her away.

A big pool of blood had formed where the man had been lying, and as the blood from the wound in his throat had stopped flowing by the time the tigress had picked him up again, and further, as she was now holding him by the small of the back whereas she had previously held him by the neck, tracking became even more difficult. The tigress kept to the contour of the hill, and as the undergrowth here was very dense and visibility only extended to a few yards, our advance was slowed down.

In two hours we covered half a mile, and reached a ridge beyond which lay the valley in which, six months previously, we had tracked down and killed a previous man-eater. On this ridge was a great slab of rock, which sloped upwards and away from the direction in which we had come. The tigress's tracks went down to the right of the rock and I felt sure she was lying up under the overhanging portion of it, or in the close vicinity.

Both Ibbotson and I had on light rubber-soled shoes - Tewari was bare-footed - and we had reached the rock without making a sound. Signing to my two companions to stand still and keep a careful watch all round, I got a foothold on the rock and inch by inch went forward. Beyond the rock was a short stretch of flat ground, and as more of this ground came into view I felt certain my suspicion that the tigress was lying under the projection was correct. I had still a foot or two to go before I could look over, when I saw a movement to my left front. A golden rod that had been pressed down had sprung erect and a second later there was a slight movement in the bushes beyond; a monkey in a tree on the far side of the bushes started calling.

The tigress had chosen the spot for her after-dinner sleep with great care, but unfortunately for us she was not asleep. When she saw the top of my head - I had removed my hat - appearing over the rock, she had risen and, taking a step sideways, had disappeared under a tangle of blackberry bushes. Had she been lying anywhere but where she was she could not have got away, no matter how quickly she had moved, without my getting a shot at her.

Our so-carefully-carried-out stalk had failed at the very last moment. There was now nothing to be done but find the kill and see if there was sufficient of it left for us to sit up over. To have followed her into the blackberry thicket would have been useless and would also have reduced our chance of getting a shot at her later.

The tigress had eaten her meal close to where she had been lying, and as this spot was open to the sky and to the keen eyes of vultures she had removed the kill to a place of safety where it would not be visible from the air. Tracking now was easy, for there was a blood trail to follow. The trail led over a ridge of great rocks and fifty yards beyond these rocks we found the kill.

I am not going to attempt to describe that poor torn and mangled thing stripped of every stitch of clothing and atom of dignity which only a few hours previously had been a man, the father of two children and the breadwinner of that wailing woman who was facing – without any illusions – the fate of a widow of India. I have seen many similar sights, each more terrible than the one preceding it, in the thirty-two years I have been hunting man-eaters, and on each occasion I have felt that it would have been better to have left the victim to the slayer than recover a mangled mass of flesh to be a nightmare ever after to those who saw it. And yet the cry of blood for blood, and the burning desire to rid a countryside of a menace of which there is none more terrible, is irresistible; and then there is always the hope, no matter how absurd one knows it to be, that the victim who has been carried off may still be alive by some miracle and in need of succour.

The chance of shooting – over a kill – an animal that has in all probability become a man-eater through a wound received over a kill, is very remote. Each succeeding failure, no matter what its cause, tends to make the animal more cautious. Eventually it reaches a state when it either abandons its kill after one meal or approaches it as silently and as slowly as a shadow, scanning every leaf and twig with the certainty of discovering its would-be slayer, no matter how carefully he may be concealed or how silent and motionless he may be.

The thicket into which the tigress had retired was roughly forty yards square and she could not leave it without the monkey seeing her and warning us. So we sat down back to back, to have a smoke and listen if the jungle had anything further to tell us while we considered our next move.

To make a machan it was necessary to return to the village and during our absence the tigress was almost certain to carry away the kill. It had been difficult when she was carrying a whole human being to track her but now, when her burden was considerably lighter and she had been disturbed, she would probably go for miles and we might never find her kill again. It was therefore necessary for one of us to remain on the spot while the other two went back to the village for ropes.

Ibbotson, with his usual disregard for danger, elected to go back, and while he and Tewari went down the hill to avoid the difficult ground we had recently come over, I stepped up onto a small tree close to the kill. Four feet above ground the tree divided in two, and by leaning on one half and putting my feet against the other, I was able to maintain a precarious seat which was high enough off the ground to enable me to see the tigress if she approached the kill. It was also high enough, if she had any designs on me, to see her before she got to within striking distance.

Ibbotson had been gone fifteen or twenty minutes when I heard a rock tilt forward, and then back. The rock was evidently very delicately poised, and when the tigress had put her weight on it and felt it tilt forward she had removed her foot and let the rock fall back into place. The sound had come from about twenty yards to my left front, the only direction in which it would have been possible for me to have fired without being knocked out of the tree.

Minutes passed, and then, when tension on my nerves and the weight of the heavy rifle were becoming unbearable, I heard a stick snap at the upper end of the thicket. Here was an example of how a tiger can move through the jungle. From the sound she had made I knew her exact position, had kept my eyes fixed on the spot, and yet she had come, seen me, stayed some time watching me, and then gone away without my having seen a leaf or a blade of grass move.

When tension on nerves is suddenly relaxed, cramped and aching muscles call loudly for ease, and though in this case it only meant the lowering of the rifle onto my knees to take the strain off my shoulders and arms, the movement, small though it was, sent a comforting feeling through the whole of my body. No further sound came from the tigress and an hour or two later I heard Ibbotson returning.

Of all the men with whom I have been on shikar, Ibbotson is far and away the best, for not only has he the heart of a lion, but he thinks of everything, and with it all is the most unselfish man who ever carried a gun. He had gone to fetch a rope and he returned with rugs, cushions, more hot tea than even I could drink and an ample lunch; and while I sat – on the windward side of the kill – to refresh myself, Ibbotson first put a man in a tree forty yards away to distract the tigress's attention and then climbed into a tree overlooking the kill to make a rope machan.

When the machan was ready, Ibbotson moved the kill a few feet – a very unpleasant job – and tied it securely to the foot of a sapling to prevent the tigress carrying it away, for the moon was on the wane and first two hours of the night at this heavily wooded spot would be pitch-dark. After a final smoke I climbed on to the machan, and when I had made myself comfortable Ibbotson recovered the man who was making a diversion and set off in the direction of Thak to pick up Mrs Ibbotson and return to camp at Sem.

The retreating party were out of sight but were not yet out of sound when I heard a heavy body brushing against leaves, and at the same moment the monkey, which had been silent all this time and which I could now see sitting in a tree on the far side of the blackberry thicket, started calling. Here was more luck than I had hoped for, and our ruse of putting a man up a tree to cause a diversion appeared to be working as successfully as it had done on a previous occasion.

A tense minute passed, a second, and a third, and then from the ridge where I had climbed on to the big slab of rock a karker came dashing down towards me, barking hysterically. The tigress was not coming to the kill but had gone off after Ibbotson. I was now in a fever of anxiety: she had abandoned her kill and gone to try to secure another victim.

Before leaving, Ibbotson had promised to take every precaution, but on hearing the karker barking on my side of the ridge he would naturally assume the tigress was moving in the vicinity of the kill, and if he relaxed his precautions the tigress would get her chance.

Ten very uneasy minutes for me passed, and then I heard a second karker barking in the direction of Thak. The tigress was still following, but the ground there was more open and there was less fear of her attacking the party.

The danger to the Ibbotsons was, however, not over by any means, for they had to go through two miles of very heavy jungle to reach camp; and if they stayed at Thak until sundown listening for my shot, which I feared they would do and which as a matter of fact they did do, they would run a very grave risk on the way down. Ibbotson fortunately realized the danger and kept his party close together, and though the tigress followed them the whole way - as her pug marks the following morning showed - they got back to camp safely.

The calling of karker and sambar enabled me to follow the movements of the tigress. An hour after sunset she was down at the bottom of the valley two miles away. She had the whole night before her and though there was only one chance in a million of her returning to the kill I determined not to lose that chance. Wrapping a rug round me, for it was a bitterly cold night, I made myself comfortable in a position in which I could remain for hours without movement.

I had taken my seat on the machan at 4 p.m. and at 10 p.m. I heard two animals coming down the hill towards me. It was too dark under the trees to see them, but when they got to the lee of the kill I knew they were porcupines. Rattling their quills, and making the peculiar booming noise that only a porcupine can make, they approached the kill and, after walking round it several times, continued on their way.

An hour later, and when the moon had been up some time, I heard an animal in the valley below. It was moving from east to west and when it came into the wind blowing downhill from the kill it made a long pause, then came on cautiously up the hill. While it was still some distance away I heard it snuffing the air, and knew it to be a bear. The smell of blood was attracting him, but mingled with it was the less welcome smell of a human being, and taking no chances he was very carefully stalking the kill. His nose,

the keenest of any animal's in the jungle, had apprised him while
he was still in the valley that the kill was the property of a tiger.
This to a Himalayan bear who fears nothing, and who will, as I
have on several occasions seen, drive a tiger away from its kill, was
no deterrent. What was, and what was causing him uneasiness, was
the smell of a human being mingled with the smell of blood and
tiger.

On reaching the flat ground the bear sat down on his haunches
a few yards from the kill, and when he had satisfied himself that the
hated human smell held no danger for him he stood erect and,
turning his head, sent a long-drawn-out cry, which I interpreted as
a call to a mate, echoing down into the valley. Then without any
further hesitation he walked boldly up to the kill and as he nosed
it I aligned the sights of my rifle on him.

I know of only one instance of a Himalayan bear eating a human
being; on that occasion a woman cutting grass had fallen down a
cliff and been killed, and a bear finding the mangled body had
carried it away and had eaten it. This bear, however, on whose
shoulder my sights were aligned, appeared to draw the line at
human flesh and after looking at and smelling the kill continued his
interrupted course to the west. When the sounds of his retreat died
away in the distance the jungle settled down to silence until
interrupted, a little after sunrise, by Ibbotson's very welcome
arrival.

With Ibbotson came the brother and other relatives of the dead
man, who very reverently wrapped the remains in a clean white
cloth and, laying it on a cradle made of two saplings and rope
which Ibbotson provided, set off for the burning ghat on the banks
of the Sarda, repeating under their breath as they went the Hindu
hymn of praise, 'Ram nam sat hai' with its refrain, 'Satya bol gat
hai'. Fourteen hours in the cold had not been without its effect on
me, but after the hot drink and food Ibbotson had brought, I felt
none the worse for my long vigil.

After following the Ibbotsons down to Chuka on the evening of
the 27th the tigress, some time during the night, crossed the
Ladhya into the scrub jungle at the back of our camp. Through this

scrub ran a path that had been regularly used by the villagers of the Ladhya valley until the advent of the man-eater had rendered its passage unsafe. On the 28th the two mail-runners who carried Ibbotson's dak on its first stage to Tanakpur got delayed in camp and to save time took, or more correctly started to take, a short cut through this scrub. Very fortunately the leading man was on the alert and saw the tigress as she crept through the scrub and lay down near the path ahead of them.

Ibbotson and I had just got back from Thak when these two men dashed into camp, and taking our rifles we hurried off to investigate. We found the pug marks of the tigress where she had come out on the path and followed the men for a short distance, but we did not see her, though in one place where the scrub was very dense we saw a movement and heard an animal moving off.

On the morning of the 29th a party of men came down from Thak to report that one of their bullocks had not returned to the cattle-shed the previous night, and on a search being made where it had last been seen a little blood had been found. At 2 p.m. the Ibbotsons and I were at this spot, and a glance at the ground satisfied us that the bullock had been killed and carried away by a tiger.

After a hasty lunch Ibbotson and I, with two men following carrying ropes for a machan, set out along the drag. It went diagonally across the face of the hill for a hundred yards and then straight down into the ravine. A few hundred yards down the bullock, which was an enormous animal, had got fixed between two rocks and, not being able to move it, the tiger had eaten a meal off its hind quarters and left it.

The pug marks of the tiger, owing to the great weight she was carrying, were splayed out and it was not possible to say whether she was the man-eater or not; but as every tiger in this area was suspect I decided to sit up over the kill. There was only one tree within reasonable distance of the kill and as the men climbed into it to make a machan the tiger started calling in the valley below. Very hurriedly a few strands of rope were tied between two branches, and while Ibbotson stood on guard with his rifle I climbed the tree and took my seat on what, during the next fourteen hours, proved to be the most uncomfortable as well as the most dangerous machan I have ever sat on. The tree was leaning away from the hill, and from the three uneven strands of rope I was sitting on there was a drop of over a hundred feet into the rocky ravine below.

The tiger called several times as I was getting into the tree and continued to call at longer intervals late into the evening, the last call coming from a ridge half a mile away. It was now quite evident that the tiger had been lying up close to the kill and had seen the men climbing into the tree. Knowing from past experience what this meant, she had duly expressed resentment at being disturbed and then gone away, for though I sat on the three strands of rope until Ibbotson returned next morning, I did not see or hear anything throughout the night.

Vultures were not likely to find the kill, for the ravine was deep and overshadowed by trees, and as the bullock was large enough to provide the tiger with several meals we decided not to sit up over it again where it was now lying, hoping the tiger would remove it to some more convenient place where we should have a better chance of getting a shot. In this we were disappointed, however, for the tiger did not again return to the kill.

Two nights later the buffalo we had tied out behind our camp at Sem was killed and through a little want of observation on my part a great opportunity of bagging the man-eater was lost. The men who brought in the news of this kill reported that the rope securing the animal had been broken, and that the kill had been carried away up the ravine at the lower end of which it had been tied. This was the same ravine in which MacDonald and I had chased an earlier tigress, and as on that occasion she had taken her kill some distance up the ravine I now very foolishly concluded that this tigress had done the same with her kill.

After breakfast Ibbotson and I went out to find the kill and see what prospect there was for an evening sit-up. The ravine in which the buffalo had been killed was about fifty yards wide and ran deep into the foothills. For two hundred yards the ravine was straight and then bent round to the left. Just beyond the bend, and on the left-hand side of it, there was a dense patch of young saplings backed by a hundred-foot ridge on which thick grass was growing. In the ravine, and close to the saplings, there was a small pool of water. I had been up the ravine several times in the past and had failed to mark the patch of saplings as being a likely place for a tiger to lie up in. I therefore did not take the precautions I should have taken when rounding the bend, with the result that the tigress who was drinking at the pool saw us first. There was only one safe line of retreat for her and she took it. This was straight up the steep hill, over the ridge, and into sal forest beyond.

The hill was too steep for us to climb, so we continued on up the ravine to where a sambar track crossed it and following this track we gained the ridge. The tigress was now in a triangular patch of jungle bounded by the ridge, the Ladhya, and a cliff down which no animal could go. The area was not large, and there were several deer in it which from time to time advised us of the position of the tigress, but unfortunately the ground was cut up by a number of deep and narrow rain-water channels in which we eventually lost touch with her.

We had not yet seen the kill, so we re-entered the ravine by the sambar track and found the kill hidden among the saplings. These saplings were from six inches to a foot in girth and were not strong enough to support a machan, so we had to abandon that. With the help of a crowbar a rock could possibly have been prised from the face of the hill and a hole made in which to sit, but this was not advisable when dealing with a man-eater.

Reluctant to give up the chance of a shot we considered the possibility of concealing ourselves in the grass near the kill, in the hope that the tigress would return before dark and that we should see her before she saw us. There were two objections to this plan: if we did not get a shot and the tigress saw us near her kill she might abandon it as she had done her other two kills; and between the kill and camp there was very heavy scrub jungle, and if we tried to go through this jungle in the dark the tigress would·have us at her mercy. So very reluctantly we decided to leave the kill to the tigress for the night and hope for the best on the morrow.

On our return next morning we found that the tigress had carried away the kill. For three hundred yards she had gone up the bed of the ravine, stepping from rock to rock and leaving no drag marks. At this spot – three hundred yards from where she had picked up the kill – we were at fault, for though there were a number of tracks on a wet patch of ground, none of them had been made while she was carrying the kill. Eventually, after casting round in circles, we found where she had left the ravine and gone up the hill on the left.

This hill up which the tigress had taken her kill was overgrown with ferns and golden rod and tracking was not difficult, but the going was, for the hill was very steep and in places a detour had to be made and the track picked up further on. After a stiff climb of a thousand feet we came to a small plateau, bordered on the left by a cliff a mile wide. On the side of the plateau nearest the cliff the ground was seamed and cracked, and in these cracks a dense growth of sal, two to six feet in height, had sprung up. The tigress had taken her kill into this dense cover and it was not until we actually trod on it that we were aware of its position.

As we stopped to look at all that remained of the buffalo there was a low growl to our right. With rifles raised we waited for a minute and then, hearing a movement in the undergrowth a little beyond where the growl had come from, we pushed our way through the young sal for ten yards and came on a small clearing, where the tigress had made herself a bed on some soft grass. On the far side of this grass the hill sloped upwards for twenty yards to another plateau and it was from this slope that the sound we had heard had come. Proceeding up this slope as silently as possible we had just reached the flat ground, which was about fifty yards wide, when the tigress left the far side and went down into the ravine, disturbing some kaleege pheasants and a karker as she did so. To have followed her would have been useless, so we went back to the kill and, as there was still a good meal on it, we noted two trees to sit in, and returned to camp.

After an early lunch we went back to the kill and, hampered with our rifles, climbed with some difficulty into the trees we had selected. We sat up for five hours without seeing or hearing anything. At dusk we climbed down from our trees and stumbling over the cracked and uneven ground eventually reached the ravine when it was quite dark. Both of us had an uneasy feeling that we were being followed, but by keeping close together we reached camp without incident at 9 p.m.

The Ibbotsons had now stayed at Sem as long as it was possible for them to do so and early next morning they set out on their twelve-days walk to keep their appointment at Askot. Before leaving, Ibbotson extracted a promise from me that I would not follow up any kills alone, or further endanger my life by prolonging my stay at Sem for more than a day or two.

After the departure of the Ibbotsons and their fifty men the camp, which was surrounded by dense scrub, was reduced to my two servants and myself - my porters were living in a room in the headman's house - so throughout the day I set all hands to collecting driftwood, of which there was an inexhaustible supply at the junction, to keep a fire going all night. The fire would not scare away the tigress, but it would enable us to see her if she prowled round our tents at night, and anyway the nights were setting in cold and there was ample excuse for keeping a big fire going all night.

Towards evening, when my men were safely back in camp, I took a rifle and went up the Ladhya to see if the tigress had crossed the river. I found several tracks in the sand, but no fresh ones and at dusk I returned, convinced that the tigress was still on our side of the river. An hour later, when it was quite dark, a karker started barking close to our tents and barked persistently for half an hour. My men had taken over the job of tying out the buffaloes, a task which Ibbotson's men had hitherto performed, and next morning I accompanied them when they went out to bring in the buffaloes. Though we covered several miles I did not find any trace of the tigress.

Again, as on the previous evening, I crossed the Ladhya, with the intention of taking up a position on a rock overlooking the open ground on the right bank of the river and watching for the tigress to cross. As I got away from the roar of the water at the junction I heard a sambar and a monkey calling on the hill to my left, and as I neared the rock I came on the fresh tracks of the tigress. Following them back I found the stones still wet where she had forded the river. A few minutes delay in camp to have a cup of tea cost a man his life, several thousand men weeks of anxiety, and myself many days of strain, for though I stayed at Sem for another three days I did not get another chance of shooting the tigress.

On the morning of the 7th, as I was breaking camp and preparing to start on my twenty-mile walk to Tanakpur, a big contingent of men from all the surrounding villages arrived and begged me not to leave them to the tender mercies of the man-eater. Giving them what advice it was possible to give people situated as they were, I promised to return as soon as it was possible for me to do so.

I caught the train at Tanakpur next morning and arrived back at Naini Tal on 9 November, having been away nearly a month.

I left Sem on 7 November and on the 12th the tigress killed a man at Thak. I received news of this kill through the divisional forest officer, Haldwani, shortly after we had moved down to our winter home at the foot of the hills, and by doing forced marches I arrived at Chuka a little after sunrise on the 24th.

It had been my intention to breakfast at Chuka and then go on to Thak and make that village my headquarters, but the headman of Thak, whom I found installed at Chuka, informed me that every man, woman and child had left Thak immediately after the man had been killed on the 12th. He added that if I carried out my intention of camping at Thak I might be able to safeguard my own life, but it would not be possible to safeguard the lives of my men. This was quite reasonable, and while waiting for my men to arrive the headman helped me to select a site for my camp at Chuka where my men would be reasonably safe and I should have some privacy from the thousands of men who were now arriving to fell the forest.

On receipt of the divisional forest officer's telegram acquainting me of the kill, I had telegraphed to the tahsildar at Tanakpur to send three young male buffaloes to Chuka. My request had been promptly complied with and the three animals had arrived the previous evening.

After breakfast I took one of the buffaloes and set out for Thak, intending to tie it up on the spot where the man had been killed on the 12th. The headman had given me a very graphic account of the events of that date, for he himself had nearly fallen a victim to the tigress. It appeared that towards the afternoon, accompanied by his grand-daughter, a girl ten years of age, he had gone to dig up ginger tubers in a field some sixty yards from his house. This field is about half an acre in extent and is surrounded on three sides by jungle, and being on the slope of a fairly steep hill it is visible from the headman's house.

After the old man and his grand-daughter had been at work for some time, his wife, who was husking rice in the courtyard of the house, called out in a very agitated voice and asked if he was so deaf that he could not hear the pheasants and other birds that were chattering in the jungle above him. Fortunately for him, he acted promptly. Dropping his hoe, he grabbed the child's hand and together they ran back to the house, urged on by the woman who said she could now see a red animal in the bushes at the upper end of the field. Half an hour later the tigress killed a man who was lopping branches off a tree in a field three hundred yards from the headman's house.

From the description I had received from the headman I had no difficulty in locating the tree. It was a small gnarled tree growing out of a three-foot-high bank between two terraced fields, and had been lopped year after year for cattle fodder. The man who had been killed was standing on the trunk holding one branch and cutting another, when the tigress came up from behind, tore his hold from the branch and, after killing him, carried him away into the dense brushwood bordering the fields.

Thak village was a gift from the Chand Rajas, who ruled Kumaon for many hundreds of years before the Gurkha occupation, to the forefathers of the present owners in return for their services at the Punagiri temples. (The promise made by the Chand Rajas that the lands of Thak and two other villages would remain rent-free for all time was always honoured by the British Government). From a collection of grass huts the village has, in the course of time, grown into a very prosperous settlement with masonry houses roofed with slate tiles, for not only is the land very fertile, but the revenue from the temples is considerable.

Like all other villages in Kumaon, Thak during its hundreds of years of existence has passed through many vicissitudes, but never before in its long history had it been deserted as it now was. On my previous visit I had found it a hive of industry, but when I went up to it on this afternoon, taking the young buffalo with me, silence reigned over it. Every one of the hundred or more inhabitants had fled taking their livestock with them – the only animal I saw in the village was a cat, which gave me a warm welcome; so hurried had the evacuation been that many of the doors of the houses had been left wide open. On every path in the village, in the courtyard of the houses, and in the dust before all the doors I found the tigress's pug marks. The open doorways were a menace for the path, as it wound through the village, passed close to them, and in any of the houses the tigress may have been lurking.

On the hill thirty yards above the village were several cattle shelters, and in the vicinity of these shelters I saw more kaleege pheasants, red jungle fowl, and white-capped babblers than I have ever before seen, and from the confiding way in which they permitted me to walk among them it is quite evident that the people of Thak have a religious prejudice against the taking of life.

From the terraced fields above the cattle shelters a bird's-eye view of the village is obtained and it was not difficult, from the description the headman had given me, to locate the tree where the tigress had secured her last victim. In the soft earth under the tree there were sign of a struggle and a few clots of dried blood. From here the tigress had carried her kill a hundred yards over a ploughed field, through a stout hedge and into the dense brushwood beyond. The footprints from the village and back showed that the entire population of the village had visited the scene of the kill, but from the tree to the hedge there was only one track, the track the tigress had made when carrying away her victim. No attempt had been made to follow her up and recover the body.

Scraping away a little earth from under the tree, I exposed a root and to this root I tied my buffalo, bedding it down with a liberal supply of straw taken from a nearby haystack. The village, which is on the north face of the hill, was now in shadow and if I was to get back to camp before dark it was time for me to make a start. Skirting round the village to avoid the menace of the open doorways, I joined the path below the houses.

This path after it leaves the village passes under a giant mango tree, from the roots of which issues a cold spring of clear water. After running along a groove cut in a massive slab of rock, this water falls into a rough masonry trough, from where it spreads onto the surrounding ground, rendering it soft and slushy. I had drunk at the spring on my way up, leaving my footprints in this slushy ground and on approaching the spring now for a second drink, I found the tigress's pug marks superimposed on my footprints. After quenching her thirst the tigress had avoided the path and had gained the village by climbing a steep bank overgrown with strobilanthes and nettles, and taking up a position in the shelter of one of the houses had possibly watched me while I was tying up the buffalo, expecting me to return the way I had gone. It was fortunate for me that I had noted the danger of passing those open doorways a second time and had taken the longer way round.

When coming up from Chuka I had taken every precaution to guard against a sudden attack, and it was well that I had done so, for I now found from her pug marks that the tigress had followed me all the way up from my camp, and next morning when I went back to Thak I found she had also followed me from where I had joined the path below the houses, right down to the cultivated land at Chuka.

Reading with the illumination I had brought with me was not possible, so after dinner that night, while sitting near a fire which was as welcome for its warmth as it was for the feeling of security it gave me, I reviewed the whole situation and tried to think out some plan by which it would be possible to circumvent the tigress.

When leaving home on the 2nd I had promised that I would return in ten days and that this would be my last expedition after man-eaters. Years of exposure and strain and long absences from home were beginning to tell as much on my constitution as on the nerves of those at home, and if by the 30th November I had not succeeded in killing this man-eater, others would have to be found who were willing to take on the task.

It was now the night of the 24th, so I had six clear days before me. Judging from the behaviour of the tigress that evening she appeared to be anxious to secure another human victim, and it should not therefore be difficult for me in the time at my disposal to get in touch with her. There were several methods by which this could be accomplished and each would be tried in turn.

The method that offers the greatest chance of success of shooting a tiger in the hills is to sit up in a tree over a kill so, if during that night the tigress did not kill the buffalo I had tied up at Thak I would, the following night and every night thereafter, tie up the other two buffaloes in places I had already selected. Failing to secure a human kill it was just possible that the tigress might kill one of my buffaloes, as she had done on a previous occasion when the Ibbotsons and I were camped at Sem in April. After making up the fire with logs that would burn all night, I turned in, and went to sleep listening to a karker barking in the scrub jungle behind my tent.

While breakfast was being prepared the following morning I picked up a rifle and went out to look for tracks on the stretch of sand on the right bank of the river, between Chuka and Sem. The path, after leaving the cultivated land, runs for a short distance through scrub jungle and here I found the tracks of a big male leopard, possibly the same animal that had alarmed the karker the previous night. A small male tiger had crossed and recrossed the Ladhya many times during the past week and in the same period the man-eater had crossed only once, coming from the direction of Sem. A big bear had traversed the sand a little before my arrival, and when I got back to camp the timber contractors complained that while distributing work that morning they had run into a bear which had taken up a very threatening attitude, in consequence of which their labourers had refused to work in the area in which the bear had been seen.

Several thousand men – the contractors put the figure at five thousand – had now concentrated at Chuka and Kumaya Chak to fell and saw up the timber and carry it down to the motor road that was being constructed, and all the time this considerable labour force was working they shouted at the tops of their voices to keep up their courage. The noise in the valley resulting from axe and saw, the crashing of giant trees down the steep hillside, the breaking of rocks with sledge hammers, and combined with it all the shouting of thousands of men, can better be imagined than described.

That there were many and frequent alarms in this nervous community was only natural, and during the next few days I covered much ground and lost much valuable time in investigating false rumours of attacks and kills by the man-eater. The dread of the tigress was not now confined to the Ladhya valley but extended right down the Sarda through Kaldhunga to the gorge, an area of roughly fifty square miles in which an additional ten thousand men were working. That a single animal should terrorize a labour force of these dimensions in addition to the residents of the surrounding villages and the hundreds of men who were bringing foodstuffs for the labourers or passing through the valley with hill produce in the way of oranges, walnuts, and chillies to the market at Tanakpur, is scarcely credible but true.

After breakfast on the morning of the 25th, I took a second buffalo and set out for Thak. The path, after leaving the cultivated land at Chuka, skirts along the foot of the hill for about half a mile before it divides. One arm goes straight up a ridge to Thak and the other, after continuing along the foot of the hill for another half-mile, zigzags up through Kumaya Chak to Kot Kindri.

At the divide I found the pug marks of the tigress and followed them all the way back to Thak. The fact that she had come down the hill after me the previous evening was proof that she had not killed the buffalo. This, though very disappointing, was not at all unusual. Tigers will on occasion visit an animal that is tied up for several nights in succession before they finally kill it, for tigers do not kill unless they are hungry.

Leaving the second buffalo at the mango tree, where there was an abundance of green grass, I skirted round the houses and found number one buffalo sleeping peacefully after a big feed and a disturbed night. The tigress, coming from the direction of the village as her pug marks showed, had approached to within a few feet of the buffalo and had then gone back the way she had come. Taking the buffalo down to the spring, I let it graze for an hour or two and then took it back and tied it up at the same spot where it had been the previous night.

The second buffalo I tied up fifty yards from the mango tree and at the spot where the wailing woman and villagers had met us the day the Ibbotsons and I had gone up to investigate the human kill. Here a ravine a few feet deep crossed the path, on one side of which there was a dry stump and on the other an almond tree in which a machan could be made. I tied up number two buffalo to the stump and bedded it down with sufficient hay to keep it going for several days. There was nothing more to be done at Thak so I returned to camp and, taking the third buffalo, crossed the Ladhya and tied it up behind Sem in the ravine where the tigress had killed one of our buffaloes in April.

At my request the tahsildar of Tanakpur had selected three of the fattest young male buffaloes he could find. All three were now tied up in places frequented by the tigress, and as I set out to visit them on the morning of the 26th I had great hopes that one of them had been killed and that I should get an opportunity of shooting the tigress over it. Starting with the one across the Ladhya, I visited all in turn and found that the tigress had not touched any of them. Again, as on the previous morning, I found her tracks on the path leading to Thak, but on this occasion there was a double set of pug marks, one coming down and the other going back. On both her journeys the tigress had kept to the path and had passed within a few feet of the buffalo that was tied to the stump, fifty yards from the mango tree.

On my return to Chuka a deputation of Thak villagers led by the headman came to my tent and requested me to accompany them to the village to enable them to replenish their supply of foodstuffs. At midday, followed by the headman, his tenants and by four of my own men carrying ropes for a machan and food for me, I returned to Thak and mounted guard while the men hurriedly collected the provisions they needed.

After watering and feeding the two buffaloes I retied number two to the stump and took number one half a mile down the hill and tied it to a sapling on the side of the path. I then took the villagers back to Chuka and returned a few hundred yards up the hill for a scratch meal while my men were making the machan.

It was now quite evident that the tigress had no fancy for my fat buffaloes, and as in three days I had seen her tracks five times on the path leading to Thak, I decided to sit up over the path and try to get a shot at her that way. To give me warning of the tigress's approach I tied a goat with a bell round its neck on the path, and at 4 p.m. I climbed into a tree. Telling my men to return at 8 a.m. the following morning, I began my watch.

At sunset a cold wind started blowing and while I was attempting to pull a coat over my shoulders the ropes on one side of the machan slipped, making my seat very uncomfortable. An hour later a storm came on and though it did not rain for long it wet me to the skin, greatly adding to my discomfort. During the sixteen hours I sat in the tree I did not see or hear anything. The men turned up at 8 a.m. I returned to camp for a hot bath and a good meal and then, accompanied by six of my men, set out for Thak.

The overnight rain had washed all the old tracks off the path, and two hundred yards above the tree I had sat in I found the fresh pug marks of the tigress, where she had come out of the jungle and gone up the path in the direction of Thak. Very cautiously I stalked the first buffalo, only to find it lying asleep on the path; the tigress had skirted round it, rejoined the path a few yards further on and continued up the hill.

Following on her tracks I approached the second buffalo, and as I got near the place where it had been tied two blue Himalayan magpies rose off the ground and went screaming down the hill. From the presence of these birds I immediately knew that the buffalo was dead and that it had been partly eaten and not carried away. I also knew that the tigress was not in the close vicinity.

On arrival at the stump to which it had been tied I saw that the buffalo had been dragged off the path and partly eaten, and on examining the animal I found it had not been killed by the tigress but that it had in all probability died of snake-bite (there were many hamadryads in the surrounding jungles), and that, finding it lying dead on the path, the tigress had eaten a meal off it and had then tried to drag it away. When she found she could not break the rope, she had partly covered it over with dry leaves and brushwood and continued on her way up to Thak. Tigers as a rule are not carrion eaters but they do on occasions eat animals they themselves have not killed.

On my way up from Chuka I had dismantled the machan I had sat on the previous night and while two of my men climbed into the almond tree to make a seat for me - the tree was not big enough for a machan - the other four went to the spring to fill a kettle and boil some water for tea. By 4 p.m. I had had a light meal of biscuits and tea which would have to keep me going until next day and, refusing the men's request to be permitted to stay the night in one of the houses in Thak, I sent them back to camp. There was a certain amount of risk in doing this, but it was nothing compared to the risk they would run if they spent the night in Thak.

My seat in the tree consisted of several strands of rope tied between two upright branches, with a couple of strands lower down for my feet to rest on. When I had settled down comfortably I pulled the branches round me and secured them in position with a thin cord, leaving a small opening to see and fire through. My 'hide' was soon tested, for shortly after the men had gone the two magpies returned, and attracted others, and nine of them fed on the kill until dusk. The presence of the birds enabled me to get some sleep, for they would give me warning of the tigress's approach and with their departure my all-night vigil started.

There was still sufficient daylight to shoot by when the moon, a day off the full, rose over the Nepal hills behind me and flooded the hillside with brilliant light. The rain of the previous night had cleared the atmosphere of dust and smoke and, after the moon had been up a few minutes, the light was so good that I was able to see a sambar and her young one feeding in a field of wheat a hundred and fifty yards away.

The dead buffalo was directly in front and about twenty yards away and the path along which I expected the tigress to come was two or three yards nearer, so I should have an easy shot at a range at which it would be impossible to miss the tigress – provided she came. There was no reason why she should not do so.

The moon had been up two hours, and the sambar had approached to within fifty yards of my tree, when a karker started barking on the hill just above the village. The karker had been barking for some minutes when suddenly a scream which I can only, very inadequately, describe as *'Ar-Ar-Arr'* dying away on a long-drawn-out note, came from the direction of the village. So sudden and so unexpected had the scream been that I involuntarily stood up with the intention of slipping down from the tree and dashing up to the village, for the thought flashed through my mind that the man-eater was killing one of my men. Then in a second flash of thought I remembered I had counted them one by one as they had passed my tree, and that I had watched them out of sight on their way back to camp to see if they were obeying my instructions to keep close together.

The scream had been the despairing cry of a human being in mortal agony, and reason questioned how such a sound could have come from a deserted village. It was not a thing of my imagination, for the karker had heard it and had abruptly stopped barking, and the sambar had dashed away across the fields closely followed by her young one. Two days previously, when I had escorted the men to the village, I had remarked that they appeared to be very confiding to leave their property behind doors that were not even shut or latched. The headman had answered that even if their village remained untenanted for years their property would be quite safe, for they were priests of Punagiri and no one would dream of robbing them. He added that as long as the tigress lived she was a better guard of their property – if guard were needed – than any hundred men could be; no one would dare to approach the village through the dense forests that surrounded it, for any purpose, unless escorted by me as they had been.

The screams were not repeated, and as there appeared to be nothing that I could do I settled down again on my rope seat. At 10 p.m. a karker that was feeding on the young wheat crop at the lower end of the fields dashed away barking, and a minute later the tigress called twice. She had now left the village and was on the move, and even if she did not fancy having another meal off the buffalo there was every hope of her coming along the path which she had used twice every day for the past few days.

With finger on trigger and eyes straining on the path I sat hour after hour until daylight succeeded moonlight, and when the sun had been up an hour my men returned. Very thoughtfully they had brought a bundle of dry wood with them, and in a surprisingly short time I was sitting down to a hot cup of tea. The tigress may have been lurking in the bushes close to us, or she may have been miles away, for after she had called at 10 p.m. the jungles had been silent.

When I got back to camp I found a number of men sitting near my tent. Some of these men had come to inquire what luck I had had the previous night, and others had come to tell me that the tigress had called from midnight to a little before sunrise at the foot of the hill, and that all the labourers engaged in the forests and on the new export road were too frightened to go to work. I had already heard about the tigress from my own men, who had informed me that, together with the thousands of men who were camped round Chuka, they had sat up all night to keep big fires going.

Among the men collected near my tent was the headman of Thak, and when the others had gone I questioned him about the kill at Thak on the 12th of the month when he so narrowly escaped falling a victim to the man-eater.

Once again the headman told me in great detail how he had gone to his fields to dig ginger, taking his grandchild with him, how on hearing his wife calling he had caught the child's hand and run back to the house – where his wife had said a word or two to him about not keeping his ears open and thereby endangering his own and the child's life – and how a few minutes later the tigress had killed a man while he was cutting leaves off a tree in a field above his house.

All this part of the story I had heard before and I now asked him if he had actually seen the tigress killing the man. His answer was 'No' and he added that the tree was not visible from where he had been standing. I then asked him how he knew that the man had been killed and he said because he had heard him. In reply to further questions he said the man had not called for help but had cried out; and when asked if he had cried out once he said, 'No, three times', and then at my request he gave an imitation of the man's cry. It was the same – but a very modified rendering – as the screams I had heard the previous night.

I then told him what I had heard and asked him if it was possible for anyone to have arrived at the village accidentally, and his answer was an emphatic negative. There were only two paths leading to Thak, and every man, woman, and child in the villages through which these two paths passed knew that Thak was deserted and the reason for its being so. It was known throughout the district that it was dangerous to go near Thak in daylight, and it was therefore quite impossible for anyone to have been in the village at eight o'clock the previous night.

When asked if he could give any explanation for screams having come from a village in which there could not – according to him – have been any human beings, his answer was that he could not. And as I can do no better than the headman it were best to assume that neither the karker, the sambar, nor I heard those very real screams – the screams of a human being in mortal agony – for which there was no natural explanation.

When all my visitors including the headman had gone and I was having breakfast, my servant informed me that the headman of

Sem had come to the camp the previous evening. He had left word for me that his wife, while cutting grass near the hut where his mother had been killed, had come on a blood trail, and that he would wait for me near the ford over the Ladhya in the morning. So after breakfast I set out to investigate this trail.

While I was fording the river I saw four men hurrying towards me, and as soon as I was on dry land they told me that when they were coming down the hill above Sem they had heard a tiger calling across the valley on the hill between Chuka and Thak. The noise of the water had prevented my hearing the call and I told the men that I was on my way to Sem and would return to Chuka shortly, and left them.

The headman was waiting for me near his house, and his wife took me to where she had seen the blood trail the previous day. The trail, after continuing along a field for a short distance, crossed some big rocks, on one of which I found the hairs of a karker. A little further on I found the pug marks of a big male leopard, and while I was looking at them I heard a tiger call. Telling my companions to sit down and remain quiet, I listened, in order to locate the tiger. Presently I heard the call again, and thereafter it was repeated at intervals of about two minutes.

It was the tigress calling and I located her as being five hundred yards below Thak and in the deep ravine which, starting from the spring under the mango tree, runs parallel with the path and crosses it at its junction with the Kumaya Chak path. Telling the headman that the leopard would have to wait to be dealt with at a more convenient time, I set off as hard as I could go for camp, picking up at the ford the four men who were waiting for my company to Chuka.

On reaching camp I found a crowd of men round my tent, most of them sawyers from Delhi, but including the petty contractors, agents, clerks, timekeepers, and gangmen of the financier who had taken up the timber and road construction contracts in the Ladhya valley. These men had come to see me in connection with my stay at Chuka. They informed me that many of the hillmen carrying timber and working on the road had left for their homes that morning and that if I left Chuka on 1 December, as they had heard I intended doing, the entire labour force, including themselves, would leave on the same day. They said they were already too frightened to eat or sleep and no one would dare to remain in the valley after I had gone. It was then the morning of 29 November and I told them that I still had two days and two nights and that much could happen in that time, but that in any case it would not be possible for me to prolong my stay beyond the morning of the 1st.

The tigress had by now stopped calling, and when my servant had put together something for me to eat I set out for Thak, intending, if the tigress called again and I could locate her position, to try to stalk her; and if she did not call again, to sit up over the buffalo. I found her tracks on the path and saw where she had entered the ravine, and though I stopped repeatedly on my way up to Thak and listened I did not hear her again. So a little before sunset I ate the biscuits and drank the bottle of tea I had brought with me, and then climbed into the almond tree and took my seat on the few strands of rope that had to serve me as a machan. On this occasion the magpies were absent, so I was unable to get the hour or two's sleep the birds had enabled me to get the previous evening.

If a tiger fails to return to its kill the first night it does not necessarily mean that the kill has been abandoned. I have on occasions seen a tiger return on the tenth night and eat what could no longer be described as flesh. On the present occasion, however, I was not sitting over a kill, but over an animal that the tigress had found dead and off which she had made a small meal. Had she not been a man-eater, I would not have considered the chance of her returning the second night good enough to justify spending a whole night in a tree, particularly when she had not taken sufficient interest in the dead buffalo to return to it the first night.

It was therefore with very little hope of getting a shot that I sat in the tree from sunset to sunrise, and though the time I spent was not as long as it had been the previous night, my discomfort was very much greater. The ropes I was sitting on cut into me, and a cold wind that started blowing shortly after moonrise and continued throughout the night chilled me to the bone. On this second night I heard no jungle or other sounds, nor did the sambar and her young one come out to feed on the fields. As daylight was succeeding moonlight I thought I heard a tiger call in the distance, but could not be sure of the sound or of its direction.

When I got back to camp my servant had tea and a hot bath ready for me, but before I could indulge in the latter - my forty-pound tent was not big enough for me to bathe under - I had to get rid of the excited throng of people who were clamouring to tell me their experiences of the night before. It appeared that shortly after moonrise the tigress had started calling close to Chuka, and after calling at intervals for a couple of hours had gone off in the direction of the labour camps at Kumaya Chak.

The men in these camps, hearing her coming, started shouting to try to drive her away, but so far from having this effect the shouting only infuriated her more and she demonstrated in front of the camps until she actually cowed the men into silence. She then spent the rest of the night moving between the labour camps and Chuka, daring all and sundry to shout at her. Towards morning she had gone away in the direction of Thak, and my informants were surprised and very disappointed that I had not met her. This was my last day of man-eater hunting and, though I was badly in need of rest and sleep, I decided to spend what was left of it in one last attempt to get in touch with the tigress.

The people not only of Chuka and Sem, but all the surrounding villages, and especially the men from Talla Des where some years previously I had shot three man-eaters, were very anxious that I should try sitting up over a live goat for, they said, 'All hill tigers eat goats, and as you have had no luck with buffaloes, why not try a goat?' More to humour them than with any hope of getting a shot, I consented to spend this last day in sitting up over the two goats I had already purchased for this purpose. I was convinced that no matter where the tigress wandered to at night her headquarters were at Thak so at midday, taking the two goats and accompanied by four of my men, I set out for Thak.

The path from Chuka to Thak, as I have already mentioned, runs

up a very steep ridge. A quarter of a mile on this side of Thak the
path leaves the ridge, and crosses a more or less flat bit of ground
which extends right up to the mango tree. For its whole length
across this flat ground the path then passes through dense brushwood, and is crossed by two narrow ravines which run east and
join the main ravine.

Midway between these two ravines, and a hundred yards from the
tree I had sat in the previous two nights, there is a giant almond
tree; this tree had been my objective when I left camp. At this
point the path passes right under the tree and I thought that if I
climbed half-way up, not only should I be able to see the two
goats, one of which I intended tying at the edge of the main ravine
and the other at the foot of the hill to the right, but I should also
be able to see the dead buffalo. As all three of these points were at
some distance from the tree, I armed myself with an accurate 275
rifle, in addition to the 450/400 rifle which I took for an emergency.

I found the climb up from Chuka on this last day very trying, and
I had just reached the spot where the path leaves the ridge for the
flat ground, when the tigress called about a hundred and fifty yards
to my left. The ground here was covered with dense undergrowth
and trees interlaced with creepers, and was cut up by narrow and
deep ravines and strewn over with enormous boulders - a very
unsuitable place in which to stalk a man-eater. However, before
deciding on what action I should take it was necessary to know
whether the tigress was lying down, as she very well might be, for
it was then 1 p.m., or whether she was on the move, and if so in
what direction. So making the men sit down behind me I listened
and presently the call was repeated; she had moved some fifty yards
and appeared to be going up the main ravine in the direction of
Thak.

This was very encouraging, for the tree I had selected to sit in was
only fifty yards from the ravine. After enjoining silence on the men
and telling them to keep close behind me, we hurried along the
path. We had about two hundred yards to go to reach the tree and
had covered half the distance when, as we approached a spot where

the path was bordered on both sides by dense brushwood, a covey of kaleege pheasants rose out of the brushwood and went screaming away. I knelt down and covered the path for a few minutes, but as nothing happened we went cautiously forward and reached the tree without further incident.

As quickly and as silently as possible one goat was tied at the edge of the ravine, while the other was tied at the foot of the hill to the right; then I took the men to the edge of the cultivated land and told them to stay in the upper verandah of the headman's house until I fetched them, and ran back to the tree. I climbed to a height of forty feet and pulled the rifle up after me with a cord I had brought for the purpose. Not only were the two goats visible from my seat, one at a range of seventy and the other at a range of sixty yards, but I could see part of the buffalo, and as the 275 rifle was very accurate I felt sure I could kill the tigress if she showed up anywhere on the ground I was overlooking.

The two goats had lived together ever since I had purchased them on my previous visit and, being separated now, were calling lustily to each other. Under normal conditions a goat can be heard at a distance of four hundred yards, but here the conditions were not normal as the goats were tied on the side of a hill down which a strong wind was blowing, and even if the tigress had moved after I had heard her, it was impossible for her not to hear them. If she were hungry, as I had every reason to believe she was, there was a very good chance of my getting a shot.

After I had been in the tree for ten minutes a karker barked near the spot from which the pheasants had risen. For a minute or two my hopes rose sky-high and then dropped, for the karker barked only three times and ended on a note of inquiry; evidently there was a snake in the scrub which neither he nor the pheasants liked the look of.

My seat was not uncomfortable and the sun was pleasingly warm, so for the next three hours I remained in the tree without any discomfort. At 4 p.m. the sun went down behind the hill high above Thak and thereafter the wind became unbearably cold. For an hour I stood the discomfort and then decided to give up, for the cold had brought on an attack of ague and if the tigress came now it would not be possible for me to hit her. I retied the cord to the rifle and let it down, climbed down myself and walked to the edge of the cultivated land to call up my men.

There are few people, I imagine, who have not experienced that feeling of depression that follows failure to accomplish anything they have set out to do. The road back to camp after a strenuous day when the game-bag is full of hill partridge is only a step compared with the same road which one plods over, mile after weary mile, when the bag is empty. If this feeling of depression has ever assailed you at the end of a single day, when the quarry has only been hill partridge, you will have some idea of the depth of my depression that evening when, after calling up my men and untying the goats, I set off on my two-mile walk to camp. My efforts had not been made only on a single day or my quarry only a few birds, nor did my failure concern only myself.

Excluding the time spent on the journeys from and to home, I had been on the heels of the man-eater from 23 October to 7 November, and again from 24 to 30 November, and it is only those who have walked in fear of having the teeth of a tiger meet in their throat who will have any idea of the effect on one's nerves of days and weeks of such anticipation.

Then again my quarry was a man-eater, and my failure to shoot it would very gravely affect everyone who was working in, or whose homes were in, that area. Already work in the forests had been stopped and the entire population of the largest village in the district had abandoned their homes. Bad as the conditions were they would undoubtedly get worse if the man-eater was not killed, for the entire labour force could not afford to stop work indefinitely, nor could the population of the surrounding villages afford to abandon their homes and their cultivation as the more prosperous people of Thak had been able to do.

The tigress had long since lost her natural fear of human beings, as was abundantly evident from her having carried away a girl picking up mangoes in a field close to where several men were working, killing a woman near the door of her house, dragging a man off a tree in the heart of a village and, the previous night, cowing a few thousand men into silence.

And here was I, who knew full well what the presence of a man-eater meant to the inhabitants and to all the people who passed through the district on their way to the markets or the temples at Punagiri, plodding down to camp on what I had promised others would be my last day of man-eater hunting. It was reason enough for a depression of soul which I felt would remain with me for the rest of my days. Gladly at that moment would I have bartered the success that had attended thirty-two years of man–eater hunting for one unhurried shot at the tigress.

I have told you of some of the attempts I made during this period of seven days and seven nights to get a shot at the tigress, but these were by no means the only attempts I made. I knew that I was being watched and followed, and every time I went through the two miles of jungle between my camp and Thak I tried every trick I have learnt in a lifetime spent in the jungles to outwit the tigress. Bitter though my disappointment was, I felt that my failure was not in any way due to anything I had done or left undone.

My men when they rejoined me said that, an hour after the karker had barked, they had heard the tigress calling a long way off but were not sure of the direction. Quite evidently the tigress had as little interest in goats as she had in buffaloes. Even so it was unusual for her to have moved at that time of day from a locality in which she was thoroughly at home, unless she had been attracted away by some sound which neither I nor my men had heard. It was quite evident that she had gone, and as there was nothing further that I could do I set off on my weary way to camp.

The path, as I have already mentioned, joins the ridge that runs down to Chuka a quarter of a mile from Thak, and when I now got to this spot where the ridge is only a few feet wide and from where a view is obtained of the two great ravines that run down to the Ladhya river, I heard the tigress call once and then again across the valley on my left. She was a little above and to the left of Kumaya Chak, and a few hundred yards below the Kot Kindri ridge on which the men working in that area had built themselves grass shelters.

Here was an opportunity, admittedly forlorn and unquestionably desperate, of getting a shot; still it was an opportunity and the last I should ever have, and the question was whether or not I was justified in taking it.

When I got down from the tree I had one hour in which to get back to camp before dark. Calling up the men, hearing what they had to say, collecting the goats, and walking to the ridge had taken about thirty minutes and, judging from the position of the sun which was now casting a red glow on the peaks of the Nepal hills, I calculated I had roughly half an hour's daylight in hand. This time factor, or perhaps it would be more correct to say light factor, was all-important: if I took the oppportunity it offered and decided to act, the lives of five men would be put at severe risk.

The tigress was a mile away and the intervening ground was densely wooded, strewn over with great rocks and cut up by a number of deep nullahs, but she could cover the distance well within the half-hour - if she wanted to. The critical question I had to decide was, whether or not I should try to call her up. If I called and she heard me, and came while it was still daylight and gave me a shot, all would be well. On the other hand, if she came and did not give me a shot some of us might not ever reach camp: we had nearly two miles to go and the path the whole way ran through heavy jungle, and was bordered in some places by big rocks, and in others by dense brushwood. It was useless to consult the men, for none of them had ever been in a jungle before coming on this trip, so the decision would have to be mine. I decided to try to call up the tigress.

Handing my rifle over to one of the men I waited until the tigress called again and, cupping my hands round my mouth and filling my lungs to their utmost limit, sent an answering call over the valley. Back came her call and thereafter, for several minutes, call answered call. She would come, had in fact already started, and if she arrived while there was light to shoot by, all the advantages would be on my side, for I had the selection of the ground on which it would best suit me to meet her. November is the mating season for tigers and it was evident that for the past forty-eight hours she had been rampaging through the jungles in search of a mate. Now, on hearing what she thought was a tiger answering her mating call, she would lose no time in joining him.

Four hundred yards down the ridge the path runs for fifty yards across a flat bit of ground. At the far right-hand side of this flat ground the path skirts a big rock and then drops steeply, and continues in a series of hairpin bends, down to the next bench. It was at this rock I decided to meet the tigress, and on my way down to it I called several times to let her know I was changing my position, and also to keep in touch with her.

I want you now to have a clear picture of the ground in your mind, to enable you to follow the subsequent events. Imagine a rectangular piece of ground forty yards wide and eighty yards long, ending in a more or less perpendicular rock face. The path coming down from Thak runs onto this ground at its short or south end and, after continuing down the centre for twenty-five yards, bends to the right and leaves the rectangle on its long or east side. At the point where the path leaves the flat ground there is a rock about four feet high. From a little beyond where the path bends to the right, a ridge of rock, three or four feet high, rises and extends to the north side of the rectangle, where the ground falls away in a perpendicular rock face. On the near or path side of this low ridge there is a dense line of bushes approaching to within ten feet of the four-foot-high rock I have mentioned. The rest of the rectangle is grown over with trees, scattered bushes, and short grass.

It was my intention to lie on the path by the side of the rock and shoot the tigress as she approached me, but when I tried this position I found it would not be possible for me to see her until she was within two or three yards, and further, that she could get at me either round the rock or through the scattered bushes on my left without my seeing her at all. Projecting out of the rock, from the side opposite to that from which I expected the tigress to approach, there was a narrow ledge. By sitting sideways I found I could get a little of my bottom on the ledge, and by putting my left hand flat on the top of the rounded rock and stretching out my right leg to its full extent and touching the ground with my toes, retain my position on it. The men and goats I placed immediately behind and ten to twelve feet below me.

The stage was now set for the reception of the tigress, who while these preparations were being made had approached to within three hundred yards. Sending out one final call to give her direction, I looked round to see if my men were all right.

The spectacle they presented would under other circumstances have been ludicrous, but was here tragic. Sitting in a tight little circle with their knees drawn up and their heads together, with the goats burrowing in under them, they had that look of intense expectancy on their screwed-up features that one sees on the faces of spectators waiting to hear a big gun go off. From the time we had first heard the tigress from the ridge, neither the men nor the goats had made a sound, beyond one suppressed cough. They were probably by now frozen with fear - as well they might be - and even if they were I take my hat off to those four men who had the courage to do what I, had I been in their shoes, would not have dreamt of doing. For seven days they had been hearing the most exaggerated and blood-curdling tales of this fearsome beast that had kept them awake the past two nights; and now, while darkness was coming one, and sitting unarmed in a position where they could see nothing, they were listening to the man-eater drawing nearer and nearer. Greater courage, and greater faith, it is not possible to conceive.

The fact that I could not hold my rifle (a D.B. 450/400) with my left hand (which I was using to retain my precarious seat on the ledge) was causing me some uneasiness, for apart from the fear of the rifle slipping on the rounded top of the rock - I had folded my handkerchief and placed the rifle on it to try to prevent this - I did not know what would be the effect of the recoil of a high-velocity rifle fired in this position. The rifle was pointing along the path, in which there was a hump, and it was my intention to fire into the tigress's face immediately it appeared over this hump, which was twenty feet from the rock.

294   MAN-EATER

The tigress, however, did not keep to the contour of the hill, which would have brought her out on the path a little beyond the hump, but crossed a deep ravine and came straight towards where she had heard my last call, at an angle which I can best describe as one o'clock. This manoeuvre put the low ridge of rock, over which I could not see, between us. She had located the direction of my last call with great accuracy, but had misjudged the distance, and not finding her prospective mate at the spot she had expected him to be, she was now working herself up into a perfect fury. Some idea of what the fury of a tigress in her condition can be like may be judged from the fact that not many miles from my home a tigress on one occasion closed a public road for a whole week, attacking everything that attempted to go along it, including a string of camels, until she was finally joined by a mate.

I know of no sound more liable to fret one's nerves than the calling of an unseen tiger at close range. What effect this appalling sound was having on my men I was scared to think. If they had gone screaming down the hill I should not have been at all surprised for, even though I had the heel of a good rifle to my shoulder and the stock against my cheek, I felt the urge to start screaming myself.

But even more frightening than this continuous calling was the fading out of the light. Another few seconds, ten or fifteen at the most, and it would be too dark to see my sights, and we should then be at the mercy of a man-eater plus a tigress wanting a mate. Something would have to be done, and done in a hurry if we were not to be massacred, and the only thing I could think of was to call.

The tigress was now so close that I could hear the intake of her breath each time before she called. She again filled her lungs. I did the same with mine. We called simultaneously. The effect was startlingly instantaneous.

Without a second's hesitation she came tramping with quick steps through the dead leaves, over the low ridge and into the bushes a little to my right front. Just as I was expecting her to walk right on top of me, she stopped. The next moment the full blast of her deep-throated call struck me in the face and would have carried the hat off my head had I been wearing one.

A second's pause, then again quick steps. A glimpse of her as she passed between two bushes. Then she stepped right out into the open and, looking into my face, stopped dead.

By great and unexpected good luck the half-dozen steps the tigress took to her right front carried her almost to the exact spot at which my rifle was pointing. Had she continued in the direction in which she was coming before her last call, my story would have had a different ending, for it would have been as impossible to slew the rifle on the rounded top of the rock as it would have been to lift and fire it with one hand.

Owing to the nearness of the tigress, and the fading light, all that I could see of her was her head. My first bullet caught her under the right eye and the second, fired more by accident than with intent, took her in the throat and she came to rest with her nose against the rock. The recoil from the right barrel loosened my hold on the rock and knocked me off the ledge, and the recoil from the left barrel, fired while I was in the air, brought the rifle up in violent contact with my jaw and sent me head over heels right on top of the men and goats. Once again I take my hat off to those four men for, not knowing but what the tigress was going to land on them next, they caught me as I fell and saved me from injury and my rifle from being broken.

When I had freed myself from the tangle of human and goat legs I took the 275 rifle from the man who was holding it, rammed a clip of cartridges into the magazine and sent a stream of five bullets singing over the valley and across the Sarda into Nepal. Two shots, to the thousands of men in the valley and in the surrounding villages who were anxiously listening for the sound of my rifle, might mean anything. But two shots followed by five more, spaced at regular intervals of five seconds, could only be interpreted as conveying one message: the man-eater is dead.

I had not spoken to my men from the time we had first heard the tigress from the ridge. On my telling them now that she was dead and that there was no longer any reason for us to be afraid, they did not appear to be able to take in what I was saying, so I told them to go up and have a look while I found and lit a cigarette. Very cautiously they climbed up to the rock, but went no further for, as I have told you, the tigress was on the other side.

Late in camp that night, with my men sitting round a camp-fire and relating their experiences to relays of eager listeners, their narrative invariably ended up with, 'and then the tiger whose roaring had turned our livers into water hit the sahib on the head and knocked him down on top of us and if you don't believe us, go and look at his face'. A mirror is superfluous in camp and even if I had had one it could not have made the swelling on my jaw, which put me on milk diet for several days, look as large and as painful as it felt.

By the time a sapling had been felled and the tigress lashed to it, lights were beginning to show in the Ladhya valley and in all the surrounding camps and villages. The four men were very anxious to have the honour of carrying the tigress to camp, but the task was beyond them; so I left them and set off for help.

In my three visits to Chuka during the past eight months I had been along this path many times by day and always with a loaded rifle in my hands and now I was stumbling down in the dark, unarmed, my only anxiety being to avoid a fall. If the greatest happiness one can experience is the sudden cessation of great pain, then the second greatest happiness is undoubtedly the sudden release from great fear. One short hour previously it would have taken wild elephants to have dragged the men from their homes and camps who now, singing and shouting, were converging from every direction, singly and in groups, on the path leading to Thak.

Some of the men of this rapidly growing crowd went up the path to help carry in the tigress, while others accompanied me on my way to camp, and would have carried me had I permitted them. Progress was slow, for frequent halts had to be made to allow each group of new arrivals to express their gratitude in their own particular way. This gave the party carrying the tigress time to catch us up and we entered the village together. I will not even attempt to describe the welcome my men and I received or the scenes of joy I witnessed at Chuka that night.

A hayrick was dismantled and the tigress laid on it, and an enormous bonfire made from driftwood close at hand to light up the scene and for warmth, for the night was dark and cold with a north wind blowing. Round about midnight my servant, assisted by the headman of Thak and Kunwar Singh, near whose house I was camped, persuaded the crowd to return to their respective villages and labour camps and told them they would have ample opportunity of feasting their eyes on the tigress the following day. Before leaving himself, the headman of Thak told me he would send word in the morning to the people of Thak to return to their village. This he did, and two days later the entire population returned to their homes.

After my midnight dinner I sent for Kunwar Singh and told him that in order to reach home on the promised date I should have to start in a few hours, and that he would have to explain to the people in the morning why I had gone. This he promised to do and I then started to skin the tigress. Skinning a tiger with a pocket-knife is a long job, but it gives one an opportunity of examining the animal that one would otherwise not get, and in the case of man-eaters enables one to ascertain, more or less accurately, the reason for the animal having become a man-eater.

The tigress was a comparatively young animal and in the perfect condition one would expect her to be at the beginning of the mating season. Her dark winter coat was without blemish and in spite of her having so persistently refused the meals I had provided for her she was encased in fat. She had two old gunshot wounds, neither of which showed on her skin. The one in her left shoulder had been caused by several pellets of home-made buckshot and had become septic; the skin, when healing, had adhered permanently to the flesh over quite a large surface. To what extent this wound had incapacitated her it would have been difficult to say, but it had evidently taken a very long time to heal and could quite reasonably have been the cause of her having become a man-eater. The second wound, which was in her right shoulder, had also been caused by a charge of buckshot, but had healed without becoming septic. These two wounds, received over kills in the days before she had become a man-eater, were quite sufficient reason for her not having returned to the human and other kills I had sat over.

After having skinned the tigress I bathed and dressed and, though my face was swollen and painful and I had twenty miles of rough going before me, I left Chuka in the best of moods while the thousands of men in and around the valley were peacefully sleeping. I counted myself fortunate in having walked out on my own feet and not been carried out on a cradle in the manner and condition of the man-eater of Thak.

CHAPTER ELEVEN

Sunderbans: The Last Refuge

THE LOWER DELTA of the river Ganges on the border between India and Bangladesh is a vast area of low lying islands, tidal rivers and creeks, covered largely with marsh and jungle, much of it impenetrable except by boat along its countless waterways. This is the Sunderbans, an area which for centuries has been known for its man-eating tigers.

No year passes without some deaths being recorded among the wood cutters, honey collectors and fishermen who, except during the monsoon season, frequent its islands and waterways.

For five or six months in the year, small parties of these people work for their livelihood in the Sunderbans travelling by boat up the creeks and rivers. At close of day, these men do not remain on shore but row their boats to a safe distance from the bank, mooring to long bamboo poles driven firmly into the river or creek bed. After dark, even today, few people will venture ashore for fear of tigers. 'Life remains insecure in the shadow of the man-eater' observes Tahawar Ali Khan, a Pakistani hunter and naturalist, of the threat which the tiger poses to man's endeavours in the Sunderbans.

Every member of a working party in the region knows the risks he runs. With typical fatalism he accepts the possibility that perhaps he or a member of his group may never return home again. His name and a few particulars will then be entered in the official records maintained by the forest department and under the column headed 'Remarks' will be entered the words 'Killed by a tiger'. The sorrowing family will receive the standard compensation of fifty rupees and the vacancy in the work party will be filled by a member of the dead man's family.

The apparent preference of the Sunderban tiger for human beings, in a region with no shortage of natural food, has been known to drive the animal to remarkable lengths: in 1960, for example, a tiger in search of human prey was reported to have swam out and attempted to board a boat moored in a river some distance offshore. In this particular case, according to Tahawar Ali Khan, a government launch had put a visiting party of officials ashore and, as a precautionary measure, then moved away from the bank to anchor in midstream.

It was late in the afternoon, and three members of the crew had remained on board engaged in odd jobs. Suddenly, to their horror, they discovered the forepaws of a tiger clinging to the gunwale. The crew rushed to the edge of the launch and saw a large tiger with his body half out of the water, trying desperately to gain a foothold on the launch which he was trying to board. Fortunately, the vessel rode fairly high in the water, and the tiger was finding it difficult to pull himself up.

After gaping incredulously for a second, the men seized bamboo mooring poles lying on the deck which they used to beat the tiger on his face and paws. He roared in protest, but did not relinquish his foothold on the launch. When the bamboo poles split and became useless, one of the men then snatched a kettle of boiling water from the galley and poured this over the tiger. Though maddened with agony, he still held on bravely and would not yield.

The three men were by this time frantic with worry and fear in face of the tiger's determination to try and haul himself aboard. Yells and further thrusts with poles proved of no avail, and it was only when a steel bar was heated red hot in the launch's boiler and used against him that the tiger finally yielded and let go his hold on the boat.

The Sunderbans have had a long history of man-eating tigers and western accounts of their activities first started to emerge with the foundation of Calcutta as an important centre of British India.

Calcutta is approached from the Bay of Bengal along the Hooghly Channel and on its eastern side there lies a jungle covered area, Sagar Island. Towards the end of the eighteenth century, a sailing vessel, having taken a longer passage than expected, ran out of provisions and water and a party of six went ashore on this island to replenish their supplies.

The party strayed a considerable distance from the shore in search of coconuts for which the island was known. Later, with darkness coming on, it was decided to lodge for the night in the ruins of an old pagoda rather than to attempt to return to the vessel. A large fire was lit and it was agreed that two men would keep guard in turns, with an engraver named Dawson taking the first watch. In the night a tiger, undeterred by the fire, rushed in and, seizing Dawson, sprang off with him in his jaws. In doing so, tiger and victim struck the side of the pagoda, rebounding upon the fire over which both rolled, before the man was carried off. In the morning a search-party from the ship found the thighs and legs of the poor victim, mangled and stripped of all flesh.

News of this tragedy was apparently reported widely, including in the official *Annual Register,* but the fate of Dawson was apparently not known to a crew from a ship, the *Ardasier Shaw*, which put ashore at Sagar Island a few years later in December 1792. Captain Consar, the ship's master and one of the party who landed to shoot deer, recorded subsequent events.

We saw innumerable tracks of tigers and deer; but still we were induced to pursue our sport and did so the whole day. About half-past three we sat down on the edge of the jungle to eat some cold meat, sent to us from the ship, and had just commenced our meal when Mr Pyefinch and a black servant told us there was a fine deer within six yards of us.

Captain Downey and I immediately jumped up to take our guns; mine was nearest, and I had just laid hold of it when I heard a roar like thunder, and saw an immense royal tiger spring on the unfortunate Munro, who was sitting down; in a moment his head was in the beast's mouth, and it rushed into the jungle with him with as much ease as I could lift a kitten, tearing him through the thickest bushes and trees, everything yielding to its monstrous force. The agonies of horror, regret, and fear rushed on me at once, for there were two tigers; the only effort I could make was to fire at the tiger, though the poor youth was still in its mouth. I relied partly on Providence, partly on my own aim, and fired a musket, saw the tiger stagger and agitated, and cried out so immediately. Captain Downey then fired two shots and I one more; we retired from the jungle and a few minutes afterwards Mr Munro came up to us all over blood, and fell.

We took him on our backs to the boat, and got every medical attendance for him from the *Valentine*, Indiaman, which lay at anchor near the island, but in vain. He lived twenty-four hours after, but in the extreme of torture; his head and skull were all torn and broken to pieces, and he was also wounded by the animal's claws all over the neck and shoulders; but it was better to take him away, though irrecoverable, than to leave him to be devoured limb by limb. We have just read the funeral service over his body and committed it to the deep.   He was an amiable and promising youth.

I must observe there was a large fire blazing close to us composed of ten or a dozen whole trees; I made it myself on purpose to keep tigers off, as I had always heard it would. There were eight or ten of the natives with us, and many shots had been fired at the place, and much noise and laughing at the time, but this ferocious animal disregarded all.

The human mind cannot form an idea of the scene; it turned my very soul within me. The beast was about four and a half feet in height and nine feet long. His head appeared as large as that of an ox, his eyes darting fire, and his roar when he first seized his prey will never be out of my recollection. We had scarcely pushed our boat from that cursed shore when the tigress made her appearance, almost raging mad, and remained on the sand as long as the distance would allow me to see her.

In the intervening years since these early events, the islands of the Sunderbans have yielded little of their potential for tragedy. Tahawar Ali Khan, who has known the area well in more recent times, relates two encounters he has had with Sunderban tigers.

I. The Man-eater of Raimangal Island

The border between India and Bangladesh follows an imaginary line from the Bay of Bengal north along the Harinbhang and Raimangal rivers. Lying between the two, extending fifteen miles by two miles in size, is Raimangal Island.

It is difficult to imagine a wilder spot on the face of the earth. Within the island's forty-five square miles of dense swamp forest, man-eating tigers have taken a heavy toll of human life, and are credited with killing more than two hundred men in just the ten years that passed after the birth of East Pakistan [later Bangladesh] in 1947.

Men were afraid to go near the island, and the forest department experienced great difficulty in leasing timber-felling and fishing rights in the area on account of its sinister reputation. Any party that returned whole from the Raimangal territory at the end of the working season considered itself exceptionally fortunate; some gangs lost two men in a single day.

Fishermen stuck to their boats as much as possible, and generally avoided the narrow creeks where there was danger from the banks. Most casualties, therefore, occurred among the wood cutters, whose profession took them inside the forests. There they worked in tight groups, and a person who strayed twenty or thirty yards from the main party courted almost certain disaster, so that even private natural functions had to be performed within a protecting ring of comrades. The men had learned from bitter experience that a person squatting still while relieving himself behind a bush was the easiest and most logical prey for a lurking man-eater.

I originally heard about the Raimangal man-eaters from the secretary to the Governor of East Pakistan at the time, during one of my periodical visits to Dacca, the provincial capital. Afterwards, I learned a little more about them from friends who had attempted to shoot the man-eaters from machans built in trees.

It seemed that about half-a-dozen tigers were operating in the territory, all of them either established or suspected man-eaters, of these one old animal in particular - a huge male with a pronounced limp in the left foreleg - was the most savage man-killer of the lot, and was responsible for most of the deaths that had occurred in the area. He was reputed to be active along the foot of the island near the sea, and although a few shikaris had sat up for him over live baits, he had never taken one and eluded all hunters' efforts. In every case, the tiger was always too suspicious and never stepped out of the dense cover into the clearing.

As a rule, man-eating tigers prefer human to other flesh and they seldom accept a live bait unless they are hungry and unable to find a human victim. But as men generally avoid Raimangal territory, human flesh was always in short supply. It was a measure of this man-eater's extreme wariness that he nevertheless still rejected baits set out for him.

In most cases, shooting from a tree over a kill or a live bait is the only way in which a man-eater can be destroyed. I must confess that I do not have the patience and iron control necessary for a successful hunt from a machan. That is why I have always preferred to hunt tigers on foot and this fact, coupled with the Raimangal tiger's disdain for baits, meant that this was the only means by which I could hope to meet up with the animal.

I was taken to Raimangal Island by the divisional forest officer's launch. We branched off from the Raimangal river into the Talpatti Khal, a creek which crosses the man-eater territory diagonally in a south-west direction till it joins the Harinbhang river on the other side, about three miles from the toe of the island. It was early in the afternoon when we dropped anchor in the Khal about a hundred yards from its mouth. Six of us, including the forest officer and Abdul Razzak, the forest guard, (together with a goat for possible use as a bait, against my better judgement), set off in a dinghy to explore the foot of the island.

We entered the Raimangal estuary and then headed into a tiny creek and stepped ashore. As we did so, the boatman drew our attention to an object about half a mile away, moving across the beach towards the jungle. It was being baited by hundreds of screaming gulls, and I saw through my binoculars that it was a tiger walking leisurely along the shore. I watched him for a couple of minutes as he came closer, but his coat seemed in perfect condition and there was no sign of a limp. It was apparently not the old man-eater that I was after but, as all tigers in the area were under suspicion, I decided to investigate the animal from closer range.

Checking my rifle and working a cartridge into the chamber, I sprinted along the beach, watching the tiger all the time. To my astonishment, the tiger suddenly disappeared from the open beach as if the ground had swallowed him up. The birds, however, clearly indicated that the animal was still there, and I concluded that he was hiding in a depression. There was a high dune ahead of me about twenty yards from the edge of the forest and, as this was an excellent observation post, I climbed it and looked over the top through my binoculars.

About five hundred yards away, a long narrow depression extended into the forest and it looked like the old bed of a creek which had silted up. In this depression, some sort of struggle seemed to be going on and, despite the noise made by the birds, I could hear the faint squealing of a pig and short angry roars of a tiger. A few moments later, the combatants came into view. A huge boar, its skin almost ripped off its back, was struggling desperately in the grip of the tiger, who had seized the boar's hindquarters between his forepaws and was backing slowly towards the jungle with his screaming victim.

The boar was resisting the pull by digging its feet into the soft ground and straining in the opposite direction, but it could not break away from the claws that held it, and was leaving deep drag marks on the channel bed. Evidently, the hold was not a satisfactory one from the tiger's point of view, because he frequently straightened his hindlegs and leaned forward over the boar for the fatal neck-hold. Recognising the deadly threat, the boar would whip round with a rapid shuffle of its front feet and lunge ferociously at the tiger's flank, making him hop sideways on his hindlegs to avoid being slashed open by the curving tusks.

After a few minutes, the badly wounded boar began to weaken from pain and loss of blood, and this gave the tiger the opportunity he was looking for. With a roar he bore down with all his weight on the stricken animal's rump till the boar's hindlegs buckled under it. Then, with a quick movement, the tiger lifted up his right leg and, reaching forward over the boar, thumped it down on its neck in a short and powerful jab like the punch of a forging hammer. The rest of the action was too fast for me to follow but, within a second, the boar was lying on its side with a twisted neck between the tiger's jaws and was then carried away into the jungle.

After examining the ground on which the grim struggle had taken place, my companions and I walked along the beach for two or three miles, and saw several sets of pug marks left by at least two different tigers. None of the prints were large enough to belong to the old man-eater, nor did the tracks indicate a limping animal. It was fairly late in the evening when eventually we turned back, so far without a sign of the tiger. Then, when we were about fifty yards from the boat, my heart missed a beat and I stopped dead in my tracks: stretching across the beach from jungle to boat were large pug prints of a tiger. No trace of them had been there when we passed earlier. Examination showed they were the Raimangal man-eater's.

Because tigers in the Sunderbans sometimes seize human prey from boats which by accident drift close to the river bank, it is a safe bet that any tiger which goes fearlessly right up to a boat - empty or otherwise - is a man-eater. In this case, the tiger had not only approached the boat, but had also made a closer inspection, placing his forepaws on a wooden seat on which he had left his muddy prints. Disappointed in his search, he cut up the soft ground with fretful pacings by the side of the boat, after which he walked a few yards along the creek and then crossed it, as shown by his tracks leading into the water.

I was quite certain that the tiger was watching us from cover somewhere and would continue to do so as long as we remained in the area. In the circumstances, sitting up for him in a tree during the night would have been a waste of time. Nevertheless, we staked the goat a short distance inside the forest by the side of the man-eater's track. Though against all expectations, if the tiger did return along the same path and make his kill during the night, he would possibly leave a trail for me to follow early in the morning.

It was nearly dark when we returned to the boat. As the tiger had crossed the creek and there was some chance of encountering him on the other side, I decided to walk back to the launch along the beach, which ran right round the foot of the island. The forest officer tried to reason with me, but finally gave me up as a madman, and wisely decided to stick to the boat. The forest guard and two other men volunteered to go with me, for which I was grateful, because the support of an additional gun would be comforting, and I also needed a man to hold the shooting lamp and another to carry a wicker basket containing the battery.

After ferrying us across the creek, the boat went down to the estuary and then followed parallel to us in shallow water close to the shore. I had fixed up the shooting lamp, and one of my men was alternately directing the powerful beam towards our left and right to guide the boat and scan the forest respectively. I kept a distance of ten to fifteen yards between ourselves and the edge of the jungle; it was short enough a distance to tempt the tiger to attack us from cover, and long enough to allow a quick shot in the event of an attack.

I walked closest to the forest. In front of me and to my left was the man with the shooting lamp, with the battery carrier walking beside him. Abdul Razzak followed immediately behind me on the left, both barrels of his gun loaded with ball cartridges. We scanned every isolated bush and depression on the beach very carefully before approaching it, but I felt really exposed to danger only when the light beam swung away from the jungle towards the boat, leaving us momentarily blinded in the gloom. Had the man-eater chosen that moment to charge out at us, we would have been at a great disadvantage.

We had gone barely a furlong from the creek, when our friend with the shooting lamp suddenly shouted 'Bacho! Sher hai !' (Look out! Tiger!) and dropped to the ground, flat on his face. The lamp flew out of his hand and landed on the soft sand with its beam pointing to the sky. I brought the rifle butt sharply to my shoulder and spun round to face the forest. Fortunately, nothing happened, and I spoke harshly to the man on the ground and told him to pick up the lamp. He recovered his wits after a few moments and pointed the beam into the jungle where, he told me in a cracked voice, the tiger had been crouched for a spring.

It would have been foolish to risk a closer investigation at that time and after a few minutes we resumed our journey. The men with the lamp and the battery were definitely panicky and I decided to stick to the shoreline instead of walking along the forest. We now felt absolutely safe and never thought of looking back over our shoulders to make sure we were not being followed. Had we done so, the Raimangal man-eater may have been killed on the beach that night. In the morning, we were shocked to discover his footprints almost superimposed on ours from the point where my friend with the lamp had seen him all the way to the mouth of the Talpatti Khal. He had followed us for more than six miles in the night over the open beach and we had been quite unaware.

Signs on the ground told us where he had shovelled out sand with his feet and concealed himself in the shallow pit about two hundred yards from the entrance to the Khal, where the dinghy had picked us up to ferry us to the launch. He then cut across the beach, entered the jungle, and came out on the Khal bank to observe the launch. The soft earth showed where his belly had rested as he sat facing the launch lying twenty yards from the bank.

The tiger then walked downstream and crossed the Khal near its junction with the river. In view of the strong tidal currents, we naturally looked for his footprints farther down the Khal on the opposite bank, but we were amazed to see them directly opposite the spot where he had entered the water. The tiger had swam straight across the fast-flowing creek as if through still water.

After crossing the Khal, the man-eater walked upstream and sat down again on the bank to observe the launch. He then recrossed the Khal and entered the jungle, where we lost his trail. Had anyone been sleeping outdoors on the deck, the tiger may have attempted to board the vessel to snatch a victim; but it was late winter, and we all slept behind closed doors and fastened shutters, and so the tiger went without a meal.

We learned all these things in the morning when we discovered and followed the tiger's footprints and other signs which he had left on the ground during the night. This evidence provided a clear picture of his activities and told us that the man-eater was a persistent, patient and extremely wary animal who knew when the odds were against him. He could, therefore, be tempted to attack only when the odds were narrowed down in his favour, and so I decided to hunt him with the assistance of only one other man, preferably Abdul Razzak.

(The goat, which figures no more in this story, was recovered unharmed in the morning and later was given away to an old woman whose husband had been killed while collecting honey in the Sunderbans).

Soon after lunch, two badly frightened men in a boat brought us news that their companion had been killed by a big tiger only a couple of hours earlier by the side of one of the creeks flowing off the Talpatti Khal. They were fishing in the creek, and had rowed to the bank to collect some dry twigs to cook their meal. Two of them remained in the boat while the third man stepped out to gather wood at the edge of the forest only half-a-dozen paces away. A couple of minutes later, the bushes parted right behind the unfortunate man and a tiger suddenly appeared. Rearing up on its hindlegs, the animal brought its paws down on the unsuspecting fisherman's shoulders, burying its teeth into the man's neck and then, lifting him off his feet, the tiger whirled round and went back into the jungle without a sound either from the tiger or its victim. The horrified men in the boat rowed for their lives and, after collecting their nets, came to report the incident to the forest officer.

In spite of the fear which the killing had inspired, the fishermen bravely volunteered to return to the spot with me and wait in midstream while I attempted to follow up the kill. Abdul Razzak and I got into their boat and after travelling upstream for a while we turned into a creek flowing south. On our right was the forest in which we had lost the man-eater's trail in the morning and, as the killing had occurred about two-and-a-half miles farther down on the same side of the creek, I felt fairly certain that the same tiger was responsible for it. Having been frustrated in his night-long search for human prey, he had attacked the first unarmed man he had seen in the morning. As we went farther down the creek it divided and sub-divided in a very confusing pattern, and it was a little past 2 p.m. when we reached the spot where the tiger had claimed his victim.

I loaded and checked my rifle and also the guard's double-barrelled 12-bore gun. After instructing the fishermen to wait in the creek, we got out of the boat and examined the ground. There was no longer any doubt that we were once again on the tracks of the Raimangal man-eater: his characteristic pug marks, which we had learned to recognise since the previous evening, showed clearly in the soft ground.

The trail led us about fifty yards into the jungle to a large pool of blood, around which some shreds of clothing were scattered. Many flies and hornets had settled on the gore, but about ten yards beyond in the heavy scrub a dense swarm of flies indicated where the kill itself was lying. The manner in which the swarm was settling down also showed that the tiger was not sitting on the kill, because when flies annoy a feeding or resting tiger, he snaps at them angrily and lashes out with his tail, causing the swarm to rise up suddenly and hover in the air before settling down again. The absence of an upward disturbance of the swarm is a clear sign that the tiger is not present.

We proceeded cautiously through the undergrowth, as the tiger might still have been lying up somewhere close by, and peered over the bushes at the body which lay in a small open depression. The tiger must have been ravenously hungry because in a little under five hours he had devoured about half the body, leaving only the portion above the lowest ribs and parts of the legs for subsequent meals. The animal was so glutted when he abandoned his kill, probably in search of water to slake his thirst, that he had been sick on the way.

Thinking that we might find the tiger asleep after his heavy meal, we took up his trail again, and had hardly taken a dozen paces forward when I noticed a slight movement in the bushes ahead of us. Signalling to my companion to watch over the top, I lay down on the ground to look through the stripped under-portion of the bushes. Less than fifteen yards away the tiger moved diagonally across us to the right, and I saw his legs through the intervening screen. There was no point in attempting a shot from that position, and so I watched the animal till he disappeared from view.

It is a matter of common observation that when an animal suspects that he is being trailed, his normal gait and behaviour will alter noticeably. His pace will quicken, he will become furtive in his movements, he will occasionally pause to look back over his shoulder and he will try to dodge his pursuer. But, as far as I could judge from what I had seen of the tiger for a couple of minutes, he was unaware that we were trailing him. This, of course, made our task easier and somewhat less dangerous. I was relying on the soft and damp ground to show up the animal's pug marks distinctly and so, after giving the tiger a start of about five minutes, we followed watchfully in his tracks.

What a chase the tiger led us. The trail turned in all directions in the forest, then ran along the banks of several creeks that forked out from each other, only to re-enter the forest on a zig-zag course till we wondered if we could find our way back to the fishermen who waited for us.

After an hour of this grim and tiring game of 'follow the leader,' I was conscious of something vaguely disturbing about our surroundings. Then, suddenly, I saw something on the ground that froze me to a standstill. About two yards on my right, and curving parallel to the track that we were following, was another set of the tiger's pug marks, and by the side of it were the prints of my rubber-soled boots and the forest guard's bare feet. This meant that the tiger had led us round in a narrowing circle, and while we were trailing him, he too was trailing us from behind. We were passing through the same portion of the jungle that we had covered minutes before.

With the sudden realisation that the guard who was following close behind me was in danger of an attack from the rear, I hissed out a warning and told him to get down. Simultaneously, I turned right about on my heels with the rifle against my shoulder, just in time to see the tip of the tiger's tail disappear behind a sprawling chest-high thicket about twenty yards away. Another minute would have been too late, and the man-eater would most certainly have crept up on the unsuspecting forest guard and killed him. My warning shout and our sudden hostile movements had upset the tiger's stalk and he had immediately tried to hide behind the nearest thicket, from where he was undoubtedly watching us. This was isolated from other bushes by ten to fifteen yards in all directions, so that it was now impossible for the tiger to get away without exposing himself on open ground. He had trapped himself, and if he could be forced to break cover, a quick shot could bring him down.

I outlined the situation to my companion without relaxing my vigilance, and told him to turn around and cover the thicket with his gun also. We waited for nearly ten minutes with weapons pointed and safety catches off, but the tiger never moved. It is quite possible that an intelligent animal like he realised that escape from his position had become difficult. The stalemate could not continue indefinitely and so I decided to force the issue. With a pincer movement in mind, I asked the guard to take the left flank while I approached the concealed tiger from the right.

The tiger uttered a low threatening growl as the distance between us and the thicket closed to about ten yards. Then I saw his tail go up behind the bush, and I braced myself for the charge. It came a second later, as the tiger sprang right over the thicket towards Razzak, who was about five yards away on my left. The whole length of the tiger's body had cleared the top of the bush when my 375 Magnum soft-nosed bullet hit him in the side.

With a roar, the tiger twisted his body sideways in the air and fell on the ground a few paces beyond the forest guard. I immediately pulled back the bolt to eject the spent cartridge, worked it forward and down in order to reload and was about to fire a second time at the tiger, who was recovered and rushing away, but was prevented by Razzak who now stood directly in the line of fire.

The tiger tore madly into heavy undergrowth, which shook violently for a few moments as he escaped through it. We raced after him to the fringe of the undergrowth and heard the tiger moaning with pain about ten yards inside. There was a large tree growing nearby and we climbed into it to spot the animal from above and shoot him if possible. The tiger may have seen us when we were climbing because, when we looked down, we saw the tops of bushes move more than fifty yards away, and then a solitary monkey sitting in a tree nearby gave an alarm call. We could see from our observation post that the undergrowth extended to the edge of a narrow creek which we had crossed earlier when we were trailing the tiger. The wounded animal was making for the water and was likely to cross over into another part of the forest.

The monkey went on calling for several minutes, and when it quietened down we descended from the tree and went about ten yards into the undergrowth where the tiger had rested. Here we saw a large pool of blood. From this point, the tiger had left a clear trail marked by blood-spattered leaves, but we turned back at this point as it was extremely dangerous to follow up a freshly wounded tiger through such heavy undergrowth. Authorities consider that at least twenty-four hours should elapse before a wounded tiger is pursued, but the forest guard and I were of the opinion that the man-eater was not likely to live another twelve hours at the rate at which he was losing blood. We therefore decided to return to the launch and come back the next morning with two or three other shikaris to track down the tiger.

We broke off two leafy branches from a tree and laid them on the ground in the form of an 'x' to mark the spot from which we could pick up the trail on the following morning, and returned to the creek together with the remains of the fisherman. The two men, who were waiting for us anxiously in the boat, buried their comrade quickly on the bank of the creek, while Abdul Razzak and I mounted guard with our guns.

The two fishermen did not turn up the next morning, and after waiting for them for more than an hour, five of us set off in a canoe – three forest guards including Abdul Razzak, a boatman and I. We went up the Khal and then about three miles down the creek flowing south before I realised that we had taken the wrong turning somewhere, and had missed the side creek which was our objective. We rowed up and down, trying one creek after another until we became hopelessly confused and lost our bearings alto-gether. Of the five men in the boat, only Razzak and I knew the site of the killing, and both of us had lost our sense of direction.

In the Sunderbans, only the rivers, key channels, important island groups and forest stations are known by name. The thousands of creeks that wiggle through the delta are unidentified except by visual recognition. They do not figure even on the maps. It is only your sense of direction, therefore, which enables you to locate a particular creek, which you then identify by sight – a case rather similar to that of a very short-sighted man who cannot look for his spectacles unless his is wearing them!

Well past noon we were still searching for the elusive creek. The boatman had become quite exhausted, and we all took turns with the oar but made little headway against the tidal current. Our rendezvous with the launch was at 4 p.m., but we decided to go back and make a fresh attempt on the following day. We seemed to be the only human beings in the wilderness and there was nobody to guide us back to the launch. The Talpatti Khal joined the Harinbhang river on the western side of the island, and so we followed the sun in our amateurish navigational effort to break out towards our starting point.

Unfortunately, the convolutions of the creeks thwarted our attempts to maintain a westerly course. We would follow a creek flowing due west by the sun, and then find that it swung north or south, or even doubled back in a U-turn. Late in the afternoon, tired and aching in every limb, we gave up the attempt for the day. We fired a few shots in the air in the hope of attracting the attention of any boatmen in the neighbourhood. There was no response, and so we passed a hungry, cold and thoroughly miserable night in the boat.

The next day, we just let our boat drift down a broad creek, hoping that we would ultimately reach the sea. To our great relief this plan succeeded and we reached the Raimangal estuary at noon. We were now in familiar waters and had only to go round the toe of the island to where our worried friends would be waiting for us.

The launch was not there when we entered the Talpatti Khal, and I learned later that, after waiting for us all night, the divisional forest officer had gone out to look for our party fully convinced that the worst had happened. He searched for us for nine hours before returning to the anchorage to await news of the disaster.

While we were discussing our next move, a party of fishermen came down the Khal, and we discovered that they knew the place we were looking for, having passed and spoken to the two fishermen who had been waiting for Razzak and me in the creek while we had been tracking the tiger. They consented to act as our guides, and so we set off once more and reached our destination by 4 p.m.

We found the crossed branches lying undisturbed on the ground, and immediately picked up the trail of the wounded man-eater. The bloodstains had darkened to a brownish black; when the tiger was on the move he had left occasional drops of blood on the ground and leaves, but the blood at the places where he had rested from exhaustion had formed pools.

Following up a wounded tiger through heavy brush is a most nerve-shattering experience, especially when the tiger is known to be a man-eater. A startled sparrow suddenly taking off from a bush in front of you can cause your heart to leap into your mouth. A beetle tapping on a root can sound like the snapping of a dry twig under a stealthy paw. A yellowing leaf shaking under the weight of a tiny butterfly can look like the twitching ear of an angry tiger. Time seems to stand still and all the human senses become intensely concentrated. The nervous tension becomes unbearable. Every inch of ground has to be probed and re-probed by anxious and suspicious eyes; every sound has to be listened for, analysed and explained; and every step has to be taken with the knowledge that a wrong one can be your last. Always expect the unexpected, otherwise you are liable to lose your life.

The old man-eater of Raimangal was dead when we found him. He had died two days earlier when the solitary monkey had given his prolonged alarm call from the tree that grew near the narrow creek. He was lying in the shallow stream with the ebb tide flowing gently past him.

II. The Chandpai Tiger

I went up to Khulna from the Sunderbans in February 1957 to replenish my stock of provisions and attend to some business affairs. Finishing my work in a few days I then set out for the Sunderbans for the five or six weeks of the working season that remained, accompanying the ranger in charge of the Chandpai forest station who was returning to his headquarters.

We stopped overnight at Chalna Port twenty miles downstream of Khulna, a deep water anchorage for ocean-going steamers which come up the Passar river from the Bay of Bengal.

Taking advantage of the outgoing tide, we resumed our journey in the morning and crossed the official forest boundary into Sunderbans proper twelve miles from Chalna. The cultivated fields and villages of the settled areas terminated suddenly at the boundary on the right bank of the river, but continued for another eight miles along the left bank to where the Chachan Ganga flows into the Passar from the north-east forming an acute angle of about thirty degrees with it.

At the junction of the two waterways, our launch turned almost right round and headed up the Chachan Ganga which flows in a semi-circular arc between the Passar and the Bhola Ganga rivers, separating the settled areas in the north from the wild forests of the south. The Chandpai forest station is situated about a mile-and-a-half up the channel on its left (or northern) bank, and almost directly opposite the station on the far bank is the entrance to the Mirgamari creek which cuts eastward through forests of goran and golpatta trees.

The Pakistan [now Bangladesh] portion of the Sunderbans contained within the forest boundary is divided into fifty-five timber felling zones called compartments, with the Chandpai forest station in compartment 28 which, for some unexplained reason, lies between compartments 26 and 27. No man-eater had ever been reported in these three compartments, and the tigers seen on rare occasions seemed content with the flesh of wild game and were easily scared away by men working in the forests. Sometimes a tiger would stray into the adjoining settled areas and kill a grazing cow or buffalo, but otherwise they caused very little trouble.

This picture was dramatically changed on the morning of 23 February when a tiger killed a man in compartment 27 - the day we arrived at Chandpai - and then crossed over to compartment 26 to kill another man on the following day.

It was about 10 o'clock in the morning when our launch left the Passar river and entered the Chachan Ganga, and the ranger and I were sitting on the tiny deck enjoying the pleasant sunshine. We were about to pass a canoe going in the same direction when we noticed that the boatman sitting in the stern was waving his oar at us and shouting something that we could not make out because of the fairly stiff cross breeze.

The pilot, too, must have noticed the agitated manner of the boatman because he tugged at the rope which rang a bell in the engine room. The launch hove to and began to drift gently with the current, while the boatman swung his canoe round and paddled towards us vigorously. Apart from him there was one other occupant who was sitting astride the prow of the boat with his bare feet almost dipping into the water. He was a tall leathery man about 50 years old, with a strikingly high and broad forehead and a white goatee. As the boat came nearer I heard the sound of this man's wailing which, in the Sunderbans, usually means one thing: that a close relative has been killed by a man–eater.

We took the weeping man by his arms and helped him aboard, and in reply to an inquiring glance the boatman said laconically: 'A tiger killed his younger brother. We were going up to the station to report and the others are following with the body.' The ranger nodded, dismissed the boatman and the launch resumed its journey.

We made the grief-stricken man drink a cup of tea and tried to soothe him, but he was inconsolable, wailing and striking his forehead with the palm of his hand. Seeing him in this state, nobody could have thought that only an hour earlier Muhabbat Ali had displayed extraordinary courage in fighting off the attack of a man-eating tiger.

Our launch made fast at the foot of a ladder attached to a rough landing stage. Scores of canoes and country barges were moored along the bank and the forest station, which was the only human dwelling in Chandpai, was crowded with men who had come to secure work permits, negotiate leases or pay royalties.

The station was the ranger's office-cum-residence and it was a pretty picture in the wilderness with its gabled, red painted corrugated iron roof and ornamental wooden railings round the verandah; its trim lawn was surrounded by a fence of golpatta matting with tamarind trees beyond growing tall and straight like coconut palms. The bungalow was built about four feet above the ground on timber piles as protection against damp, high tides and, to some extent, wild animals.

Half an hour after our arrival, the body of the man-eater's victim was brought by his relatives in a sheet of cloth and placed before us on the lawn. Examination revealed that the neck had been seized and broken by the tiger. Both shoulders bore claw marks and the right collar bone had been fractured. The body, however, was whole, which indicated that it had been recovered before the tiger could start his meal. After formal identification the corpse was removed and covered with a sheet to await burial, while two elderly kinsmen sat near it and recited verses from the Quran in low tones.

Detailed questioning of the men who were eye-witnesses to the attacked followed, and then the ranger and I left with a few people to investigate the site of the incident for supporting evidence. We had with us two expert trackers, and with their help we filled in the gaps in the stories of the witnesses and built up a complete picture of the events that preceded the actual attack.

Muhabbat Ali and his brother Afsar Ali, who was only 27 years old when he died, were sons of Zahiruddin, a veteran wood cutter of Kandapara village near Bagerhat. The elder son was a wood cutter like his father, but the younger looked after the land and cattle owned by the family. He was respected and admired by the villagers because he had learned to read and write from a moulvi who led the prayers in the mosque of a large neighbouring village. When the father became too old to wield the axe, the youngest son stepped into his place while the old man stayed behind to tend the fields with the help of his son-in-law. The two brothers, accompanied by a few relatives and fellow villagers, arrived at the Chandpai forest station on 18 February 1957, and began to cut golpatta fronds in compartment 27 after securing the necessary work permits.

They worked hard for five days till Thursday evening when they knocked off in a happy mood because Friday was the day of rest and would be spent in reconnoitring the creeks for good work sites. Early in the morning the brothers set out, the elder sitting in the rear of their canoe and plying the oar, with his brother up forward. Their companions had gone ahead of them and the two men were following about a quarter of a mile behind.

Less than half an hour later, Afsar Ali saw a big tiger standing on the creek's left bank a stone's throw away. He called out to his brother, standing up in the boat waving his dao (jungle-cutting knife) and yelling at the top of his voice. Muhabbat Ali also joined in and they laughed when the tiger slunk away into the forest. The tiger then preceded the boat to a spot about three hundred yards away, keeping inside the forest on a track parallel to the creek. The brothers did not realise that the man-eater had by then marked down his next victim.

From the clear evidence of the tiger's pug marks and other signs on the ground, I was later able to establish the movements of the man-eater after his disappearance into the forest with the help of two expert trackers. I came to the conclusion that the tiger was originally drawn to the bank by the sounds of the party that had gone ahead of the brothers, and reached there in time to see the last canoe in the procession.

The animal then marked down Afsar Ali who had drawn attention to himself by standing up in the boat, waving his dao and yelling loudly. The tiger probably chose not to attack the boat in that area because the bank was very soft and narrow which made it difficult for him to spring into the boat which was in the middle of a ten-yard wide creek. He therefore hid himself and followed the creek through the forest till he reached a good spot from which he could attack. The tiger's selection of this piece of ground and the method of attacking was almost scientific, and I believe is the only recorded example of its kind.

The selected ground was a narrow clearing in the forest, curtained off from the creek by a large and leafy sundri tree that grew on the edge of the bank and leaned outwards a little. Its trunk forked out four feet above the ground and formed a wide 'v'. Near the other end of the clearing, about ten yards from the tree, was a gently sloping grass-covered mound eight to nine feet high. The tiger climbed this mound and lay down in the grass directly facing the tree. From this position he could only look into the creek through the 'v'.

As soon as he sighted the prow of the boat, the tiger charged from the mound and sprang through the 'v'. His hindlegs slipped on the damp ground when he leaped upwards, however, and instead of going clean through the 'v' he struck against the left fork (from which we later recovered some hairs and a shred of his skin). This deflected his course and, missing Afsar Ali sitting in the bow, he fell in the middle of the boat.

After a moment of stunned surprise Muhabbat Ali, who was seated in the rear, brought his oar crashing down on the tiger. The confused and badly shaken animal collected himself, turned round and leaped back to the bank with such force that he overturned the canoe, spilling both men into the water. He then stood on the bank, roaring angrily at the terrified brothers who yelled back and rapped the boat hull with their hands until, to their great relief, the tiger went away.

They righted the canoe and pulled away as fast as they could, shouting at the top of their voices for their friends who had heard the commotion and hailed them. The brothers were exhausted when they rejoined their comrades, describing what had befallen them on the way. After resting and smoking for a while, the entire party moved on and entered a wider creek on the left which was lined with dense clumps of golpatta. Not wishing to return with empty boats, the men then decided to work for a couple of hours. The recent incident initially made them cautious; they stuck close together and posted a man as look-out. But the animal had been scared away on two separate occasions by the brothers, when they were practically unarmed, and as time passed, the men relaxed their vigilance. The tiger was therefore able to approach them undetected.

Baulked of his prey on the first attempt, the tiger had retired in disappointment and rage but he was determined to make up for his failure. Later examination of the ground showed that after jumping back from the boat, the tiger went into the forest and prowled about restlessly, as shown by his tracks crossing each other several times in both directions over a length of about twenty yards. He then followed the boat, sat down behind cover while the men were bunched together to hear the story of the attack, and when the party moved into the wider creek the tiger was close behind in the forest. He first hid in the undergrowth while the men deployed for work and then worked his way round in a wide arc to within eight or nine yards of the spot where Afsar Ali was working. Here he sat on his haunches in a depression behind the stump of a tree felled by a storm, probably watching his quarry through the narrow clearance between the stump and the ground.

Muhabbat Ali was working only three or four paces away from his brother and he glanced at the young man as he casually placed his dao on the ground and straightened up to remove a thorn from his finger. In that brief interval, the tiger bounded silently over the trunk of the tree. Muhabbat Ali heard a strangled shout which sounded like *bhaiyya* (brother) and saw the tiger stand on his hindlegs with his forepaws on Afsar Ali's shoulders and his jaws fastened round his neck.

Yelling with terror, the victim's kinsmen and friends scattered in all directions, flinging away their heavy daos and axes, diving into their boats or climbing the nearest trees. The only man who did not waver for an instant was the elder brother. He gazed in horror as Afsar Ali struggled vainly in the grip of the tiger, and then a demonic fury seized him and in a voice of thunder he roared in Bengali: 'Leave him!' Simultaneously, he rushed forward with upraised dao and, grabbing his brother round the waist, struck the tiger a heavy blow on the side of his neck.

The tiger uttered a deafening roar as the blood spurted from him and, relinquishing his death-hold, withdrew a few paces towards some bushes. Muhabbat Ali laid his dying brother gently on the ground and then rose to meet the tiger who had turned around to seize his victim once more. Grasping the handle of his blood-stained dao with both hands and shouting '*Yaa Ali* ', the age-old battle-cry of the Muslims, he advanced on the tiger who first took a couple of steps towards him and then stood, uncertainly, snarling and tail twitching. The gap between man and beast closed to less than a yard and Muhabbat Ali's dao swung in a blow which could have cut the head clean from the body, but the tiger stepped backwards and then withdrew, roaring, as he went deep into the jungle. Muhabbat Ali immediately rushed to his brother's side, while the other men descended from the trees and returned from their boats, shouting to each other with anxious enquiries. Muhabbat

Ali knelt down and lifted his brother's head tenderly to his bosom. Life was ebbing from Afsar Ali who, feeling his brother's touch, tried to speak. No sound came, but his lips shaped themselves weakly for the Bengali word 'jal ' (water).

But all the drinking water was stored in large earthen pitchers on their barge more than two miles away. Muhabbat Ali's reason seemed to desert him momentarily as he dashed about aimlessly like a mad person, whimpering 'Jal! Jal! Jal! ' He then sat down by his dead brother's side, tearless and wordless, perhaps remembering the happy days when the family was whole, and thinking of his aged parents and a widowed girl.

The tiger disappeared deep into the forest, crossing or leaping over several minor creeks, and we lost his trail after following it for over a mile. Blood from the dao wound led to the edge of a broad creek, indicating that the tiger had crossed over. We could not, however, pick up the trail on the other bank as the incoming tide had swamped the area. When the chase was abandoned, the tiger was travelling south-west towards Mirgamari creek, beyond which was the boundary of compartment 26.

At 8 o'clock on the following morning, Abdul Jabbar, a brawny middle-aged man from Noakhali, was cutting golpatta by the side of a narrow creek in compartment 26 when he looked up and saw a tiger gazing at him from the other bank. He shouted a warning to his four companions and they all took refuge in nearby trees. The tiger crossed the creek and, as he turned to go along the bank to the right, a raw dao wound showed clearly on the left side of his neck.

When the men recognised the tiger, they shouted loudly from the trees to frighten the animal away. The man-eater stood on the bank for a few minutes, looking towards the trees and growling. He then went away along the bank, but the men waited in the trees for another hour before they dared to descend and make for their boats. As a precautionary measure they decided to pass the morning in their canoes, only returning to work after the midday meal.

The men were very watchful and bunched together while working in the afternoon and, as a precaution, they decided to knock off for the day at about 4 o'clock. While the others were wiping their sweaty bodies and putting on their shirts, Abdul Jabbar moved away four or five paces to pass water. Just then, the wounded tiger stepped out of a thicket and pounced on him.

The man screamed and put his hands out in a futile attempt to ward off the attacker, but the raking claws tore his face to shreds and Jabbar fell on the ground with the tiger on top of him. His terror-stricken companions first ran for their lives, but after covering a hundred yards or so they stopped. They then plucked up courage and went back towards their comrade. They were horrified to see that the tiger was devouring his victim on the spot where he had killed him. Standing a hundred feet away, the men yelled and brandished their axes, but the tiger paid them scant attention, snarling occasionally as he tore large lumps of flesh from his victim's buttocks.

When their attempts to drive away the tiger proved unsuccessful, the wood cutters climbed into a large tree and shouted to attract the attention of some passing boatmen. In due course, one of these boatmen arrived at the Chandpai forest station and gave us news of the latest tragedy.

On seeing us arrive, the frightened men descended from the tree and ran towards us shouting that the tiger had carried away the partly eaten body of their comrade into the jungle a quarter of an hour earlier, and they pointed out the route taken by him. We heard a brief account of the tragedy and told the men to report later at the station for detailed questioning. It was too late in the evening to follow up the tiger in the dense forest and so we decided to pick up the trail early next day. We reasoned that as the tiger was suffering from a bad wound and was very hungry, he would lie up near his kill after a heavy meal and we might succeed in tracking him down in the morning.

From the ranger and the forest guards who knew the territory well, I gathered that we stood on a small island which was shaped roughly like an elongated leaf, encircled by a large creek. The wood cutter had been killed about a hundred yards from the western tip of the island. To check this information, we circled the island in our boats on a quick reconnaissance. I noticed that the forest ended up about two hundred yards short of the eastern tip at the edge of an extensive shallow depression which was over-grown with tall grass standing shoulder high. Near the tip itself was a large mound of clay covered with bushes.

A plan began to take shape in my mind and I discussed it with the ranger as we bent over a forest department map of the area after dinner. It was agreed that three parties would assist in the morning to hunt the tiger – two of them covering the forest from the encircling creek, and the third party covering the grass patch at the eastern end of the island from the mound near the tip, thus cutting off all escape routes of the tiger. I would then follow the man-eater's trail into the jungle in the hope of at least driving him out towards the waiting guns in case I could not kill him myself.

Accordingly, when morning came, armed men in boats were posted in the two creeks at roughly one hundred yard intervals, and four men were placed behind the bushes on the mound so that they could look down into the depression and command the entire grass patch with their guns. The trap was set and it remained for me to close it.

I picked up the trail from the spot where Abdul Jabbar had been killed, and followed it for more than a hundred yards into the forest where the tiger had beaten a recognisable path through heavy undergrowth. Dense thickets limited visibility on the ground to only three or four yards and I found the going very difficult. I imagined a wounded man-eater waiting for me behind every bush, and my eyes ached with the strain of watching every inch of ground. With the rifle held in the crook of my arm, I used the barrel to part the bushes gently before stepping forward.

It took me almost half an hour to cover barely a hundred yards. Then I was suddenly aware of a faint, sickly smell. I stood perfectly still, perhaps for a couple of minutes, and then crept forward very cautiously until I reached some tall bushes which had arched over to meet at the top, leaving a kind of tunnel at the bottom a little over two feet high. The tiger had forced himself and his human burden through the gap and the sides of the tunnel showed traces of blood and lumps of flesh. I dropped on my hands and knees to look through. There was a small clearing at the other end five yards away. The man-eater was breakfasting on a human leg and looking straight into my eyes.

I instantly threw myself flat on the ground and brought up the rifle to point along the tunnel, but the tiger was too quick for me. With a fierce growl, he sprung to his feet and leaped sideways out of my sight. One second faster and I might have dropped him by the side of the man he had killed. But one second is a long time in the jungle, and a tenth of it can make all the difference between success and failure, and frequently between life and death.

The rustling of bushes told me that the tiger had gone away diagonally towards the left, and I consoled myself with the thought that he would walk into the trap which I had laid for him outside the forest. Making a wide detour to the right to avoid the dense undergrowth to which the tiger could possibly return, I stepped into the clearing where the abandoned body lay. It was safer there because the tiger would have to come at me across a stretch of open ground if he decided to return to his kill. I thought of climbing a tree to sit over the kill but decided against it. When I was fairly satisfied that there was no immediate danger, I collected the remains of the wood cutter in his shirt, snapped off a branch from a tree, and suspended the gory bundle from the stump so that it could be easily located and recovered later on.

When I had finished this unpleasant task, I heard shouts and the sound of several gunshots from the direction in which the man-eater had gone, followed immediately by a tremendous roar from the tiger. He then roared three or four times more at short intervals, giving me a rough fix on the direction in which he was moving, which appeared to be from north to south in front of me across the width of the island.

The roars indicated that the tiger had been painfully wounded by the gun-fire and I ran forward across the clearing with the rifle tucked against my side. I stopped short of where I expected the tiger to cross and sat down between two dense thickets with the rifle at the ready against my shoulder. In this position I was quite safe from attack from either flank and was absolutely confident of meeting any attack from the front. Only my back was exposed, but I was reasonably certain that there was no danger from that quarter, though I did look behind me occasionally to satisfy myself.

Later examination of the ground revealed that the wounded tiger dragged himself to within eighteen yards of me when I was waiting for him so confidently between the thickets. I have never been able to understand how he came so close without my knowing it. The tiger had been hit in the front knee when the ranger and his men fired at him from the northern creek. Yet, crippled as he was, he limped in the direction of his kill, saw me from a distance of eighteen yards, and turned right around in his tracks to make for the eastern tip of the island. And I did not see him, or even suspect his presence. What masterly use of cover despite the agonising pain from his disabled leg.

And so it happened that the Chandpai Tiger, after killing two men on two successive days, limped painfully into the final trap.

As he came out of the forest and dragged himself into the depression to rest and lick his wounds in the tall grass, four guns fired simultaneously from the mound. He turned round to face the mound and, lifting his head, roared with pride and defiance. Another volley then crashed out, and the Chandpai Tiger slowly toppled over on his side and lay still.

Epilogue

A SMALL UNIT of British soliders once made a journey through the Aberdare mountain region of Kenya. At night they slept in the open without cover and, rashly, were apparently not in the habit of building a thorn fence or fire for their protection.

One night towards the end of their trek, with no guard posted, their camp was visited by a full-grown lioness. She stalked silently up to the sleeping men and, after carefully stepping over several prostrate figures, then attacked one of the soldiers, Jason James, seizing him by the right thigh and prepared to drag him away. 'I thought it was cramp,' he said later, recalling the severe pain as he was suddenly awakened. 'I poked my head out of my sleeping bag and saw the lioness. I just yelled and she ran off.'

For the rest of that long, sleepless night a full guard was mounted around the camp-site but the lioness did not return to the scene of her attack. Jason James' injuries, made by the lioness' tusks as they took hold of his thigh, were prevented from being any more severe by a book which the soldier had had in a pocket of his trousers as he slept. The wounds nevertheless required three weeks treatment in hospital before they were free of the danger of infection and had satisfactorily healed.

There was no evidence to link the lioness in this incident with any other attacks on human beings but, accidentally or not, she had taken her first step in the descent towards a man-eating career.

Nothing was particularly notable about the circumstances of this attack: its equivalent or worse has been repeated countless times in east Africa over the years. As such it is, perhaps, barely worthy of mention – except that this camp night attack by a lioness is not taken from the annals of man-eater encounters which occurred a generation or more ago.

It took place in January, 1991.

Bibliography

Aflalo, F.G.A: A Book of the Wilderness and Jungle (London, 1926)

African Wild Life, Vol 1, No. 1, October 1946 [Stevenson-Hamilton J.:
    Lions – as I Knew them]

African Life, Vol. 2., No.10. May 1959 [McCaffery, Jean:
    Mgori's Man-eater]

Allen, H: The Lonely Tiger (London, 1960)

Anderson, Kenneth: Man-eaters and Jungle Killers (London,1957)

  This is the Jungle (London, 1964)

  Tales from the Indian Jungle (London,1970)

  Man-eaters and Memories (London, 1970)

Ansorge, W.J: Under the African Sun (London, 1899)

Apponyi, H: My Big Game Hunting Diary (London, 1937)

Baines, Thomas: The Northern Goldfield Diaries. Oppenheimer Series
    N.3, (London, 1946)

Baker, E.: Sports in Bengal (London, 1887)

Baker, Sir Samuel W.: Wild Beasts and their Ways (London, 1890)

Baldwin, J.: The Large and Small Game in Bengal and the
    North-western Povinces of India (London, 1883)

Baldwin, William Charles: African Hunting – from Natal to the
    Zambesi (London, 1863)

  African Hunting and Adventure (London, 1894)

Ball, V: Jungle Life in India (London, 1880)

Barth, Henry: Travels and Discoveries in North and Central Africa
    (London, 1890)

Bazé, W.: Tiger! Tiger! (London, 1957)

Beaton, K. de P.: A Warden's Diary, 2 Vols (Nairobi, 1949)

Best, J.W.: Tiger Days (London, 1931)

  The Marked Man-Eater (London, 1934)

  Forest Life in India (London, 1935)

Bradley, M.H: Trailing the Tiger (London, 1930)

Brander, A.D.: Wild Animals in Central India (London, 1923)

Brown, C.A.: Claws, the Tale of a Lion (London, 1938)
Burchell, William J.: Travels in the Interior of South Africa
        (London, 1953)
Burke, R.St.G: Jungle Days (London, 1935)
Burton, R.G: A Book of Man-Eaters (London, 1931)
    The Book of the Tiger (London, 1934)

Cameron, V.L.: Across Africa (London, 1877)
Campbell, Dugald: Wanderings in Wildest Africa (London, 1931)
Campbell, Walter: The Old Forest Ranger (London, 1853)
Cardinall, A.W.: In Ashanti and beyond (London, 1927)
Carrington Turner, J.E: Man-Eaters and Memories (London, 1959)
Casserly, G: In the Green Jungle (London, 1927)
    Dwellers in the Jungle (London, 1925)
Chaillu, P.B. du: Explorations and Adventures in Equatorial Africa
        (London, 1861)
Chanler, W.A: Through Jungle and Desert. Travels in Eastern Africa
        (London, 1896)
Chapman, Abel: Memories of four-score years less two, 1851-1929
        (London, 1930)
Christy, C.: Big Game and Pygmies (London, 1924)
Clark, James L.: Trails of the Hunted (London, 1929)
Cloudsley-Thompson : Animal Twilight (London, 1967)
Comyn, D.C.E.Ff: Service and Sport in the Sudan (London, 1911)
Cooch Behar, Maharajah of: Thirty-seven Years' Big Game Shooting
        (London, 1908)
Corbett, J: Man-Eaters of Kumaon (London, 1944)
    The Man-eating Leopard of Rudraprayag (London, 1948)
    The Temple Tiger (London, 1952)
    My India (London, 1952)
    Jungle Lore (London, 1953)

Daly, M: Big Game Hunting and Adventure 1897-1936 (London,
    1937)
Davies, D (Gouldsbury, C.E): Tiger Slayer by Order (London, 1916)
Dewar, D: Beasts of an Indian Village (London, 1923)
Dickinson, F.A.: Big Game Shooting on the Equator (London, 1908)
    Lake Victoria to Khartoum (London, 1910)
Digby, D: Tigers, Gold and Witchdoctors (London, 1928)

Donaldson-Smith, A.: Through unknown African Countries
(London, 1897)

Dugmore, A. Radcliffe: African Jungle Life (London, 1928)

Dunbar-Brunton, James: Big Game Hunting in Central Africa
(London, 1912)

Dunton, S: Hold That Tiger (London, 1959)

Eardley-Wilmot, E: The Life of a Tiger (London, 1911)

Elliott, J.G: Field Sports in India (n.d.)

Field, D: Jungle Jottings (London, 1936)

Fitzpatrick, D: Jock of the Bushveld (London, 1907)

Fletcher, F.W.F.: Sport on the Nilgiris and in Wynaad
(London, 1911)

Foa, E: After Big Game in Central Africa (London, 1899)

Foran, W.R: Kill or be Killed (London, 1933)

Forsyth, J.: The Highlands of Central India (London, 1872)

Gee, E.P.: The Wild Life of India (London, 1964)

Gibbons, A.S.H: Exploration and Hunting in Central Africa
(London, 1898)

Gilmore, P: Encounters with Wild Beasts (London, 1905)

Glasford, A.I.R: Leaves from an Indian jungle (Bombay, 1903)
    Rifle and Romance in the Indian Jungle (London, 1905)

Gordon-Cumming, Col. R.G.: Wild men and wild beasts
(London, 1871)
    Five Years of a Hunter's Life (London, 1850)

Gouldsbury, C.E: Tiger Slayer by Order (London, 1916)

Guggisberg, C.A.W.: Game Animals of Eastern Africa (Nairobi, 1949)

Hamilton, D.: Records of Sport in Southern India (London, 1892)

Handley, L.M.H: Hunter's Moon (London, 1933)

Hanley, P.: Tiger Trails in Assam (1961)

Herbert, Agnes: Two Dianas in Somaliland (London, 1908)

Hewett, J.: Jungle Trails in Northern India (London, 1938)

Hicks, F.: Forty years among the wild animals of India (Allahabad, 1910)

Hinde, S.L. and H.: The last of the Masai (London, 1901)

Hill, M.F.: Permanent Way, the Story of the Kenya Uganda Railway
(Nairobi, n.d.)

Hodson, A.W.: Trekking the Great Thirst (London, 1912)
    Where Lion reign (London, 1920)
Hoefler, Paul: Africa speaks – a story of Adventure (London, n.d.)
Hornaday, W.T: Two Years in the Jungle (London, 1885)
Horthy, Eugene de: The Sport of a Lifetime (London, 1939)
Hubbard, W.D: Ibamba (London, 1963)
Hutchinson, Horace G. (Ed): Big Game Shooting (London, 1905)
    [Bryden H.A.: The Lion]
Huxley, E: Forks and Hope. An African Notebook (London, 1964)

Inglis, James: Tent Life in Tigerland (London, 1888)
Irby, A.H: The Diary of a Hunter (London, 1863)

Jeary, Bertram F.: Pride of Lions (London, 1936)
Johnson, D.: Sketches of Indian field sports with observations on the
    animals (London, 1827)
Johnson, Martin: Over African Jungles (London, 1935)
Johnston, H.H.: The Uganda Protectorate (London, 1902)

Kearton, Cherry: In the Land of the Lion (London, 1929)
Kenya Game Department: Annual Reports 1951, 1953/4
Khan, Tahawar Ali: Man-eaters of Sunderbans (Lahore, 1961)
Kipling, L: Beasts and Man in India (London, 1891)
Kirby, F. Vaughan: Sport in East Central Africa (London, 1899)
Kittenberger, Kalman: Big Game Hunting and collecting in East Africa
    (London, 1929)
Knowles, G.H: Terrors of the Jungle (London, 1932)
Koch-Isenburg, L: Through the Jungle Very Softly (London, 1963)
Krapf, J.L: Travels, Researches and Missionary Labours (London, 1860)

Landor, A. Henry Savage: (or Savage-Landor, A. Henry):
    Across Wildest Africa (London, 1907)
Leveson, H.A: Sport in Many Lands (London, 1877)
Locke, Colonel A: The Tigers of Trengganu (London, 1954)

Maydon, H.C.: Big Game Shooting in Africa (London, 1932)
Medway, Lord: The wild mammals of Malaya and offshore islands
    including Singapore (Kuala Lumpur, 1969)
Meikle, R.S: After Big Game (London, n.d.)

Meinertzhagen, R: Kenya Diary 1902-1906 (Edinburgh and
        London, 1959)
Mellis, C.J.: Lion hunting in Somaliland (London, 1895)
Mitchell, K.W.S: Tales from Some Eastern Jungles (London, 1928)
Mockler-Ferryman, A.F: The Life Story of a Tiger (London, 1910)
Moray Brown, J: Shikar Sketches (London, 1887)
Mosse, A.H.E.: My Somali Book (London, 1913)

Ness, B: Ten Thousand Miles in two Continents (London, 1929)

Okeden, W.P: Diary and Sporting Journal of India: 1821-41
        (London, 1928)
Oswell, W. Edward: William Cotton Oswell, Hunter and Explorer
        (London, 1900)

Peacock, E.H.: A game book for Burma and adjoining territories
        (London, 1933)
Pease, A.E.: Travel and Sport in Africa (London, 1902)
Percival, A. Blainey: A Game Ranger's Note Book (London, 1927)
Perry, R.: The World of the Tiger (London, 1964)
Pienaar, A.A.: The Adventures of a Lion Family and other Studies of
        Wild Life in East Africa (London, 1923)
Pierce, Francis B: Rambles in Lion Land (London, 1898)
Pitman, C.R.S: A Game Warden among his Charges (London, 1931)
        Game Warden in Uganda (London, 1942)
Pollock, F.T: Incidents of Foreign Sport and Travel (London, 1894)
        Fifty Years' Reminiscences of India (London, 1896)
Powell-Cotton, P.H.G.: A Sporting Trip to Abyssinia (London, 1902)
        In Unknown Africa (London, 1904)
Powell, A.N.W.: The Call of the Tiger (London, 1957)
Prater, S.H.: The Book of Indian Animals (Bombay, 1971)

Rainsford, W.S. The Land of the Lion (London, 1909)
Rice, W.: Hunting experiences on foot in Rajpootana (London, 1857)
Roscoe, John: The Soul of Central Africa (London, 1922)

Sanderson, G.P: Thirteen Years among the Wild Beasts of India
        (London, 1878)
Schaller, G.: The Deer and the Tiger (Chicago, 1967)

Selous, Frederick C.: A Hunter's Wanderings in Africa (London, 1895)
    Travels and Adventures in South East Africa (London, 1893)
    African Nature Notes and Reminiscences (London, 1908)
Shakespeare, Capt. Henry: From the Wild Sports of India (London,1860)
'Silver Hackle': Man-eaters and other Denizens of the Indian Jungle
        (London, 1928)
Singh, Arjan: Tiger Haven (London, 1973)
Singh, Colonel K: The Tiger of Rajasthan (London, 1959)
Sirgnja, R.S.S: Tiger Shooting (London, n.d.)
Smythies, E.: Big game shooting in Nepal (London, 1942)
Southworth, A.S: Four thousand miles of African Travel
        (New York, 1875)
Stebbing, E.P: Jungle Byways in India (London, 1911)
Stebbing, J.: Diary of a Sportsman and Naturalist in India (London, 1920)
Stevenson-Hamilton, J: Animal Life in Africa (London, 1912)
    Wild Life in South Africa (London, 1954)
Stewart, A.E.: Tiger and Other Game (London, 1927)
Stigand, C.H., and Lyell, D.D.: Central African Game and its Spoor
        (London, 1906)
Stigand, C.H.: The Game of British East Africa (London, 1913)
Strachan, A.: Mauled By a Tiger (London, 1933)
Stuart Baker, E.C: Mishi The Man-Eater (London, 1928)
Sutherland, James: Adventures of an Elephant Hunter (London, 1912)

Taylor, John: Pondoro – Last of the Ivory Hunters (London, 1956)
    Man-Eater and Marauders (London, 1959)
Taylor, M.L: The Tiger's Claw (London, 1956)
Temple-Perkins, E.A.: Kingdom of the Elephant (London, 1955)
Thomas, H.B., and Scott, Robert: Uganda (London, 1949)

Vaidhya, S: Ahead Lies the Jungle (London, 1958)

Wardrop, A.E.: Days and Nights with Indian Big Game (London, 1923)
Watteville de, Vivienne: Speak to the Earth (New York, 1935)
Webber, T.W: The Forests of Upper India (London, 1902)
Wells, Eric F.V.: Lions wild and friendly (London, 1933)
Weinholt, Arnold: The Story of a Lion Hunt (London, 1922)
Willoughby, Sir John C.: East Africa and its Big Game (London, 1889)
Wilmot, E. Cronje: Always lightly tread (Cape Town, n.d.)

Wolhuter, Harry: Memoirs of a Game Ranger (South Africa, 1948)
Woodyat, N.: Sporting Memories (London, 1923)

Ylla, and Leakey, L.S.B.: Animals of Africa (London, 1953)
Ylla: Animals in India (London, 1958)

Index

Vita Sackville-West
Passenger to Teheran

with a new introduction by Nigel Nicolson

In the spring of 1926 Vita Sackville-West travelled to Persia to visit her husband, Harold Nicolson, who was at the British Legation, going by way of Egypt, India and Iraq and returning later that year through Russia, newly communist, and revolution-torn Poland. The route was circuitous and the pace leisurely, though not without excitement, and the result is a lively and reflective book of travels.

The author begins with the provocative statement that 'there is no greater bore than the travel bore' and then by her own account of the journey disproves it. She is eloquent about her journey and adventures, drawn towards the geographic remoteness and simplicity of life she encounters, but is humorous too, her reactions often less than discreet.

Her son, Nigel Nicolson, reveals many personal details of the journey omitted from the original 1926 edition in his engaging introduction to this classic of travel literature. He has also selected the photographs, almost all previously unpublished, from V Sackville-West's album of her journey.

£17.95   160 pp (hardback)   83 illustrations
ISBN 1 873054 00 9

In the introduction to this new edition, Nigel Nicolson once again lifts the veil of his mother's evasive past and selects unpublished photographs from her personal album...Vita made a good job of her first travel book...she has a distinctive knack of description. Daily Mail, 25 October, 1990.

William Makepeace Thackeray
Notes of a Journey from Cornhill to Grand Cairo

New edition introduced by Sarah Searight
Illustrations compiled by Briony Llewellyn

This is William Thackeray's lively account of a journey he made in 1844 on the first commercial steamboat service to the Eastern Mediterranean, which took him via Spain, Malta, Rhodes and Athens to visit the newly fashionable extensions to the Grand Tour of Constantinople, Jerusalem and Cairo.

Written before the literary success of *Vanity Fair*, this little-known volume from Thackeray's early career gives us impressions of the people, places and antiquities encountered, mixing reflective and acute observation with wit and humour. The result is a highly engaging style of travelogue which commends itself to the attention of today's reader, and travel writer too.

The text, rich in allusions and references, is annotated throughout and the new Introduction puts Thackeray's journey in the context of mid-Victorian attitudes towards, and difficulties with, travel in the East. The illustrations, many in colour, are by leading orientalist painters of whom some, like J.F. Lewis, were abroad at the time of Thackeray's visit and whose adopted eastern lifestyle Thackeray vividly portrays.

£16.50   160 pp (hardback)   145 illustrations (colour, b&w)
ISBN 1 873054 01 7

It is a delight to read this new edition of a little-known volume written in Thackeray's early career, with a new introduction by Sarah Searight. The imagery is unforgettable... And that is only the half of it. This book also contains dozens of 19th-century master paintings to accompany Thackeray's words... The result is a sensual and aesthetic treat: an intellectual, culinary, meteorological, maritime masterpiece. Country Life, 11 July, 1991.

Robert Louis Stevenson
An Inland Voyage
with a travel guide by Andrew Sanger

As a young man, Robert Louis Stevenson made a canoe voyage along the rivers and canals of Belgium and Northern France, continuing on foot in the Loire region.

This is the great story-teller's little-known account of that journey, with a glimpse of the changing scenery along the route admirably captured in the specially commissioned water-colour and ink illustrations by Michael Reynolds.

For to-day's traveller retracing RLS's journey, the route has been divided into four itineraries, each with maps, recommended hotels and places of interest, as part of a practical travel guide compiled by the writer Andrew Sanger.

£14.95   160 pp (hardback)   78 illustrations (colour, b&w)
ISBN   1 873054 02 5

...with illustrations by Michael Reynolds and a travel guide to the route by Andrew Sanger. It makes for a delightful present for a lover of either Stevenson or France or both. ·
The Independent, 30 November, 1991

Titles in the Literary Travellers' Series may be ordered
at any good bookshop worldwide
or details may be obtained by contacting:

Cockbird Press Limited, P O Box 356
Heathfield, East Sussex TN1 9QF, United Kingdom
Tel: (0435) 830430 Fax: (0435) 830027